KISSINGER'S SHADOW

KISSINGER'S SHADOW

THE LONG REACH OF AMERICA'S MOST CONTROVERSIAL STATESMAN

GREG GRANDIN

METROPOLITAN BOOKS

HENRY HOLT AND COMPANY   NEW YORK

Metropolitan Books
Henry Holt and Company, LLC
Publishers since 1866
175 Fifth Avenue
New York, New York 10010
www.henryholt.com

Metropolitan Books® and ® are registered trademarks of
Henry Holt and Company, LLC.

Library of Congress Cataloging-in-Publication data is available.

Library of Congress Cataloging-in-Publication Data

Grandin, Greg, 1962–
   Kissinger's shadow : the long reach of America's most controversial statesman /
Greg Grandin.
      pages cm
   Includes bibliographical references and index.
   ISBN 978-1-62779-449-7 (hardcover)—ISBN 978-1-62779-450-3 (ebook)
1. Kissinger, Henry, 1923—Influence.   2. United States—Foreign relations—
1945–1989.   3. United States—Military policy—20th century—History.   4. United
States—Politics and government—20th century.   5. Statesmen—United States—
Biography.   6. Militarism—United States.   7. Exceptionalism—United States.
8. National security—United States—Political aspects.   9. United States—Military
policy—Decision making.   10. United States—Foreign relations—Philosophy.
I. Title.
   E840.8.K58G695 2015
   327.2092—dc23
   [B]   2015003553

First Edition 2015

Designed by Kelly S. Too

Printed in the United States of America
1   3   5   7   9   10   8   6   4   2

For Eleanor and Manu, again

There are two kinds of realists: those who manipulate facts and those who create them. The West requires nothing so much as men able to create their own reality.

—Henry Kissinger, 1963

CONTENTS

KISSINGER'S SHADOW

On Not Seeing the Monster

Thomas Schelling, a Harvard economist and future Nobel Laureate, once asked Henry Kissinger what was more terrifying: seeing the monster or not seeing the monster?

It was early May 1970, just a few days after Richard Nixon appeared on TV and told the nation that the United States had sent ground troops into Cambodia. Nixon said that the operation was necessary to clear out enemy sanctuaries along the border with Vietnam. But his speech also made clear that something much more profound than military strategy had led to his decision to send ground troops into a neutral country. "We live in an age of anarchy," the president said. "We see mindless attacks on all the great institutions which have been created by free civilizations in the last 500 years." Nixon suggested that he had invaded Cambodia not just in response to a foreign threat but to domestic disorder: "It is not our power but our will and character that is being tested tonight." For months, Nixon and Kissinger, his national security adviser, had said they had a plan to get the United States out of Vietnam. Now, suddenly, they were widening the war into a neighboring country. Four days after Nixon's speech, National Guardsmen opened fire at Kent State, killing four students who were protesting the invasion. Nine more were wounded. Two weeks later, at Jackson State, police shot into a group of protesting African American students, killing two and wounding twelve.

Schelling bore some intellectual responsibility for America's involvement in Vietnam. He had a mind like a computer, which he used to apply mathematical formulas to military strategy. Whether one was "deterring the Russians" or "deterring one's own children," he said, the problem was the same: to figure out the proper ratio of threat to incentive. Lyndon B. Johnson and his secretary of defense, Robert McNamara, directly applied Schelling's theories, bombing North Vietnam as a form of behavior modification. Schelling also had a large influence on the men who would take over America's Vietnam policy from Johnson and McNamara, particularly on Henry Kissinger. Kissinger had taught at Harvard before he joined the Nixon White House and he considered Schelling a friend. He had adopted the economist's insights, especially the idea that "bargaining power . . . comes from the capacity to hurt," to cause "sheer pain and damage." It was a sentiment that Kissinger would try to operationalize in Southeast Asia.[1]

By 1970, though, Schelling had turned against the war, and the US invasion of Cambodia prompted him, along with eleven other prominent Harvard professors, to travel to Washington to meet with Kissinger and register their objections.[2] This was no ordinary group of antiwar intellectuals. Over the years, different labels have been applied to the kind of men who moved easily between Washington and Cambridge, between the classroom and the war room: the Eastern establishment, the best and the brightest, the power elite. These were them. The Harvard delegation included two Nobel laureates, a future Nobel laureate (Schelling), physicists, chemists, economists, and political scientists. Many of them were former advisers to presidents going back to Harry Truman. A number of the group had been involved in executing policies that led to early American involvement in Vietnam.

Serious men, they took their break with the administration seriously. "This is too much," one told a reporter, referring to the invasion. Others were disturbed about the coarsening of public discourse brought on by the war. "'Professors' and 'liberals'—same thing," was how Nixon's undersecretary of defense, David Packard, dismissed the delegation. One member, Ernest May, a Harvard dean and military historian with close ties to the Pentagon, told Kissinger: "You're tearing the country apart domestically."

Kissinger's former colleagues weren't aware that Nixon and Kissinger had already been secretly bombing Cambodia and Laos for over a year (and would continue to bomb for three more before Congress put an end to it). They knew only about the invasion, and that was bad enough. "Sickening," Schelling said. Today in the United States, a shared and largely unquestioned assumption, irrespective of political affiliation, holds that Washington has the right to use military force against the "safe havens" of terrorists or potential terrorists, even if those havens are found in sovereign countries we are not at war with. This assumption was the premise of George W. Bush's 2002 invasion of Afghanistan and Barack Obama's expansion of drone attacks in Somalia, Yemen, and Pakistan, along with his most recent military operations against Islamic State militants in Syria and Iraq. This reasoning was not widely held in 1970. Schelling's Harvard delegation rejected Kissinger's attempt to justify the invasion by citing the need to destroy communist "sanctuaries." As one reporter summed up the group's objections, violation of a neutral country's sovereignty "could be used by anyone else in the world as a precedent for invading another country, in order, for example, to clear out terrorists." Even if the invasion succeeded on its own terms and cleared out enemy sanctuaries, Schelling later told a journalist, "it still wouldn't have been worth the invasion of another country."

The meeting with Kissinger took place in the old Situation Room in the White House basement. Schelling began by introducing the group and stating its purpose, but Kissinger interrupted him: "I know who you are . . . you're all good friends from Harvard University." "No," said Schelling, "we're a group of people who have completely lost confidence in the ability of the White House to conduct our foreign policy and we have come to tell you so. We are no longer at your disposal as personal advisers." Kissinger, Schelling recalled later, "went gray in the face, he slumped in his chair. I thought at the time that he suffered serious depression." At one point, Kissinger asked if someone could tell him what "mistakes" the administration had made. It was then that Schelling asked Kissinger the question about monsters: "You look out the window, and you see a monster. And you turn to the guy standing next to you at the very same window, and say, 'Look, there's a monster.' He then looks out the window and doesn't see a monster at all. How do you explain to him that there really is a monster?"

Schelling continued: "As we see it, there are two possibilities: Either, one, the President didn't understand when he went into Cambodia that he was invading another country; or two, he did understand."

"We just don't know which one is scarier," Schelling said.

An Obituary Foretold

Henry Kissinger has been accused of many bad things. And when he dies, his critics will get a chance to rehearse the charges. Christopher Hitchens, who made the case that the former secretary of state should be tried as a war criminal, is himself gone. But there's a long witness-for-the-prosecution list—reporters, historians, and lawyers eager to provide background on any of Kissinger's actions in Cambodia, Laos, Vietnam, East Timor, Bangladesh, against the Kurds, in Chile, Argentina, Uruguay, and Cyprus, among other places.

There have been scores of books published on the man over the years, but it is still Seymour Hersh's 1983 *The Price of Power* that future biographers will have to top. Hersh gave us the defining portrait of Kissinger as a preening paranoid, tacking between ruthlessness and sycophancy to advance his career, cursing his fate and letting fly the B-52s. Small in his vanities and shabby in his motives, Kissinger, in Hersh's hands, is nonetheless Shakespearean because the pettiness gets played out on a world stage with epic consequences.

Denunciations will be balanced by more favorable views. Kissinger has many devotees. And once his detractors and admirers are dispensed with, the obituary will move on to those who urge balance. Transgressions, they'll say, need to be weighed against accomplishments: détente with the Soviet Union, opening up Communist China, negotiating arms treaties with Moscow, and his shuttle diplomacy in the Middle East. It's at this moment that the consequences of many of Kissinger's policies will be redefined as "controversies" and consigned to matters of opinion, or perspective, rather than fact. On the heels of George W. Bush's reckless hubris and Barack Obama's reactive pragmatism, Kissinger's sober statesmanship is, as a number of commentators have recently claimed, needed more than ever.

There'll be color commentary, colleagues and acquaintances who will reminisce that he had a wry sense of humor and a fondness for intrigue, good food, and high-cheeked women. We'll be reminded that he dated Jill St. John and Marlo Thomas, was friends with Shirley MacLaine, and was affectionately known as Super K, Henry of Arabia, and the Playboy of the West Wing. Kissinger was brilliant and had a temper. He was vulnerable, which made him vicious, and his relationship with Richard Nixon was, as one reporter put it, "deeply weird." They were the original frenemies, with Kissinger flattering Nixon to his face and bitching about him behind his back. "The meatball mind," he called his boss as soon as the phone was back on the hook, a "drunk."[1] Nixonger, Isaiah Berlin called the duo.

Born in Fürth, Germany, in 1923, Kissinger came to America when he was fifteen, and summaries of his life will stress his foreignness. "Jewboy," Nixon called him. Kissinger's view of the world, conventionally described as valuing stability and the advance of national interests above abstract ideals like democracy and human rights, is often said to clash with America's sense of itself as innately good, as an exceptional and indispensable nation. "Intellectually," his biographer, Walter Isaacson, writes, his "mind would retain its European cast." Kissinger, notes another writer, had a worldview that a "born American could not have." And his Bavarian accent did grow deeper as he grew older.[2]

But reading Kissinger as alien, as out of tune with the chords of American exceptionalism, misses the point of the man. He was in fact the quintessential American, his cast of mind perfectly molded to his place and time.

As a young man, Kissinger embraced the most American of conceits: self-creation, the notion that one's fate is not determined by one's condition, that the weight of history might impose limits to freedom, but within those limits there is considerable room to maneuver. Kissinger didn't express these ideas in an American vernacular, the way, say New World poets and writers like Walt Whitman and Herman Melville did. "The Past is dead, and has no resurrection," Melville wrote, "but the Future is endowed with such a life, that it lives to us even in anticipation. . . . Those who are solely governed by the Past stand, like Lot's wife, crystallized in the act of looking backward. . . . It is for America to make precedents, and not to obey them." Rather, Kissinger tended to express his philosophy in the heavy prose of German metaphysics. But the ideas were largely the same: "Necessity," he wrote in 1950, "describes the past but freedom rules the future."[3]

That line is from a thesis that Kissinger submitted as a Harvard senior, a nearly four-hundred-page journey through the writings of a number of European philosophers.[4] "The Meaning of History," as Kissinger titled the work, is dense, melancholy, and often overwrought, easy to dismiss as the product of youth. But Kissinger has repeated many of its premises and arguments, in different forms, to this day. Besides, by the time of his arrival at Harvard, the author had extensive real-world, wartime experience thinking about the questions his thesis raised, including the relationship between information and wisdom, being and nothingness, and the way the past presses on the present.

Kissinger escaped the Holocaust. But at least twelve family members didn't. Drafted into the army in 1943, he spent the last year of the war back in Germany, working his way up the ranks of military intelligence. As administrator of the occupied Rhine River town of Krefeld, with a population of 200,000, Kissinger purged Nazis from municipal posts. He also distinguished himself as an intelligence agent, identifying, arresting, and interrogating Gestapo officers and securing confidential informants. He won a Bronze Star for his effectiveness and bravery. In other words, the tension between fact and truth, a central preoccupation of his thesis—which, as one observer points out, reads like a "personal statement"—was not an abstract question for Kissinger. It was the stuff of life and death, and Kissinger's subsequent diplomacy was, writes one of Kissinger's Harvard classmates, a "virtual transplant from the world of thought into the world of power."[5]

Kissinger's metaphysics, as they evolved from his thesis to his most recent book, published at the age of ninety-one, comprised equal parts gloom and glee. The gloom was reflected in his acceptance that experience, life itself, is ultimately meaningless and that history is tragic. "Life is suffering, birth involves death," he wrote in 1950, "transitoriness is the fate of existence. . . . Experience is always unique and solitary."[6] As to "history," he said he believed in its "tragic element." "The generation of Buchenwald and the Siberian labor camps," he wrote, "cannot talk with the same optimism as its fathers." The glee came from embracing that meaninglessness, from the realization that one's actions were neither predetermined by historical inevitability nor governed by a higher moral authority. There were "limits" to what an individual could do, "necessities," as Kissinger put it, imposed by the fact that we live in a world filled with other beings. But individuals possess will, instinct, and intuition—qualities that can be used to expand their arena of freedom.[7]

It's difficult to work one's way through Kissinger's brooding thesis. But it is worth the effort, for it reveals him as a far more interesting thinker than he is conventionally described as being. Kissinger is inevitably called a "realist," which is true if realism is defined as holding a pessimistic view of human nature and a belief that power is needed to impose order on anarchic social relations. But if realism is taken as a view of the world that holds that reality is transparent, that the "truth" of facts can be arrived at from simply observing those facts, then Kissinger was decidedly not a realist. Rather, Kissinger in his thesis was declaring himself in favor of what today the Right denounces as radical relativism: there is no such thing as absolute truth, he argued, no truth at all other than what could be deduced from one's own solitary perspective. "Meaning represents the emanation of a metaphysical context," he wrote. "Every man in a certain sense creates his picture of the world." Truth, Kissinger said, isn't found in facts but in the questions we ask of those facts. History's meaning is "inherent in the nature of our query."[8]

This kind of subjectivism was in the postwar air, and Kissinger in his thesis sounds not unlike Jean-Paul Sartre, whose influential lecture on existentialism was published in English in 1947 and is cited in Kissinger's bibliography. Sartre, like Kissinger, would soon use the phrase "dialectical unity of freedom and necessity." And when Kissinger insists that individuals have the "choice" to act with "responsibility" toward others, he seems absolutely Sartrean: since morality isn't something that is imposed from without but comes from within, each individual "is responsible for the world." Kissinger, though, would take a very different path than Sartre and other dissenting intellectuals, and this is what made his existentialism exceptional: he used it not to protest war but to justify waging it.

Kissinger wasn't alone among postwar policy intellectuals in invoking the "tragedy" of human existence and the belief that life is suffering, that the best one can hope for is to establish a world of order and rules. George Kennan, a conservative, and Arthur Schlesinger, a liberal, both thought human nature's "dark and tangled aspects," as Schlesinger put it, justified a strong military.[9] The world needed policing. But both men (and many others who shared their tragic sensibility, like Reinhold Niebuhr and Hans Morgenthau) eventually became critical, some extremely so, of American power. By 1957, Kennan was arguing for "disengagement" from the Cold War and by 1982 he was describing the Reagan administration as "ignorant, unintelligent, complacent and arrogant."[10] Vietnam provoked Schlesinger to advocate stronger legislative power to rein in what he came to call the "imperial presidency."

Not Kissinger. At every single one of America's postwar turning points, moments of crisis when men of good will began to express doubts about American power, Kissinger broke in the opposite direction. He made his peace with Nixon, whom he first thought was unhinged; then with Ronald Reagan, whom he initially considered hollow; and then with George W. Bush's neocons, despite the fact that they all rose to power attacking Kissinger. Fortified by his uncommon mix of gloom and glee, Kissinger never wavered. The gloom led him, as a conservative, to privilege order over justice. The glee led him to think he might, by the force of his will and intellect, forestall the tragic and claim, if only for a fleeting moment, freedom. "Those statesmen who have achieved final greatness did not do so through resignation, however well founded," Kissinger wrote in his 1954 doctoral dissertation. "It was given to them not only to maintain the perfection of order but to have the strength to contemplate chaos, there to find material for fresh creation."[11]

Kissinger's existentialism laid the foundation for how he would defend his later policies. If history is already tragedy, birth death, and life suffering, then absolution comes with a world-weary shrug. There isn't much any one individual can do to make things worse than they already are.

Yet before it was an instrument of self-justification, Kissinger's relativism was a tool of self-creation and hence self-advancement. Kissinger, who admittedly believed in nothing, was skilled at being all things to all people, particularly people of a higher station: "I won't tell you what I am," he said in his famous interview with Oriana Fallaci, "I'll never tell anyone."[12] The myth about him is that he disliked the messiness of modern interest-group politics, that his talents would have been better realized had they been unencumbered by the oversight of mass democracy. Really, though, it was only because of mass democracy, with its near endless opportunities for reinvention, that Kissinger was able to climb the heights.

A product of a new postwar meritocracy, Kissinger quickly learned how to use the media, manipulate journalists, cultivate elites, and leverage public opinion to his advantage. And within a remarkably short period of time and at a stunningly young age (he was forty-five when Nixon named him his national security adviser in 1968) he had seized the national security apparatus from the establishment "Eastern men." The gentile Wasps with their inner-directed egos, like Nixon's first secretary of state, William Rogers, whom Kissinger eventually pushed out, had no idea what they were up against. "What amazed" his colleagues, David Halberstam once wrote, was "not the dishonesty or ruthlessness, but the fact that what was at issue was frequently stunningly inconsequential."[13]

This book, though, focuses not on Kissinger's outsized personality but rather on the outsized role he had in creating the world we live in today, which accepts endless war as a matter of course. Since the end of World War II and the beginning of the Cold War, there have been many versions of the national security state, a quasi-covert warfare establishment that the political theorist Michael Glennon has recently described as a "double government."[14] But a transformative moment in the evolution of that state occurred in the late 1960s and early 1970s, when Henry Kissinger's policies, especially his four-year war in Cambodia, hastened its disintegration, undermining the traditional foundations—elite planning, bipartisan consensus, and public support—on which it stood. Yet even as the breakup of the old national security state was proceeding apace, Kissinger was helping with its reconstruction in a new form, a restored imperial presidency (based on ever more spectacular displays of violence, more intense secrecy, and an increasing use of war and militarism to leverage domestic dissent and polarization for political advantage) capable of moving forward into a post-Vietnam world.

America's failed war in Southeast Asia destroyed the public's ability to ignore the consequences of Washington's actions in the world. The curtain was being drawn back, and everywhere, it seemed, the relationship of cause and effect was coming into view— in the reporting by Hersh and other investigative journalists on US war crimes, in the scholarship of a new questioning generation of historians, in the work of documentary filmmakers like Emile de Antonio's *In the Year of the Pig* and Peter Davis's *Hearts and Minds*, among apostate former true believers, like Daniel Ellsberg, and in the forensic logic of dissident intellectuals like Noam Chomsky. Worse, the sense that the United States was the source of as much bad as good in the world began to seep out into popular culture, into novels, movies, and even comic books, taking the shape of a generalized, even if not always political, skepticism and antimilitarism—a "critical disposition," as one writer put it, that "has become a cultural belief, entirely taken for granted and now part of conventional wisdom."[15]

There are many ways Kissinger helped the national security

state adapt to what the first generation of neoconservatives began, by 1970, to identify as an entrenched, permanent "adversary culture."[16] But key was the restoration of a denial mechanism, a way to neutralize the torrent of information becoming available to the public regarding US actions in the world, and the often unhappy results of those actions. What we could call Kissinger's imperial existentialism helped pull the curtain closed once more, blinding many to the monster outside. Reporters and academics might have been obsessively digging up facts that proved the United States overthrew this democratic government or funded that repressive regime, but he persevered in insisting that the past shouldn't limit the country's range for options in the future.

In doing so, Kissinger provided a new generation of politicians a template for how to justify tomorrow's action while ignoring yesterday's catastrophe. The present can learn from the past, he said, but not through an obsessive reconstruction of "cause and effect." Kissinger dismissed "causal" reasoning as a false, or lower-order and deterministic, form of comprehension. Rather, history teaches "by analogy." And each generation has the "freedom" to "decide what, if anything, is analogous."[17] In other words, if you don't like the lesson Richard Nixon and Vietnam teaches, don't worry about it. There's always Neville Chamberlain and Munich.

America's exceptional sense of itself depends on a similarly ambiguous relationship to the past. History is affirmed, since it is America's unprecedented historical success that justifies the exceptionalism. Yet history is also denied, or at least what is denied is an understanding of the past as a series of causal relationships. That is, the blowback from any given action—arming anti-Soviet jihadists in Afghanistan, for example, or supplying Saddam Hussein with the sarin gas he used on Iran—is rinsed clean of its source and given a new origin story, blamed on generalized chaos that exists beyond our borders.

This evasion has been on full display of late, as the politicians who drove us into Iraq in 2003 tell us that decisions made at the time that facilitated the rise of Islamic State militants shouldn't hinder America from taking bold action in the future to destroy Islamic State militants. "If we spend our time debating what happened eleven or twelve years ago," former vice president Dick Cheney today says, "we're going to miss the threat that is growing and that we do face."[18] The United States, Cheney insists, needs to do "what it takes, for as long as it takes."

Kissinger perfected this type of dodge. He was a master of advancing the proposition that the policies of the United States and the world's violence and disorder are entirely unrelated, especially when it came to accounting for the consequences of his own actions. Cambodia? "It was Hanoi," Kissinger writes, pointing to the North Vietnamese to justify his four-year bombing campaign of that neutral nation. Chile? That country, he says in defense of his coup-plotting against Salvador Allende, "was 'destabilized' not by our actions but by Chile's constitutional President." The Kurds? "A tragedy," says the man who served them up to Saddam Hussein, hoping to turn Iraq away from the Soviets. East Timor? "I think we've heard enough about Timor."[19]

Obituaries, already on file and waiting to run, will mention how conservative hostility toward Kissinger's policies—détente with Russia, opening to China—helped propel Ronald Reagan's first real bid for the presidency in 1976. And they will draw a distinction between his brand of supposed hardheaded power politics and the neoconservative idealism that led us into the fiascos of Afghanistan and Iraq. But they'll likely miss the way Kissinger served not just as a foil but as an enabler for the New Right. Over the course of his career he advanced a set of premises that would be taken up and extended by neoconservative intellectuals and policy makers: that hunches, conjecture, will, and intuition are as important as facts and hard intelligence in guiding policy, that too much knowledge can weaken resolve, that foreign policy has to be wrested out of the hands of experts and bureaucrats and given to men of action, and that the principle of self-defense (broadly defined to cover just about anything) overrules the ideal of sovereignty. In so doing, Kissinger played his part in keeping the great wheel of American militarism spinning ever forward.

Henry Kissinger is, of course, not singularly responsible for the evolution of the United States' national security state into the perpetual motion machine that it has become today. That history, starting with the 1947 National Security Act and running through the Cold War and now the War on Terror, is comprised of many different episodes and is populated by many different individuals. But Kissinger's career courses through the decades like a bright red line, shedding spectral light on the road that has brought us to where we now find ourselves, from the jungles of Vietnam and Cambodia to the sands of the Persian Gulf.

At the very least, we can learn from Kissinger's long life that the two defining concepts of American foreign policy—realism and idealism—aren't necessarily opposing values; rather, they reinforce each other. Idealism gets us into whatever the quagmire of the moment is, realism keeps us there while promising to get us out, and then idealism returns anew both to justify the realism and to overcome it in the next round. So it goes.

Back in 2004, the journalist Ron Suskind reported a conversation he had with a top aide to George W. Bush who many now believe was Karl Rove. Studying "discernible reality" was not the way the world worked any more, Rove said: "We're an empire now, and when we act, we create our own reality. And while you're studying that reality—judiciously, as you will—we'll act again, creating other new realities, which you can study too, and that's how things will sort out. We're history's actors."[20] The quote circulated widely, interpreted as the blind ideology of the Bush administration taken to its conceited conclusion, the idea that reality itself could bend to neocon will.

But Kissinger said it four decades earlier. Inspired by John F. Kennedy's facing down of the Soviets during the Cuban missile crisis, Kissinger, then still a Harvard professor, urged foreign policy experts to escape the restraints imposed by reality and embrace a similar élan: An "expert," he wrote in 1963, "respects 'facts' and considers them something to be adjusted to, perhaps to be manipulated, but not to be transcended. . . . In the decades ahead, the West will have to lift its sights to encompass a more embracing concept of reality. . . . There are two kinds of realists: those who manipulate facts and those who create them. The West requires nothing so much as men able to create their own reality."[21]

Nothing so much as Henry Kissinger.

1

A Cosmic Beat

History [is] an endless unfolding of a cosmic beat that expresses itself in the sole alternatives of subject and object, a vast succession of catastrophic upheavals of which power is not only the manifestation but the exclusive aim; a stimulus of blood that not only pulses through veins but must be shed and will be shed.

—Henry Kissinger

You can almost hear Wagner's "Ride of the Valkyries" in the background. Henry Kissinger wrote the above passage in his 1950 Harvard thesis, submitted at nearly the exact moment Harry Truman announced that the United States would support the French in Vietnam and send troops to Korea, thus putting the country on the road to war in Southeast Asia. "The Meaning of History" focused almost exclusively on European philosophy, but reading through its pages knowing the role its author would later play in expanding the conflict into Laos and Cambodia, one can't but think of napalm and cluster bombs and wonder whether America's catastrophe in Southeast Asia was inevitable, if there was something in the very life-being of the United States, a will-to-infinity, for example, that drove it toward ruin in the jungle. Was there an inner historical logic that would manifest itself at My Lai, a bloodline that traced back to the first Puritan massacres of Native Americans?

Kissinger doesn't believe in historical inevitability. So were he to be asked this question, he would surely answer no. More importantly, Kissinger was offering the above definition of history—as a reflexive, pulsating projection of power without any intelligible objective other than the projection of power—not as a recommendation but as a warning, a cautionary description of the fate that often befalls great civilizations when they lose their sense of purpose, when they forget why they are projecting their power and only know that they can project their power. He was urging statesmen *not* to succumb to history's cosmic beat, *not* to fall into a "repetition" of the kind of unforced "cataclysmic wars" that brought down past great civilizations. It was advice more easily given than followed.

Many have pointed out the influence of the Prussian historian Oswald Spengler's best-selling *The Decline of the West* on the future statesman. Kissinger, Harvard's Stanley Hoffmann remarked, "walked, in a way, with the ghost of Spengler at his side."[1] "Kissinger was a Spenglerian," another Harvard colleague, Zbigniew Brzezinski, said.[2] Spengler, like Kissinger, is often associated with political realism, his deep pessimism regarding human nature reflected in the realpolitik of a number of prominent postwar intellectuals and policy makers such as George Kennan, Hans Morgenthau, and Samuel Huntington.

But Spengler also waged a relentless assault on the very idea of reality. He insisted that there existed a higher plane of experience that was inaccessible to rational thought, a plane where instinct and creativity reigned. "We have," Spengler thought, "hardly yet an inkling of how much in our reputedly objective values and experiences is only disguise, only image and expression."[3] To get behind image and expression, to penetrate perceived material power and interests and grasp what Spengler called destiny, one needed not information but intuition, not facts but hunches, not reason but a soul sense, a world feeling. "Often enough a statesman does not 'know' what he is doing," Spengler wrote, "but that does not prevent him from following with confidence just the one path that leads to success."[4]

Kissinger was captivated by this metaphysical and quasi-mythological Spengler, more so than other postwar defense realists such as Kennan, Morgenthau, and Huntington. "All of life is permeated by an inner destiny that can never be defined," Kissinger wrote. "History discloses a majestic unfolding that one can only intuitively perceive, never causally classify."[5] Spengler, he said, "affirmed that there are certain ultimate goals, which no hypothesis can prove, and no sophistry ever deny, expressed in such words as hope, love, beauty, luck, fear."[6]

Most of Kissinger's thesis stayed at that level of romantic abstraction. But at different points in "The Meaning of History," and then later throughout his scholarly and public career, he fixed his sights on a specific target: the growing influence of positivism on postwar social science. Increasingly, at Harvard (as well as at other universities and think tanks, like the RAND Corporation), political scientists, economists, and international relations scholars were applying mathematics, formal logic, and methods associated with natural science to assess human behavior. Economistic formulas such as rational choice and game theory were used to describe and predict everything from individual behavior to nuclear strategy.

It would be an overstatement to say that Kissinger rejected these methods. Game theory calculations, especially those worked out by Kissinger's Harvard colleague Thomas Schelling, influenced both his dissection of Eisenhower's nuclear defense strategy and conduct of the Vietnam War. At the same time, however, Kissinger strongly criticized the idea of objectivity, that society is "governed by objective laws that have their roots in human nature"

and that these laws are knowable through observation.[7] Kissinger
was particularly drawn to Spengler's criticism of the "causal principle" as applied to historical interpretation. Spengler believed that
cause-and-effect analysis was (as Spengler's intellectual biographer
Stuart Hughes wrote) a "ridiculous simplification of the inextrica-
ble medley of converging elements that went to make up even the
least important item of history."[8]

Kissinger too dismissed what he called "mere causal analysis"
as a kind of superstition akin to primitives trying to explain what
causes a steam engine to move forward. Such a "magic attitude," he
said, is an effort to escape the meaninglessness of existence by finding meaning in "data."[9] Causal reasoning focuses on the "typical"
and the "inexorable," affirming the false doctrine of "eternal
recurrence"—that is, the belief in historical inevitability. If something happened once it was bound to happen again, and again.
Kissinger rejected this idea. Instead, he affirmed the existence of a
realm of consciousness that superseded the material world, a realm
that Spengler called "destiny" but Kissinger preferred to describe
as "freedom." "Reality that is subject to the laws of causality,"
Kissinger wrote, represents only the outer, surface appearance of
things. But "freedom is an inward state" and "our experience of freedom testifies to a fact of existence which no thought-process can
deny."

According to Spengler and Kissinger, it is at the moment when
the "causality-men" (Spengler's term) and the "fact-men" (Kissinger's term) take over that a civilization is in most danger. As the
dreams, myths, and risk taking of an earlier creative period fall
away, intellectuals, political leaders, and even priests become pre-
dominantly concerned with the question not of *why* but of *how*. "A
century of purely extensive effectiveness," Spengler wrote (referring to the rationalism of modern society, which strives for ever
more efficient ways of doing things), "is a time of decline." The intuitive dimensions of wisdom get tossed aside, technocratic proce-

dure overwhelms purpose, and information is mistaken for wisdom. "Vast bureaucratic mechanisms," Kissinger said, develop "a momentum and a vested interest of their own."

Western culture was history's highest expression of technical reason: it "views the whole world," Kissinger wrote, "as a working hypothesis." The "machine" was its great symbol, a "perpeteum mobile"—a perpetual motion machine that asserted relentless "mastery over nature." And the vastly powerful and obsessively efficient United States was the West's vanguard. As such it was especially vulnerable to falling prisoner to what Spengler called the "cult of the useful." At Harvard, the Vatican of American positivism, filled with the country's high priests of social science, Kissinger looked around and asked: Would American leaders command or fall slave to their own technique? "Technical knowledge will be of no avail," the twenty-six-year-old student-veteran warned, "to a soul that has lost its meaning."*

For all of that, Brzezinski and Hoffmann were only half right when they labeled Kissinger a Spenglerian. Spengler wrote as if decline was inevitable, as if the cycle he described—in which each civilization experiences its spring, summer, autumn, winter—were as unavoidable as the spinning of the earth. Once societies pass their great creative stage and the logicians, rationalists, and bureaucrats arrive on the scene, there is no turning back. Having lost a sense of purpose, civilizations lurch outward to find meaning. They get caught up in a series of disastrous wars, propelled forward to doom by history's cosmic beat, power for power's sake, blood for blood's. "Imperialism is the inevitable product" of this

---

* Kissinger wrote his thesis long before the United States fully committed to Vietnam, but over the years he'd return again and again to many of its premises to explain why that war, along with others that followed, went wrong. His most recent book, *World Order*, cites T. S. Eliot's "Choruses from the Rock": "Where is the wisdom we have lost in knowledge? / Where is the knowledge we have lost in information?"

final stage, Kissinger wrote, summing up *The Decline of the West*'s argument, "an outward thrust to hide the inner void."

Kissinger accepted Spengler's critique of past civilizations but rejected his determinism. Decay was not inevitable. "Spengler," Kissinger said, "merely described a fact of decline, and not its necessity." "There is a margin," he would write in his memoirs, "between necessity and accident, in which the statesman by perseverance and intuition must choose and thereby shape the destiny of his people." There were limits to what any political leader could do, he said, but to hide "behind historical inevitability is tantamount to moral abdication."[10]

Based on his reading of Spengler (and other philosopher-historians, such as Arnold Toynbee, who warned of the "suicidal-ness of militarism"), Kissinger might have come to the conclusion that the best way to avoid decline was to avoid war altogether, to put America's great resources to building a sustainable society at home rather than squander them in adventures in places far and wide. But Kissinger took a different lesson from Spengler: it wasn't war that was to be avoided but war fought without a clear political objective. He in fact advocated fighting wars far and wide—or at least advocated for a willingness to fight wars far and wide—as a way of preventing the loss of purpose and wisdom that Spengler identified as taking place during civilization's final stage.[11]

By late 1950, Kissinger, having finished his undergraduate studies and started the doctoral program in Harvard's Department of Government, had advanced a searing critique of "containment," a policy associated with another "realist," George Kennan, which committed Washington to limiting the global spread of Soviet influence. Kissinger conceded, in a series of memos he composed in December 1950 and March 1951 for his adviser, the intellectual historian William Y. Elliott, that "our 'containment' policy contained the germs of a profound idea."[12] But Washington's "timidity" prevented those germs from sprouting. The problem, according to Kissinger, was that containment was applied in too literal a fashion as an effort to "physically counter every Soviet threat where it occurred." Such an application had the effect of both fragmenting the United States' strength and granting Moscow the power to decide where and when Washington would fight. Thus containment, Kissinger wrote, had effectively become "an instrument of Soviet policy."

The Soviets, Kissinger argued, had to be disabused of their idea that "any adventure could be localized at their discretion." The United States should make it clear that it might retaliate anywhere in the world. Importantly, Washington should reserve the right to wage war "not necessarily" at "the point of aggression."* Rather than fighting in Korea, say, Washington could hit Russia at the place and time of its choosing, preferably with "highly mobile" strike forces. Moscow also had to be convinced that "a major war with the United States"—which he called "the only *real* deterring threat" (Kissinger's emphasis)—was a significant possibility.

Kissinger composed these memos just a few months after he had completed "The Meaning of History," at a moment when Washington's three-year-old Cold War stance was being tested in Korea. In them, Kissinger was essentially applying Spengler's criticism of the risk aversion inherent in bureaucratic structures to a concrete policy: containment. One of the problems of bureaucracies, Kissinger pointed out, is that they tend to compartmentalize functions, which in the case of foreign relations meant severing diplomacy from war-

---

* Fifty years later, George W. Bush's undersecretary of defense for policy, Douglas Feith, an important player in the 2003 invasion of Iraq, proposed that Washington should respond to 9/11 by attacking South America, along with "other targets outside the Middle East in the initial offensive," in order to "surprise the terrorists." (Feith's memo is discussed in the 9/11 Commission report and reported on in *Newsweek*, August 8, 2004.)

fare. For the rest of his career, Kissinger would insist that you can't practice the first without the possibility of the second; diplomats needed to be able to wield threats and incentives equally. Here, in analyzing the weaknesses of containment, Kissinger was arguing that statesmen had to overcome their caution and think of containment as *both* a military and a political doctrine, remaining alive to putting into place whatever combination of war and diplomacy was required to check Soviet expansion, to see the whole globe and be willing to act in any part of it, and not in reaction but proactively. They cross a line in Korea, we strike in Baku. "Hit-and-run actions" aimed "to disperse their armies," Kissinger said.

By the middle of the 1950s, Kissinger, having finished his doctorate, had established himself among an influential cohort of defense intellectuals. At Harvard during these years, he published a lively journal, *Confluence,* and helped run a prestigious International Seminar, which afforded him the opportunity to build a network of intellectuals and politicians, including Hannah Arendt, Sidney Hook, Arthur Schlesinger, Daniel Ellsberg, and Reinhold Niebuhr, among others.* As a member of the Council of Foreign

---

* Letters exchanged between Henry Kissinger and Hannah Arendt regarding a submission capture something essential about the two correspondents. Kissinger (on August 10, 1953) alternates between obsequiousness, condescension, and pedantry: "I hope you will not feel that I have done violence to any of your intentions in some of my editorial changes. Your article is one of the most substantial ones we have printed since we have started *Confluence* and I have worked on it with the greatest sympathy spending a whole weekend going over it several times. I did make a few cuts not because it was too long but because it seemed to me to ramble. I am convinced that the essence of a good article is also to keep some proportion between what one must say to support one's argument and what might be excellent in itself but what detracts from the main force of the argument." Arendt's response (August 14, 1953) dispensed with courtesies: "I fear you will be disappointed to see from the galleys all sentences which you wrote were eliminated and quite a few of my own sentences re-instated.... I realize that your editorial methods—re-writing to the point of writing your own sentences—are quite current.... I happen to object to them on personal grounds and as a matter of principle. If we had given this matter a little more thought, you might have decided not to want this, or any of my manuscripts, which I would have regretted. But it cer-

Relations, he researched nuclear strategy and advised the liberal Republican patrician Nelson Rockefeller. He maintained his contacts in the military intelligence community, serving on a number of government committees related to covert operations and psychological warfare: the Operations Research Office, the Psychological Strategy Board, and the Operations Coordinating Board. In 1953, Kissinger also approached the Boston Division of the FBI, telling one of its agents that he was "strongly sympathetic to the FBI" and was willing to pass along information on his Harvard colleagues. "Steps will be taken," the interviewing agent wrote in his report, "to make Kissinger a Confidential Source of this Division."[13]

In a series of essays and his 1957 book, *Nuclear Weapons and Foreign Policy*, Kissinger expanded his earlier critique of containment to cover Eisenhower's doctrine of massive nuclear retaliation.[14] The problem with that doctrine, Kissinger argued, was its "all-or-nothing" absolutism, which posited using nuclear weapons only in retaliation against a Soviet or Chinese strike. Such a policy "makes for a paralysis of diplomacy," Kissinger said, for as time went on, the advantage would steadily tilt away from the United States toward its adversaries: "As Soviet nuclear strength increases, the number of areas that will seem worth the destruction of New York, Detroit or Chicago will steadily diminish."[15] There was very little Moscow or Peking could do over which Washington would risk total nuclear war (as, Kissinger said, the impasse in Korea demonstrated).

Washington, Kissinger wrote, had to find a way to divide the unified risk of massive retaliation into smaller, credible units of

---

tainly would have saved us both some time and trouble." The rest of the correspondence, found in the Hannah Arendt Papers at the Library of Congress, suggest that Kissinger published the manuscript as per Arendt's wishes.

threats. Kissinger here was drawing directly from his Harvard colleague Thomas Schelling, who argued that if a threat "can be decomposed into a series of consecutive smaller threats, there is an opportunity to demonstrate on the first few transgressions that the threat will be carried out on the rest."

One way to do so was to overcome a reluctance to use nuclear weapons. Here's Kissinger in 1957: to convey the "maximum credible threat, limited nuclear war seems a more suitable deterrent than conventional war"; the United States needs "a diplomacy" that can "break down the atmosphere of special horror which now surrounds the use of nuclear weapons, an atmosphere which has been created in part by skillful Soviet 'ban-the-bomb' propaganda."[16] Another way was to demonstrate a willingness to fight "little wars" in the world's "grey areas"—that is, those parts of the globe outside of the Eurasian heartland, which for Kissinger by the mid-1950s included Indochina, as the French had renamed Laos, Cambodia, and Vietnam.[17]

In the wake of the Korean stalemate, Kissinger wasn't alone in making the case that Washington needed to develop a strategy to wage "little wars"—he was part of a shift among a cohort of hawkish defense intellectuals including General Maxwell Taylor, General James Gavin, Robert Osgood, and Bernard Brodie. But the totality of Kissinger's vision set him apart. His assessment of the inadequacies of Eisenhower's defense strategy was just the tip of a broader analysis of American society: insulated by two oceans and exhilarated by two victories in world wars fought on foreign soil, the United States, Kissinger said, lacked the self-awareness required of a world power. An absolutist sense of morality—"so purist and abstracted"—absolved American leaders from having to make "decisions in ambiguous situations." American politicians didn't know how to conduct the "minutiae of day-to-day diplomacy." Everything was "all-or-nothing." Kissinger believed that the United States needed to be willing to fight a "major" war. That, though, was impossible since all that its leaders could imagine was a "massive" conflict of total destruction. Added to the problem was the country's technological fetishism, its tendency to respond "to every Soviet advance in the nuclear field by what can best be described as a flight into technology, by devising ever more fearful weapons."

This dependence on weapons reinforced the fundamental "dilemma" faced by the United States. Washington could dot the globe with strategic air bases. It could sign defense treaties with two-thirds of the world's nations. And it could build more than enough nuclear warheads to destroy the planet many times over. But "the more powerful the weapons," Kissinger wrote in 1956, "the greater becomes the reluctance to use them."[18] By telegraphing its refusal to deploy its atomic warheads in a limited strike and its unwillingness to engage in small wars, Washington had turned America's strength (its nuclear supremacy) into a weakness. This impotence was captured in a phrase used by Eisenhower that seemed to particularly grate on the Harvard professor: "there is no alternative to peace." It was clear to Kissinger that if the West was to triumph in the Cold War, more than technological strength was needed.

By this point, Kissinger had begun to invest the word *doctrine* with a Spenglerian mysticism, with the idea that civilizations need to be self-aware, that they need to know their "purpose" in order to transform brute force and material dominance into an effective diplomacy. "It is the task of strategic doctrine," he wrote in 1957, "to translate power into policy." Kissinger continued: "Whether the goals of a state are offensive or defensive, whether it seeks to achieve or to prevent a transformation, its strategic doctrines must define what objectives are worth contending for and determine the degree of force appropriate for achieving them."[19] Without a strategic doctrine that encapsulated America's larger purpose, Washington's reactions to crises would always be both tentative and overreactive.

———————

There was a problem with this formulation. Already in his early writings, well before he had a chance to apply his ideas as a government official, a close reading finds Kissinger struggling to break out of his own circular reasoning. He repeatedly urged America's leaders to state their vision and make clear what they meant to accomplish with any given policy or action—to not, as he put it, exalt the technique of American power over the purpose of American power.* But he found it difficult to define what he meant by purpose. At times, Kissinger appears to mean the ability to play a long geostrategic game, to imagine where one wants to be, in relation to one's adversaries, in ten years' time and to put into place a policy to get there. At other times, he seems to mean the need to figure out ways to divide the threat of massive nuclear retaliation into more manageable, credible units of deterence, to be able to better balance punishments and incentives. And at still other times, purpose might refer to the need to create "legitimacy," demonstrate "credibility," or establish a global "balance of power." But these are all instrumental definitions of purpose. They still beg the question, why? If the projection of power is the means, what is the end?

It was not to accumulate more objective power, for he had consistently argued that there was no such thing. Kissinger is perhaps most well known for the concept "balance of power." But there's a fascinating and rarely cited passage in his 1954 doctoral dissertation where he insists that what he means by this is not "real" power: "a balance of power *legitimatized* by power would be highly unstable and make unlimited wars almost inevitable, for the equilibrium is achieved not by the *fact* but by the *consciousness* of balance" (Kissinger's emphasis). He goes on to write that "this consciousness is never brought about until it is tested."[20]

---

* "When technique becomes exalted over purpose, men become the victims of their complexities. They forget that every great achievement in every field was a vision before it became a reality," he wrote in 1965 (*The Troubled Partnership*, p. 251).

In order to "test" power—that is, in order to create one's conscious-ness of power—one needed to be willing to act. And the best way to produce that willingness was to act. On this point at least, Kissinger was unfailingly clear: "inaction" has to be avoided so as to show that action is possible. Only "action," he wrote, could void the systemic "incentive for inaction."[21] Only "action" could overcome the paralyzing fear of the "drastic consequences" (that is, nuclear escalation) that might result from such "action." Only through "action"—including small wars in marginal areas like Vietnam—could America become vital again, could it produce the awareness by which it understands its power, breaks the impasse caused by an overreliance on nuclear technology, instills cohesion among allies, and reminds an increasingly ossified foreign policy bureau-cracy of the purpose of American power.

By the mid-1950s, then, Kissinger had come full around to embrace the object of his criticism: power for power's sake. He had built his own perpetual motion machine; the purpose of American power was to create an awareness of American purpose. Put in Spenglerian terms, "power" is history's starting and ending point, history's "manifestation" and its "exclusive objective." And since Kissinger held to an extremely plastic notion of reality, other con-cepts he was associated with, such as "interests," were also pulled into the whirlpool of his reasoning: we can't defend our interests until we know what our interests are and we can't know what our interests are until we defend them.*

---

* Kissinger directly linked his call for action to his earlier critique of "American empir-icism," arguing that it was only willed action—action taken instinctively, with incom-plete information—that can prevent such empiricism from becoming a rigid dogma. In his first book, *Nuclear Weapons and Foreign Policy* (1957), pp. 424–26, he wrote: "Policy is the art of weighing probabilities; mastery of it lies in grasping the nuances of possibilities. To attempt to conduct it as a science must lead to rigidity. For only the risks are certain; the opportunities are conjectural. One cannot be 'sure' about the implications of events until they have happened and when they have occurred it is too late to do anything about them. Empiricism in foreign policy leads to a penchant for *ad hoc* solutions." Americans might pride themselves on being undogmatic but that

For most of the 1960s, Kissinger was on the margins of formal power, serving as a part-time adviser to the National Security Council, first during Kennedy's administration and then Johnson's. But his hawkish positions lowered the public debate, feeding the anti-Communism that propelled deeper involvement in Vietnam.

Kissinger contributed to the false idea that Moscow was poised to overtake Washington in the nuclear arms race. Indeed, that it had already done so. "There is no dispute about the missile gap as such," he wrote in 1961, helping to justify the Pentagon's massive arms buildup that year, including thousands of Minuteman and Polaris missiles. Alarmism was then, as it is today, a good career move: "We must not delude ourselves about the gravity of our position," he said, for "our margin of survival has narrowed dangerously."[22] Such "extravagant claims," notes a review of Kissinger's scholarship from this period, were reinforced by other hard-liners and in time "became part of the intellectual baggage of

---

they "postpone committing themselves until all facts are in" is itself a form of dogmatism. By the time they do act, "a crisis has usually developed or an opportunity has passed." The result, Kissinger argued, is an inability to bridge the gap between "grand strategy" and the "particular tactics" taken in response to any given crisis. He goes on: "The paradoxical result is that we, the empiricists, often appear to the world as rigid, unimaginative, and even somewhat cynical, while the dogmatic Bolsheviks exhibit flexibility, daring, and subtlety." But, he said, "the willingness to act need not derive from theory." One can and should act based on intangibles: on "tradition," past experiences, instinct, imagination, and "a feeling for nuance." To do so will help sharpen our leaders' consciousness regarding those intangibles: "A power can survive only if it is willing to fight for interpretations of justice and its conception of vital interests:" but, importantly, it would be a disaster to wait to act until one has a fully formed interpretation of justice and conception of interests, or until the situation allows for a perfect application of that interpretation and conception. Rather, in a complex world, ideals and interests can only be known by testing them, by acting. Confronting the Soviet threat "presupposes above all a moral act: a willingness to run risks on partial knowledge and for a less than perfect application of one's principles. The insistence on absolutes either in assessing the provocation or in evaluating possible remedies is a prescription for inaction." Inaction would lead to a dogmatic loss of imagination, and loss of imagination would hinder future action.

the Kennedy Administration, and they explain in part the willingness of the United States to overcommit its power and prestige in Vietnam."[23]

Kissinger had hopes for Kennedy. He told Arthur Schlesinger a few months before the 1960 election that what the country needed more than anything was "someone who will bring about a big jump—not just an improvement of existing tendencies, but a shift into a new atmosphere, a new world." Someone, he said, who will not just "manipulate the status quo" but create a new reality.[24] Once in office, JFK disappointed Kissinger, who complained that the new president proved too cautious and too ad hoc in his response to crises.

There was, though, one event that captured his imagination. In August 1962, the White House received intelligence that the Soviets had placed long-range nuclear missiles in Cuba, leading Kennedy, in a speech broadcast to the nation on TV, to announce that he was sending warships to blockade the island. Kissinger was entranced. He called the speech, in an essay published immediately after the crisis had passed in late 1962, a brilliant "stroke": Kennedy "boldly seized an opportunity given few statesmen: to change the course of events by one dramatic move." In forcing Khrushchev to back down, the president achieved much more than the dismantling of Soviet missiles: he "exploded the myth that in every situation the Soviets were prepared to run greater risks than we."[25] Again, note the importance of avoiding "inaction," having less to do with advancing hard interests (the removal of missiles from Cuba) than with proving that "action" was possible.

We now know that the resolution of the Cuban missile crisis, which brought the world to the brink of the nuclear abyss, was settled not with dramatic televised displays of resolve but with back-channel compromises. No matter. For Kissinger, the lesson to be drawn from the crisis was twofold: first, "initiative creates its

own consensus," and, second, statesmen shouldn't wait until all
the facts are in before they seize that initiative.* "Conjecture,"
Kissinger wrote in his tribute to Kennedy, is a preferable foundation for action than data and facts, for an overreliance on information can be paralyzing. "The dilemma of any statesman is that
he can never be certain about the probable course of events."
Kissinger continued: "In reaching a decision, he must inevitably
act on the basis of an intuition that is inherently unprovable. If
he insists on certainty, he runs the danger of becoming a prisoner
of events."

Here, then, in the early winter of 1962, is an almost perfect
exposition of what after September 11, 2001, would become known
as the "one-percent doctrine," as expressed by Vice President Dick
Cheney. Cheney declared that if there is even the slightest chance
that a threat will be realized, the United States would act as if that
threat were a foregone conclusion: "It's not about our analysis, or
finding a preponderance of evidence," he said. "It's about our
response."

"In the decade ahead, the West will have to lift its sights to
encompass a more embracing concept of reality," Kissinger wrote
in 1963, hoping momentum resulting from Kennedy's bold actions
in Cuba could carry over into other areas of foreign policy and
build that "new world" he talked about with Schlesinger.[26]

---

* We also now know that Moscow's bid to place nuclear missiles in Cuba was prompted
by Washington's involvement in the 1961 Bay of Pigs invasion and Kennedy's stagger-
ing arms escalation. Also key to understanding Cuban motives in wanting the missiles was Operation Mongoose (a covert CIA operation put into place following the
failed Bay of Pigs invasion designed to topple the Cuban government), ongoing acts
of sabotage carried out by Washington-backed anti-Castro proxies, and the fear of
another invasion.

Kissinger's first visit to South Vietnam was in October 1965, less than a year after Lyndon Baines Johnson decided to escalate the war with ground troops. There, he was briefed by Daniel Ellsberg, then stationed at the US embassy in Saigon. Kissinger took Ellsberg's advice to not waste time talking to top officials but seek out Vietnamese or Americans who had been in the country for a long time. "I was impressed that Kissinger actually acted on my advice," Ellsberg recalls.[27] And what Kissinger learned troubled him deeply: Washington was relying on corrupt, unpopular, and incompetent Saigon allies, North Vietnamese sanctuaries in Laos and Cambodia made a military solution impossible, and the one pressure tactic the United States did have—the bombing of North Vietnam—would soon "mobilize world opinion against us."*

---

* If Kissinger had the soon-to-be dissident Ellsberg perched on his left shoulder, Edward Lansdale, an unrepentant Cold Warrior, sat on his right. Lansdale, an old Asia hand, also briefed Kissinger on his trips to Vietnam; his experience in the Pacific dated back to World War II and ran through the counterinsurgency in the Philippines and the Korean War. Lansdale was somewhat marginalized by the time Kissinger established regular contact with him in 1965, serving as the assistant to the US ambassador in the Saigon embassy. But earlier, during the covert years of deepening American involvement in South Vietnam in the mid-1950s, Lansdale was one of the key figures who took "black bag" counterterrorism and psychological warfare tactics learned in the Philippines and applied them in Vietnam. Such tactics were later incorporated into Phoenix, the CIA's infamous assassination program. Lansdale sent his South Vietnamese contacts Kissinger's way when they were visiting the United States, so as to "revive your faith in your fellow man in the good fight." And as it became clear that Johnson wouldn't fully commit to what Kissinger thought was needed to win in South Vietnam, Kissinger commiserated with Lansdale, writing in a June 2, 1967, letter: "You have been much on my mind in the recent months. What a tragic process to have our bureaucracy clash with the aspirations of a shattered society." Lansdale is a good example of the many-headed-hydra US national security state: between his tours in Vietnam, he was in charge of the program of destabilization against the Cuban government authorized by Kennedy on November 30, 1961, following the failed Bay of Pigs invasion, which in turn set off the chain of reactions that led to the Cuban missile crisis. Kissinger and Lansdale shared a common mentor, Fritz Kraemer, a refugee from Nazi Germany who tutored a number of influential military and intelligence officers. For Lansdale's connection with Kraemer, see Kraemer's obituary, *New York Times*, November 19, 2003. For Kissinger's correspondence with Lansdale, see Hoover Institution Archives, Edward G. Lansdale Papers, box 53.

Upon his return, Kissinger privately told Cyrus Vance and Averill Harriman, top Johnson officials, that "we couldn't win."[28] But he continued to publically support the war effort. Why? It is impossible, of course, to answer that question definitively, to judge what mix of ambition, considered opinion, and moral judgment moved Kissinger to brush away his doubts and push on. But conceptually at least, he got caught in the vortex of his own circular argument: inaction has to be avoided in order to show that action is possible. The purpose of not questioning the projection of American power in Vietnam was to avoid weakening American purpose.

Upon returning from his first visit to South Vietnam in late 1965, Kissinger threw himself into a campaign to build public support for ongoing intervention. In early December, he joined 189 other scholars from Harvard, Yale, and fifteen other New England universities in an open letter expressing confidence that Johnson's policies would help the "people of South Vietnam . . . determine their own destiny."[29] "A Vietcong victory will spell disasters," said the letter. Then, later that month, he led a Harvard team against a group of Oxford opponents of the war in a debate held in Great Britain and broadcast nationally in the United States on CBS. Kissinger passionately defended the bombing of North Vietnam, insisting that it was not a violation of international law. He also invoked the analogy of World War II, saying Washington's actions in Indochina were as righteous and justified as they were in Nazi Germany.[30]

Bob Shrum, who went on to become a Democratic political consultant, was on Kissinger's team and says that when he today watches a recording of the debate he is "amazed by two things: how young we look, even Kissinger, and how wrong we were."[31]

———

Wrong or right, it didn't much matter. For Kissinger it was win-win. If Vietnam had gone well, he could have claimed it as validation of his "little war thesis." The war didn't, of course, go well, leading Kissinger to confirm his original belief that America lacked the resolve necessary to fight either small or major wars. "I'm absolutely unreconstructed on that subject," he said in 2011, referring to the United States' defeat in Southeast Asia. "I believe that most of what went wrong in Vietnam we did to ourselves."*

---

* For someone who has insisted that it is only in retrospect that historical events seem inevitable, that at the time statesmen have the "freedom" to choose a range of responses to any given crisis, Kissinger often presents his support for the Vietnam War as predetermined by the moment's political and intellectual climate. But others of equal position and similar worldview chose differently. Born in Germany in 1904, Hans Morgenthau is considered the founder of America's postwar realist approach to international relations, one of the most influential diplomatic scholars of the twentieth century. Like Kissinger, Morgenthau, educated at the University of Frankfurt before moving into the US academy, was influenced by Continental philosophy (including Spengler). Like Kissinger, he rejected the fetish for deductive formulas to explain human events, offering, as one scholar describes, a "sweeping denunciation of all rationalized political science." He believed "facts have no social meaning in themselves": "our sensual experience," our "hopes and fears, our memories, intentions and expectations" create "social facts." Like Kissinger, he was a realist who didn't think reality was objective. "The social world itself," he wrote, "is an artifact of man's mind as the reflection of his thoughts and the creation of his actions." And like Kissinger, he defined power not as an objective condition but as a "psychological relation," based on the "expectations of benefits" and "the fear of disadvantages." Unlike Kissinger, however, Morgenthau didn't let his critique of postwar positivism lead to a position of radical relativism; he insisted on the need to distinguish right from wrong. His very early pragmatic opposition to US involvement in Vietnam in the 1950s evolved, by the mid-1960s, into a strong moral critique of Washington's policy. For Morgenthau on Vietnam, see Ellen Glaser Rafshoon, "A Realist's Moral Opposition to War: Hans J. Morgenthau and Vietnam," *Peace and Change* (January 2001).

2

Ends and Means

What one considers an end, and what one considers a mean, depends
essentially on the metaphysics of one's system, and on the concept
one has of one's self and one's relationship to the universe.

—Henry Kissinger

At Harvard as a graduate student, Henry Kissinger and his doctoral
adviser, William Yandell Elliott, often took long Sunday walks
together in Concord. On one of these outings, Elliott—described
by the *Harvard Crimson* as "a large, flamboyant Virginian . . . a
grandiose, hulking figure who often wore a white plantation suit
and a Panama hat"—urged his protégé to live his life by Imman-
uel Kant's famous ethical imperative: "Treat every human being,
including yourself, as an end and never a means." That dictum
was a response to the utilitarian calculus influential during Kant's
life that promoted the greatest good for the greatest number of
people over the interests of the individual. Kant was especially
appealing to arch–Cold Warriors like Elliott, who saw Soviet
Communism as a vast, monstrous application of instrumental
morality.

Kissinger was very familiar with Kant, having grappled, in his

1950 undergraduate thesis, with the paradox that is at the heart of
Kantian philosophy: human beings are entirely free *and* history is
inevitably advancing according to God's divine plan toward a world
of perpetual peace. Kissinger accepted Kant's idea of freedom but,
as a child of the Holocaust and an observer of the Gulag, couldn't
accept Kant's theology, especially the belief that existence had a
transcendent purpose. For Kissinger, the past was nothing but "a
series of meaningless incidents." History had no significance in
itself. Whatever "meaning" human beings might assign to past
events came not from the working out of a higher, external and
objective moral plan, Kissinger argued, but subjectively, from
within: "The realm of freedom and necessity can not be reconciled
except by an inward experience."[1]

Kissinger, as a diplomat, is often described as amoral, as believing that values such as universal human rights have no role to play
in the implementation of foreign policy. He reportedly once said,
paraphrasing Goethe, that if he "had to choose between justice and
disorder, on the one hand, and injustice and order, on the other,"
he would "always choose the latter."[2] This vision, though, isn't
amoral. Rather, contrary to Elliott's injunction, it suggests a utilitarian, or relative, moralism: a greater good can be achieved for the
greatest number of people when great powers do what they need to
do to create an orderly, stable, and peaceful interstate system, which,
in turn, might nurture whatever fragile justice human beings are
capable of achieving.

Kissinger's embrace of a relative, rather than an absolute,
morality is suggested in another story from his graduate school days
at Harvard. In 1953, during a seminar, Elliott pushed Kissinger
to acknowledge that "reality," and hence ethics, must exist.[3] "Well,
now wait a minute, Henry," the professor said, in reaction to
Kissinger's lengthy exposition that argued that there was no such
thing as truth. "There must be a metaphysical structure of reality
which is the true structure."

Kissinger's response effectively used Kantian existentialism (the idea that human beings are radically free) to undermine Kantian morality. "We can hardly insist," he said, "on both our freedom and on the necessity of our values." We can't, in other words, be both radically free and subject to a fixed moral requirement. Kissinger admitted that some people might find such a position a "counsel of despair," since it rejects the possibility of any foundational truth. But, he said, it was actually liberating since it allowed men to escape, however fleetingly, the misery of existence: "Our values are indeed necessary, but not because of an order of nature; rather, they are made necessary by the act of commitment to the metaphysics of a system. This may be the ultimate meaning of personality, of the loneliness of man, and also of his ability to transcend the inevitability of his existence," Kissinger said.

Then, a bit later in the discussion, Kissinger quoted Kant's moral imperative back to Elliott, with an addendum: "What one considers an end, and what one considers a mean, depends essentially on the metaphysics of one's system, and on the concept one has of one's self and one's relationship to the universe."*

Elliott didn't seem to quite grasp the radical existentialism of Kissinger's position. When you talk about "contingent values," he responded to Kissinger's comment, you are referring to "that realm of freedom in which man has not learned that there is a plan

---

* I asked Maureen Linker, a philosopher at the University of Michigan, Dearborn, her opinion of this reading of Kant's categorical imperative. She answered: "Kissinger's point that what one considers an end and a means is dependent on one's metaphysical system is a distortion of Kant. Kant would say that the life of any rational agent is the only acceptable ends. Kant argued for a universal and absolute moral system against relativism. . . . He would have no part of Kissinger's interpretation." In his undergraduate thesis, as well, Kissinger in effect uses Kant's notion of freedom against Kant's ethical absolutism, in a way that equates his critique of historical causality with fixed morality. "Values," he wrote, "are, at best, a mode of causality." Just as trying to find the true meaning of history always "exhausts itself in the riddle of the first cause," trying to find the foundation on which to base one's ethical position always exhausts itself in the riddle of first principles.

beyond his own plan which he dimly and imperfectly recognizes that orients him toward God." Elliott here was holding to a more standard interpretation of Kant, one that accepted the paradox that individuals were both radically free and that there was a divine "plan." How, he asked Kissinger, could one "reconcile this demonic freedom . . . with a return to a divine will, through which man, through prayer, submits himself?" Kissinger didn't answer, but a story told by the late journalist David Halberstam suggests that perhaps Kissinger's relativism eventually rankled Elliott. At the professor's retirement party, as colleagues gathered to say goodbye, Elliott "visited each with parting words. Almost all his comments were generous, until he came to Kissinger: 'Henry,' he began, 'you're brilliant. But you're arrogant. In fact you're the most arrogant man I've ever met.' Kissinger became ashen-faced. 'Mark my words,' Elliott continued, 'your arrogance is going to get you in real trouble one day.' "4

The details of Henry Kissinger's political ascendance, how in a remarkably short period of time he became one of the most power-ful men in American history, have been told before. And when they have, it has usually been to highlight their sordidness, to establish the transgression that made Kissinger's rise possible: In late 1968, Democrat Hubert Humphrey and Republican Richard Nixon were locked in a close race for the White House. The war in Vietnam was the critical issue of the election. With both candi-dates claiming to be the best chance for "peace," any progress in informal talks then taking place in Paris between Washington and Hanoi would benefit Humphrey. Kissinger, still a Harvard profes-sor, used his contacts in the outgoing Johnson administration, including a former student, to acquire information about the negotiations, which he then passed on to Nixon's campaign. In turn, Nixon's people used the intelligence to preempt a possible truce. Nixon won the election and, in gratitude, gave Kissinger the job of national security adviser.[5]

But the events need to be told again, not to rehearse culpability but because they capture nearly perfectly Kissinger's philosophy of history. Kissinger in the fall of 1968 was applying in practice what he had long argued for in theory: an insistence that individuals have a degree of freedom in shaping historical events, that they are not bound by any "true structure," that risk is a requirement of real statesmanship, that initiative creates its own reality, and that political leaders shouldn't wait on the facts to seize that initiative. Transcendence was possible, despair could be avoided, and ends could be means or means could be ends. Quite so: negotiations to end the Vietnam War became the means of Kissinger's ascent. Thus what William Elliott described as a "demoniac" individual freedom was reconciled to the metaphysics of the system—that is, to the national security state. Kissinger was working out his "relationship to the universe."

The story of Kissinger's involvement in the 1968 campaign starts with a question: Why did Kissinger—a close associate of the liberal Republican Nelson Rockefeller and occasional adviser to Democratic administrations—decide to throw in with Nixon, whom he considered a resentful right-winger?

"Richard Nixon is the most dangerous, of all the men running, to have as President," Kissinger said just before the Republican National Convention in Miami.[6] Kissinger was stunned, therefore, when Rockefeller lost to Nixon at that convention, according to the journalists Marvin and Bernard Kalb. "He wept," they wrote.[7] "Now the Republican Party is a disaster," Kissinger said.[8] "That man Nixon is not fit to be president." He knew of what he spoke, for Kissinger had been in charge of keeping Rockefeller's "shit files" on Nixon, "several filing cabinets" containing what today is called oppositional, or negative, research.[9] After Nixon's nomination, Kissinger slept through the morning, woken only by a telephone call from a friend. Kissinger, the friend later remarked, sounded "more shaken, more disappointed, more generally depressed than I had ever known him." "That man Nixon," Kissinger said, "doesn't have the right to rule."

Kissinger himself, at a public conference organized in 2010 by the State Department on American involvement in Vietnam, cited his opposition to Nixon as evidence that he couldn't have been involved in schemes to get him elected: "I had never met Richard Nixon when he appointed me. And I had spent 12 years of my life trying to keep him from becoming President. I was the principal foreign policy advisor of Nelson Rockefeller. So when I read some of these books of how carefully I plotted my ascent to that office, I think it is important to keep—to remember that I was a close friend of Nelson Rockefeller and, actually, I knew Hubert Humphrey a lot better. Well, I didn't know Nixon at all."[10]

At that same conference, however, the diplomat Richard Holbrooke told a story that helps explain Kissinger's accommodation. Holbrooke spoke immediately after Kissinger, reminiscing about 1968, the assassinations of Martin Luther King and Robert F. Kennedy and the protests and riots over race and war. "There's never been a year like '68 in our lives," he said. Then Holbrooke described how that summer he and Kissinger were in Martha's Vineyard, watching the Chicago Democratic Convention on TV. The police were beating protesters outside and Democrats were savaging each other inside. Nixon had already won his party's nomination, and, with the "destruction of the Democratic Party" being broadcast to the nation, Kissinger turned to Holbrooke and said, "This is the end of me." "You remember?" Holbrooke asked, gesturing to Kissinger in the audience. Kissinger is off camera, but the crowd laughed and maybe he did too.

Holbrooke sets an evocative scene: Kissinger, on a warm late August in Martha's Vineyard, the summer heartland of America's

Eastern establishment, watching the televised disintegration of that establishment and experiencing one of the longest and darkest nights of his soul. He cried: "Nelson Rockefeller and Hubert Humphrey are being destroyed. I'll never serve in the government again."

The despair was fleeting. Kissinger acted immediately, positioning himself as useful to both the autumnal New Deal Democrats and the rising Republican Right. A few days after the Democratic Convention, Kissinger, still on the Vineyard and now sitting on a beach in West Tisbury, offered Rockefeller's Nixon files to another summering Harvard professor, Samuel Huntington, who was working for the Humphrey campaign. "It was a wonderful offer," Huntington later recalled.[11]

One that Kissinger never made good on. Even as he was running down Nixon to the Democrats ("I've hated Nixon for years," he said, stalling Zbigniew Brzezinski, who was trying to get Kissinger to turn over the files), he was reaching out to Richard V. Allen, one of Nixon's top foreign policy advisers, to say that he would soon be traveling to Paris to assess the status of talks between Washington and Hanoi and would be available to advise the campaign on the matter. In Paris Kissinger cultivated contacts on Johnson's negotiating team, including a lawyer named Daniel Davidson. Davidson admitted he was "charmed and enchanted" by Kissinger. As he put it, "he had an intelligence, a sense of humor, and a conspiratorial manner that swept you into his camp."[12]

Holbrooke was also in the delegation: "Henry was the only person outside of the government we were authorized [by the White House, because of his past position as an adviser] to discuss the negotiations with," he told Kissinger's biographer, Walter Isaacson. "We trusted him. It is not stretching the truth to say that the Nixon campaign had a secret source within the U.S. negotiating team."[13] When Kissinger returned to Cambridge two weeks later, he called the Nixon campaign again, reporting that "something big was afoot regarding Vietnam." Kissinger advised that Nixon keep any statement on the war he might make vague, so as not to be "undercut by negotiations." Diplomats in Paris were working on a deal: Johnson would halt the bombing of North Vietnam, and Hanoi would reciprocate by agreeing to enter into formal negotiations with South Vietnam.

Kissinger contacted Nixon's staffers a number of times thereafter, speaking most often with Allen. It was Allen who first described, to Seymour Hersh, Kissinger's role in derailing the talks and over the years he has elaborated: "Henry Kissinger, on his own, volunteered information to us through a spy, a former student, that he had in the Paris peace talks, who would call him and debrief, and Kissinger called me from pay phones and we spoke in German. The fact that my German is better than his did not at all hinder my communication with Henry and he offloaded mostly every night what had happened that day in Paris."[14]

Kissinger placed his last call at the end of October. "I've got important information," he said: the North Vietnamese had agreed to participate in official peace talks, scheduled to begin November 6, one day after the presidential vote. They had "broken open the champagne" in Paris, Kissinger reported. A few hours after Kissinger's call to the Nixon campaign, Johnson suspended the bombing.[15] Announcement of a deal between Washington, Saigon, and Hanoi might have pushed Humphrey, who was closing in on Nixon in the polls, over the top. But there would be no deal: the South Vietnamese scuttled the settlement, after hearing from Nixon's campaign that they could get better terms from a Republican administration: "Saigon Cannot Join Paris Talks under Present Plan," ran the above-the-fold November 2 headline of the *New York Times*.

Later that day, Nixon, campaigning in Austin, Texas, said: "In view of early reports this morning, prospects for peace are not as bright as they were even a few days ago."[16]

Nixon's people had acted fast. Using Kissinger's intelligence and working through Anna Chennault (the Chinese-born widow of a World War II lieutenant general and a prominent conservative activist), they urged the South Vietnamese to derail the talks, promising better conditions were Nixon to be elected. President Johnson was informed of the meddling. Through wiretaps and intercepts, he learned that Nixon's campaign was telling the South Vietnamese that Nixon was going to win and "to hold on a while longer." If the White House had gone public with the information, the outrage might also have swung the election to Humphrey. But Johnson hesitated. He feared that "Nixon's conniving" was just too explosive. "This is treason," he said. "It would rock the world."[17]

Johnson stayed silent, Nixon won, and the war went on.

The fact that Kissinger participated in an intrigue that extended the war for five pointless years—seven, if you count the fighting between the 1973 Paris Peace Accords and the 1975 fall of Saigon—is undeniable.* Adding to the evidence is Kissinger himself. He's been caught on tape twice, on recordings recently released, admitting he passed on useful information to Nixon.

The first recording is of a meeting held by Nixon, Kissinger, and Bob Haldeman in the Oval Office on June 17, 1971. The three men were trying to come up with a plan to contain the fallout from

---

* The historian Ken Hughes, in his recent *Chasing Shadows: The Nixon Tapes, the Chennault Affair, and the Origins of Watergate* (2014), pp. 175–77, cites a Nixon campaign memo that describes Kissinger as a "top diplomatic source who is secretly with us and has access to the Paris talks and other information."

Daniel Ellsberg's leaking of the Pentagon Papers to the *New York Times*. One idea, suggested by Haldeman and seconded by Nixon, was to "blackmail" Lyndon Johnson and force him to issue a public statement condemning Ellsberg's leak. Nixon believed that a file existed—the so-called "bombing halt" file—that held proof that Johnson stopped bombing North Vietnam to help Humphrey win the election.* The material was thought to be in a safe at the Brookings Institution, a Washington think tank, and Nixon, in this meeting, ordered Haldeman to use "thievery" to get it. This was the beginning of the black-bag group known as the "plumbers," who would go on to burgle the Democratic Party headquarters at the Watergate Hotel.[18] "Goddamn it, get in and get those files. Blow the safe and get it," Nixon instructed.

It's a disreputable scene: a president and his top advisers, including Kissinger, sitting around discussing blackmailing a former president and blowing up safes.† For our purposes here, what is important is that Kissinger reveals that he knew that Johnson

---

* A secret file with damning information did in fact exist. It had been compiled by Johnson's advisers and secreted out of the White House upon Nixon's victory. Ken Hughes argues that Nixon wanted it because it contained evidence not of Johnson's perfidy (since Johnson, according to Hughes, didn't time the bombing halt to benefit Humphrey) but of Nixon's sabotage of the peace talks. On May 14, 1973, just after Johnson's death, Walt Rostow, Johnson's national security adviser, deposited the bombing halt file in the LBJ Presidential Library in Austin, Texas. He appended a note that, in part, read: "The attached file contains the information available to me and (I believe) the bulk of the information available to President Johnson on the activities of Mrs. Chennault and other Republicans just before the presidential election of 1968." Rostow wanted the file to remain classified indefinitely: "After fifty years the Director of the LBJ Library . . . may, alone, open this file. . . . If he believes the material it contains should not be opened for research [at that time], I would wish him empowered to re-close the file for another fifty years when the procedure outlined above should be repeated." Rostow's instructions notwithstanding, the library began declassifying the file in 1994. Despite renewed attention to the Watergate break-in on its fortieth anniversary, scholars and reporters, aside from Ken Hughes and journalist Robert Parry, have mostly ignored its contents.

† Richard Goodwin, JFK's speechwriter, described Nixon's inner circle, including Henry Kissinger, as the "bureaucratization of the criminal class."

didn't time the bombing halt to help Humphrey because, contrary to his latter statements, he had access to classified information about the Paris negotiations:

> KISSINGER: I used to give you info—I used to—you remember, I used to give you information about it at the time so I have no—
>
> NIXON: I know.
>
> KISSINGER: I mean, about the timing.
>
> NIXON: Yeah.
>
> KISSINGER: But I, to the best of my knowledge, there was never any conversation in which they said we'll hold it until the end of October. I wasn't in on the discussions here. I just saw the instructions to Harriman.

The reference is to Averell Harriman, who headed the US Paris delegation. Kissinger is admitting not only that he passed on information to Nixon's campaign but that he had access to specific, classified negotiating instructions—that is, the terms the White House was willing to accept, the concessions it was offering, and the timeline it was proposing for drawing down hostilities.

Kissinger's second admission, which came nearly a year later, on April 19, 1972, is more succinct. It was in response to Nixon's opinion that the North Vietnamese would begin to soften their negotiating position in the period prior to the 1972 presidential elections. The reason he thought this was because that's what they did in 1968, compromising with Johnson's envoys in Paris prior to the presidential elections. "They are quite aware of American political things," Nixon told Kissinger. Kissinger agreed: "As I told you all that fall, what the game was."[19] "Only eleven words," the historian Jeffrey P. Kimball writes, "but with these words Kissinger affirmed that in the fall of 1968 he had passed to 'you'—that is, not only the Nixon camp but Nixon himself—information about the looming diplomatic breakthrough in Paris."[20]

Guardians of Kissinger's legacy say his accusers misread or overstate the importance of such evidence: Nixon would have won the election anyway; the information Kissinger passed on wasn't very specific; the Nixon campaign had other sources, so sabotage of the talks would have taken place even without Kissinger's participation; and the South Vietnamese didn't want a Humphrey presidency and would have balked of their own accord, without any prompting from Nixon. Intentionally or not, these excuses mimic the approach to the past Kissinger outlined in his undergraduate thesis. Truth is not found in "the facts of history" but from a "construct" of hypotheticals, counterfactuals, and conjectures.

Yet, in a way, Kissinger's defenders are right. Not that Kissinger wasn't implicated in Nixon's preelection machinations. He was. But focusing too intently on the search for evidence establishing culpability can miss the episode's larger meaning, its importance in Kissinger's ascent, how it allowed him to perform a trial run of his philosophy of politics.

Four years earlier, Kissinger had elaborated on the importance of political imagination in his discussion of JFK's response to the Cuban missile crisis. The "essence" of good foreign policy, Kissinger wrote, "is its contingency; its success depends on the correctness of an estimate which is in part conjectural."[21] The problem, though, is that successful nation-states rationalize their foreign policy. They create a foreign service, with protocols, guidelines, clear procedures, and grades for promotion, administered by functionaries who depend on experts deeply versed in the particularities of their particular region. The whole system is set up to strive for "safety" and "predictability," to work for the maintenance and reproduction of the status quo. "The attempt to conduct policy bureaucratically leads to a quest for calculability which tends to become a prisoner of events." Routinization leads to caution, caution to inaction, inaction to atrophy. Success is measured by "mistakes avoided rather than by goals achieved."[22]

In contrast, great statesmen, the ones who will truly make a difference, never let themselves become paralyzed by a "pre-vision of catastrophes." They are agile, thriving on "perpetual creation, on a constant redefinition of goals."[23]

This was a good description of Kissinger in late 1968, nimble and fleet-footed, acting incisively on conjecture and seizing the spirit of the moment. No matter how many contacts he cultivated, no matter how many late nights he spent in Parisian cafes whispering into the ears of young staffers or how many German conversations he had from street-corner pay phones, his defenders probably are right. Even with access to Johnson's negotiating instructions, he couldn't have had exact information about the decisions being made at the White House. He had to have been winging it, at least to some degree, guessing at what others knew, imagining what others would do with that guess, playing the angles, sussing out the chance, all the while giving the appearance of composure and certainty. Nixon himself called the information Kissinger passed on "uncomfortably vague." Though he was impressed by his flair for the covert: "One factor that had most convinced me of Kissinger's credibility was the length to which he went to protect his secrecy."[24]

Sailing to Europe shortly after the start of Harvard's fall term, Kissinger might have feared that the trip was time wasted, a fool's errand. And once back, he took an enormous risk. If things had broken a different way, he could have been burned with both political parties or, even worse, brought up on charges. It is illegal for private citizens to interfere in the foreign relations of the United States. "Kissinger had proven his mettle by tipping us," Richard

Allen told Hersh. "It took some balls to give us those tips"; it was a "pretty dangerous thing for him to be screwing around with national security."

Brushing aside any "pre-visions of catastrophes" he might have had, Kissinger leveraged a high-stakes, dead-heat presidential campaign, using the anxieties of those around him as the raw material of "fresh creation." Rather than fall "prisoner of events," as he feared he might during that moment of weakness on the Vineyard, Kissinger busted out. He wasn't so much seizing an opportunity as creating one. After Nixon's victory, Kissinger did what he could to keep Nixon's attention, including starting the false rumor that the outgoing Johnson administration planned to either depose or assassinate the president of South Vietnam, Nguyen Van Thieu, before leaving office. He then arranged, via William F. Buckley, to have the rumor passed on to Nixon. Kissinger said he wanted the incoming president to know that "if Thieu meets the same fate as Diem [an earlier South Vietnam leader who was deposed and executed in a coup that the Kennedy administration helped initiate], the word will go out to the nations of the world that it may be dangerous to be America's enemy, but to be America's friend is fatal." The historian Stephen Ambrose says that what Kissinger was doing was playing to Nixon's keenness for "secrecy, rumor, intrigue, and circuitous communication, all covered by a veneer of concern for high principle (America must stick by its friends) and highlighted by Kissinger's dramatic phraseology."[25]

Kissinger wanted a top spot in Nixon's White House, but even in his wildest dreams he couldn't have imagined the reward his risk taking would bring. A victorious Nixon not only made him the head of the National Security Council but instructed him to reorganize that institution so as to take control of foreign policy from the State Department and the Defense Department.

It's worth pausing a moment to consider the above narrative in truncated, chronological form, since it conveys just how fast

Kissinger's wheel of fortune was spinning, the quickness with which he went from hopelessness, from believing his career was collapsing along with the middle ground of American politics—from being confused with Professor Schlesinger!—to being anointed Nixon's national security adviser.

August 5–8	Republican Convention. Rockefeller loses nomination to Richard Nixon. Kissinger is devastated.
August 9	Kissinger gives interview on New York radio voicing "grave doubts" about Nixon. A few days later, Kissinger calls Nixon a "disaster."
August 26–29	In Chicago, Humphrey wins Democratic nomination. In Martha's Vineyard, Kissinger, watching the protests outside the convention center on TV, despairs that American politics is radicalizing and he will have no place in it.
Late August	A few days after the convention, Kissinger offers Rockefeller's oppositional files on Nixon to Humphrey's campaign. He never delivers.
September 10	Kissinger calls Allen, saying he is going to Paris and offering to relay information he obtains on the negotiations.
September 17	Kissinger arrives in Europe on the SS Île de France. Harvard's fall semester will soon begin. Kissinger scheduled to teach two classes: an undergraduate lecture course, Principles of International Relations, and his graduate seminar.
September 26	Back in Cambridge from Paris, Kissinger calls John Mitchell and says "something big was afoot."
October	Kissinger has at least two more conversations with Nixon's people, according to the historian Robert Dallek, warning of the possibility of a bombing halt. He continues, though, to disparage the Republican candidate, describing him in mid-October as "paranoiac."

October 31	Kissinger calls Allen: "I've got some important information." Twelve hours later, Johnson halts bombing.
November 2	South Vietnam's president, Nguyen Van Thieu announces that his country will not participate in peace talks under the terms agreed on by Washington and Hanoi.
November 5	Nixon beats Humphrey. Kissinger (around November 12) arranges to have a false report passed on to Nixon that the outgoing Johnson administration planned to depose or assassinate Thieu.
November 22	Nixon summons Kissinger to his headquarters at the Pierre Hotel in Manhattan. The meeting takes place three days later, on November 25. The men discuss the importance of setting up a centralized, strong National Security Council that will run foreign policy from the White House.
November 26	Kissinger officially offered job of national security adviser.
December 16	Kissinger's last class at Harvard.
Late December	Kissinger submits detailed plan to reorganize the NSC, investing enormous power in the council and its director.
December 27	Nixon approves the plan.

Nixon's inauguration was still a month away and Kissinger was already one of the most powerful men on the planet.

Having now lived a very long life, first acting in the name of the strongest state in world history and then moving into a realm of unparalleled private privilege, Kissinger has enjoyed great luxury, wealth, and public acclaim. He even won a Nobel Peace Prize for ending a war that he encouraged in its inception and helped extend in its duration. That he was able to pull off the original gambit that brought such attainment—that, instead of being banished to Harvard or indicted, he became the most powerful national security adviser in American history—proved the validity of his theories, that with imagination certain individuals could grasp the inner movement of history and manipulate it to their advantage.

From this point forward, every single policy that Henry Kissinger advocated as being good, both materially and morally, for the long-run, strategic ends of the United States also happened to be good for the personal advancement of Henry Kissinger.

3

Kissinger Smiled

Oh no, we won't stop the bombing. Absolutely not.

—Henry Kissinger

Richard Nixon was inaugurated on January 20, 1969. A month later, on February 24, Henry Kissinger and his military aide, Colonel Alexander Haig, met with Colonel Ray Sitton, to begin the planning of Menu, the code name for the B-52 bombing of Cambodia. Extreme secrecy was required. Nixon, elected promising to end the conflict, feared the public backlash that an escalation of the war into Cambodia might provoke. And the White House wanted to circumvent Congress, which exercised its power over the armed services largely through the appropriations of funds needed to conduct specific missions. Many, including Nixon and Kissinger, felt that Congress wouldn't have approved the bombing of Cambodia, since Cambodia was a neutral country that the United States wasn't at war with.

Kissinger, Haig, and Sitton came up with a simple but

comprehensive deception.* Sitton, based on recommendations he received from General Creighton Abrams, the commander of military operations in Vietnam, would work up a number of targets in Cambodia to be struck. Then he would bring them to Kissinger and Haig in the White House for approval. Kissinger was very hands-on, revising some of Sitton's work. "I don't know what he was using as his reason for varying them," Sitton later recalled. "Strike here in this area," Kissinger would tell him, "or strike here in that area." Once Kissinger was satisfied with the proposed target, Sitton would backchannel the coordinates to Saigon, and from there a courier would pass them on to the appropriate radar stations, where an officer would make the last minute switch. The

---

* It wasn't until 1973 that Congress and the public became aware of the secret Menu bombing of Cambodia, after a whistleblower named Major Hal Knight wrote a letter to Senator William Proxmire informing him of his involvement, while stationed at Ben Hoa Air Force in South Vietnam in 1970, in the deceit. At the time, congressional investigators and journalists couldn't find the link connecting what Knight was doing in South Vietnam—burning documents and writing false reports—to the White House. General Abrams, for instance, gave detailed testimony to the Senate Armed Services Committee, but insisted that he didn't know who came up with the protocols for deception: "The instructions on precisely how this would be handled at the time it was approved all emanated from Washington." "Who ordered the falsification of the records?" one senator asked Abrams. "I just do not know," he answered. Later, though, after Kissinger was out of office, Seymour Hersh (in his 1983 book *The Price of Power*, pp. 59–65) identified Colonel Sitton as that missing link. There has been very little follow-up to Hersh's success in establishing Kissinger as the architect of the so-called duel reporting system. But I've located a lengthy and, as far as I can tell, largely unknown oral history conducted with Sitton in 1984. Now deceased, Sitton discusses the details of the deception and confirms the veracity of Hersh's account: "I was in shock," Sitton said, referring to being confronted by Hersh with leaked documents indicating his role in plotting the bombing of Cambodia, "I couldn't believe he was able to get those things." Hersh was wrong about some of the bombing's technical details, Sitton says, but those "inaccuracies" aren't "all that important." "He made a lot of assumptions, thinking he was so smart he knew that much about it," Sitton said. "He didn't do too badly," Sitton acknowledges. For the interview, see LTG Ray B. Sitton, interview by Marcus J. Boyle, transcript, K239.0512-1570, United States Air Force Oral History Collection, Archives Branch, Air Force Historical Research Agency, Maxwell Air Force Base, Alabama (see especially pp. 152–64 for Sitton's description of working with Haig and Kissinger to develop the double-bookkeeping protocol). For Abrams's testimony and quotations, see *Bombing in Cambodia: Hearings before the Committee on Armed Services, United States Senate* (1973), pp. 343, 360, 363.

B-52 would be diverted from its "cover" target in South Vietnam into Cambodia, where it would drop its bomb load on the real target. When the run was complete, the officer in charge of the deception would burn whatever documents—maps, computer printouts, radar reports, messages, and so on—that might reveal the actual flight. Then he would write up false "post-strike" paperwork, indicating that the South Vietnam sortie was flown as planned. This way, Congress and Pentagon administrators would be provided "phony target coordinates" and other forged data, so as to account for actual expenditures—of fuel, bombs, and spare parts—without ever having to reveal that Cambodia was being bombed.

Sitton, an expert on B-52s who was assigned to the Joint Chiefs of Staff, said he did often wonder what he was doing participating in a shadow chain of command, bypassing superiors in the Department of Defense, plotting bombing targets in a vaulted room deep in the bowels of the Pentagon and then secreting them into Kissinger's office for approval. "I kind of felt I was way out on a limb and skating on some pretty thin ice with all my trips to the west basement of the White House." But whenever he expressed these concerns to higher-ups, he was told: "Whatever you are doing, keep on doing it. It seems to be working. Do just what you are doing. When you get a call to go to the White House, go, because you don't really have any choice."

That's *how* an illegal, covert war came to be waged on a neutral country, a war run out of a basement by a presidential appointee who a few months earlier was a Harvard professor.

Why Nixon and Kissinger felt they needed to wage a secret, illegal war on a desperately poor country of rice farmers and water buffalos is another story.

Richard Nixon wanted a tough line against North Vietnam, believing it would force Hanoi to make the concessions necessary to bring the conflict to a face-saving conclusion. Already, before the November election, Nixon had shared with Bob Haldeman what has come to be known as the "madman theory." Walking along a Key Biscayne beach, Nixon told his future chief of state that he wanted the North Vietnamese "to believe I've reached the point where I might do anything to stop the war. We'll just slip the word to them that, 'for God's sake, you know Nixon is obsessed about Communists. We can't restrain him when he's angry—and he has his hand on the nuclear button'—and Ho Chi Minh himself will be in Paris in two days begging for peace."[1]

Kissinger was more than willing to oblige. "Toughness," after all, was a leitmotif that ran through much of his statecraft, the idea that war and diplomacy are inseparable and that, to be effective, diplomats need to be able to punish and persuade in equal, unrestricted measure. In fact, the madman theory was an extension of Kissinger's philosophy of the deed—that power wasn't power unless one was willing to use it, that the purpose of action was to neutralize the inertia of inaction.*

Within days of Nixon's January 20 inauguration, Kissinger

---

* To let "slip" the fact that Nixon was obsessed with Communists, that he can't be restrained, was itself a form of action, a good example of what the philosopher of language J. L. Austin called a "performative utterance." By this, Austin meant that most examples of language do not *represent* an objective action and therefore can't be evaluated in terms of whether they are true or false. Speech itself *is* the action. In arguing against the "true/false fetish," Austin, writing in the 1950s, wasn't making any claims about morality and politics. But his work on language was part of a broader intellectual reaction to postwar positivism similar to Kissinger's reflections on the relativeness of truth and metaphysics of reality. In fact, Austin's insistence that performative utterances are always "hollow or void" captures the emptiness at the center of Kissinger's relativism. That emptiness has led to a kind of consistency: from his undergraduate thesis to his most recent books, Kissinger has argued for the importance of creative and unexpected responses to crises—in effect, performative utterances that telegraph to adversaries his seriousness of purpose. Yet despite this call for constant innovation, the arguments he has made for any given escalation (to establish credibility, to back up diplomatic overtures with military might, to strengthen resolve, to avoid inaction so to demonstrate that action is possible), be it in Southeast Asia in the 1960s or, thirty years later, in the Middle East, have been predictably similar.

asked the Pentagon to tell him what his bombing options were. He and Nixon wanted to start striking North Vietnam again but that would be hard to pull off given domestic support for Johnson's bombing halt. The next best option was to bomb Cambodia. There were two stated reasons why Nixon and Kissinger decided to launch what turned out to be a four-year bombing campaign in that country. First, the peace talks that Nixon, with an assist from Kissinger, had derailed were going to start again, and the White House wanted a show of resolve that would force Hanoi to make the concessions it believed were needed in order to wind down US operations.

The second expressed reason for the bombing was to destroy the supply lines, depots, bases of North Vietnamese forces, and command center of the National Liberation Front (NLF, or the Vietcong, South Vietnam's Communist insurgency), which was supposedly located in Cambodia, near its border with Vietnam. The United States had in fact started targeting Cambodia (and Laos) in 1965, but the Joint Chiefs of Staff wanted to accelerate the air assault, especially after the early 1968 Tet Offensive revealed just how effective Hanoi was in running troops and arms into South Vietnam from Cambodia. Johnson, however, having escalated the war in 1965 refused to further escalate it in 1968. By then, he was trying to figure a way out.*

---

* The wars in Laos and Cambodia—which included bombing and cross-border raids— can be considered but two fronts in a long, often covert campaign that started during the Johnson administration and ended in 1973, each entailing a major invasion (Cambodia, with US troops, in 1970; Laos, with South Vietnamese troops and US air support, in 1971). In both cases, the main objective of US actions was to disrupt the Ho Chi Minh trail and destroy the chain of command and control of the Vietcong. Nixon and Kissinger greatly intensified (in terms of bombing rate and amount of munitions dropped) and expanded (in terms of extent of territory targeted) the bombing in both countries. But it was Cambodia that became an obsession for Nixon and Kissinger, because it reportedly housed the headquarters of the National Liberation Front and served as the primary gateway of North Vietnamese supplies and troops into South Vietnam.

Nixon, too, wanted out. But he believed that if he were to have any chance of "Vietnamizing" the conflict—that is, withdrawing US troops while building up the South Vietnamese army—the logistical and communication infrastructure of North Vietnam and the NLF would have to be neutralized. Hanoi and the Vietcong had launched offensives in South Vietnam shortly following Nixon's inauguration, and Nixon and Kissinger wanted to retaliate in a way that would both send a message and curtail their ability to conduct similar operations in the future.

"Hit them," Kissinger told Nixon, ten days before the bombing started, and then ask North Vietnam "for private talks."[2]

Nixon and Kissinger's bombing of Cambodia began on March 18, 1969, and tracks, almost perfectly, two domestic phenomena: the political ascent of Henry Kissinger and the quickening dissolution of America's political consensus.*

---

* Broadly speaking, the Cambodia bombing campaign between 1969 and 1973 comprised two named operations. The first, Operation Menu, ran from March 18, 1969, to May 1970. The second, Operation Freedom Deal, ran from May 1970 to August 1973. Menu was the phase that was most secret, carried out with the deception protocol designed by Sitton, Kissinger, and Haig. Most (but not all) of the Menu strikes took place along the border with Vietnam, targeted at destroying the logistics and command and control of the North Vietnamese army and the South Vietnamese Communist insurgents. That bombing, as we shall see, had the effect of dispersing North Vietnamese and insurgent activity further into Cambodia, spilling the American war deeper into the country and helping to destabilize the country. This crisis, which Menu helped escalate, was then used by Nixon and Kissinger to justify further escalation, including a major US invasion launched in the spring of 1970. After that invasion failed, the bombing operation called Freedom Deal was launched. Freedom Deal included both tactical (jet fighter) assaults and strategic (B-52) bombing and was more widespread, aimed at targets located throughout the whole of the country, including heavily populated areas well west of the Mekong River. Menu stayed secret for longer than anyone in the administration thought possible. It wasn't until 1973 when Congress, tipped off by Hal Knight became aware of some of Menu's extent (although a few members of Congress, including Gerald Ford, had earlier been informed). Freedom Deal was not technically "secret." Nevertheless, its extent and intensity were underre-

When Kissinger entered the White House, he found adversaries everywhere, including career officers in the Pentagon, increasingly pessimistic experts entrenched in the foreign service bureaucracy, and rivals in his inner circle, both those needing to be kept close, such as the ambitious Alexander Haig, and those whom Kissinger would immediately betray, like Morton Halperin. And then there were the cabinet members Melvin Laird at Defense and William Rogers at State, who once they realized the threat of Kissinger's pumped-up National Security Council, began to plot ways to undercut him.

The National Security Council, or NSC, was established in 1947 under Harry Truman as a consultative body. Much like the Council of Economic Advisers (established in 1946), which brokered ideas and suggestions regarding prices, employment, monetary policy, and so on, the NSC was meant to advise the president on all matters related to national security and expedite the cooperation of established offices and agencies like the State Department and the Pentagon. It wasn't meant to be a decision-making, much less a decision-executing, body. But as the Cold War unfolded, the NSC under Eisenhower, Kennedy, and Johnson accumulated more and more autonomy and power. Kissinger, though, presided over a qualitative leap forward. Under his leadership, the NSC represented the most advanced expression of the postwar imperial presidency (before it was shattered by Vietnam and Watergate and put back together along new lines, as we shall see in later chapters).

Kissinger's NSC became the central hub of the foreign policy of

---

ported in the US press, which was often fed confusing and mixed messages by the administration. For instance, on July 1, 1970, Nixon appeared on TV and said the United States was providing small arms and moral support to the Cambodian government but no significant military aid. This was not true: Washington was providing direct air support deep in Cambodia.

the United States: the vast amount of information churned out by the bureaucracy—memos, country reports, embassy cables, option papers, and so on—now first passed through Kissinger's office, where it was vetted, culled, and repackaged, before moving on to the Oval Office. "Henry's Wonderful Machine," as Marvin and Bernard Kalb described Kissinger's command center, was nearly a platonic realization of the maxim: information is power. "Since Kissinger controlled the system, he controlled the decision-making process," the Kalbs wrote. "Everyone reports to Kissinger and *only* Kissinger reports to the president."[3] His NSC became "the only forum for reviewing and making policy at the highest level and would concentrate control over the execution of policy almost exclusively in the White House."[4] But even this description underplays Kissinger's reorganizational achievement. Under Nixon, Kissinger didn't just exercise "control over the execution of policy"— he *executed* policy. In addition to planning and running the covert bombing of Cambodia, Kissinger organized a number of other clandestine operations, including arms deals (thus foreshadowing Iran-Contra), destabilization campaigns against foreign governments, and hush-hush diplomatic missions to Vietnam, Berlin, China, and the Soviet Union.

Nixon, however, was mercurial. He had approved Kissinger's plan to reorganize the NSC in December 1968. But Kissinger was afraid the president might reverse himself. Nixon often shied away from direct confrontations with his staff, cabinet members, and other high officials, including those who wanted to rein Kissinger in. Kissinger was constantly on guard to defend his territory.

For Kissinger, beyond bringing (he hoped) Hanoi to heel, bombing Cambodia was both the means and end of this power struggle. "Kissinger's primary source of power," Nixon's speechwriter, William Safire, said in his memoir of his time in the White

House, "was in his tuning-fork relationship with the President on matters that mattered to them the most."[5] Cambodia was one of the matters that mattered most to Nixon, understood as the key both to gaining an advantage over North Vietnam and winning (as we will see in a later chapter) his reelection. Kissinger, according to Marvin and Bernard Kalb, "knew, almost instinctively, that he would be able to control the bureaucracy—and thus help reorder American diplomacy—only to the degree that he became indistinguishable from the President and his policies."[6]

Rogers at State was opposed to the idea of escalating the war into Cambodia. Laird at the Pentagon was for it, but thought it needed to be done aboveboard, legally and publicly through the normal chain of command. This gave Kissinger an opening, letting him stake out a ne plus ultra position. He wanted to bomb. He wanted to bomb in a way that inflicted the most pain. And he wanted to bomb in absolute secrecy, completely off the books. He grasped the nettle, showing the White House, especially the tough-minded "Prussians" on Nixon's staff, Bob Haldeman and John Ehrlichman, and the militarists at the Pentagon that he was the "hawk of hawks."

For Kissinger, the extreme secrecy in which the bombing of Cambodia and Laos was conducted proved personally useful, creating an atmosphere of distrust that allowed him to undercut his rivals. Within the NSC, Colonel Alexander Haig, who was Kissinger's top military aide, competed with the civilian Morton Halperin for Kissinger's favor. Kissinger leveraged this competition to his advantage in his own rivalry for Nixon's attention: Nixon liked the hard-line Haig and distrusted Halperin, who came to represent the defeatism that, Nixon believed, derived from having too much intelligence and expertise. Knowing that support for Halperin would, in his words, "tag" him as a "softy," Kissinger began, as Seymour Hersh writes, to "savage" him "behind his back."[7]

By the fall of 1969, Halperin was gone and Kissinger would soon purge the NSC of anyone else Nixon didn't like.* The causes of displeasure were diverse, but they nearly all included some variation of either being too soft, too pessimistic, too halfhearted, or too accurate about US prospects in Southeast Asia. As it became increasingly clear that the bombing of Cambodia would not achieve its stated effect—neither forcing concessions from the North Vietnamese nor seriously curtailing the operational ability of the enemy—the madman theory became a self-performance, meant to convince neither Hanoi nor Saigon but Washington that it had an option other than capitulation. According to the general in charge of providing logistical support to the campaign, bombing Cambodia was the "one sacrosanct absolute" for those, like Nixon, who refused to admit that it would be impossible to end the war and save Saigon.[8] Cambodia was a test of purity. Kissinger passed.

"It's an order, it's to be done," Kissinger later told Haig, referring to yet another Nixon order to launch a massive bombing raid on Cambodia. "Anything that flies on anything that moves."[9]

The bombing galvanized Kissinger. The first raid occurred on March 18. Halperin recalls being in conversation with Kissinger when Haig interrupted with a note indicating the sortie was a success. "Kissinger smiled."[10] Kissinger then brought the information

---

* Halperin was among the first targets of the first round of illegal wiretaps put into place to keep the bombing of Cambodia a secret. After a May 1969 story in the *New York Times* appeared reporting on the bombing (a story that *didn't* result in a wider exposure of the campaign), Kissinger, thinking that Halperin might have been the inside source for the journalist who wrote the report, goaded Nixon to wiretap him. FBI director J. Edgar Hoover's May 9 memo of his phone call with Kissinger notes that Kissinger "hoped I would follow it up as far as we can take it and they will destroy whoever did this if we can find him, no matter where he is." It's doubtful that Kissinger believed that tapping Halperin's home phone would provide evidence of wrongdoing. But support for the taps, not just of Halperin but of other government officials and journalists, had a value in itself: it gave Kissinger yet another chance to show the White House that "he could be trusted." This was the first of many such illegal bugs to come, putting Nixon on the road to disgrace.

to the Oval Office: "Historic day. . . . K really excited . . . he came beaming in with the report," Haldeman wrote in his diary.[11]

Kissinger supervised every aspect of the bombing, overruling generals, rolling out maps, and picking his own targets for the bombing raids. Seymour Hersh writes that "when the military men presented a proposed bombing list, Kissinger would redesign the missions, shifting a dozen planes, perhaps, from one area to another, and altering the timing of the bombing runs." Kissinger seemed to enjoy "playing the bombardier."[12] (The joy wasn't limited to Cambodia: when the bombing of North Vietnam finally got started again, Kissinger, according to Woodward and Bernstein, "expressed enthusiasm at the size of the bomb craters").[13] "Not only was Henry carefully screening the raids," one general remembers, "he was reading the raw intelligence." That intelligence said that one target, Area 704, was home to "sizable concentrations" of Cambodian civilians.[14] B-52s flew at least 247 bombing missions over Area 704. A Pentagon report, released in 1973, stated that "Henry A. Kissinger approved each of the 3,875 Cambodia bombing raids in 1969 and 1970 as well as the methods for keeping them out of the newspapers."[15]

The bombing "did not bring psychological pressure to bear on negotiations, as hoped," the historian Joan Hoff writes, and it "did not result in destruction of the [NLF's] headquarters."[16] Worse than failing to achieve its two stated goals, the campaign took on an escalating logic of its own.

By March 1970, a year of bombing contributed to the shattering of Cambodia's neutrality, leading to a military coup against Cambodia's leader, Prince Sihanouk, which was probably sanctioned by Kissinger and Haig.* General Lon Nol deposed Sihanouk and joined

---

* Kissinger had an extreme "personal animus" for Sihanouk because of his "neutralism," according to one embassy official in Cambodia. And it was Kissinger's military aide, Haig, who pushed the coup. Mark Pratt, the State Department desk officer for Laos and Cambodia, reports that Haig (through the Military Assistance Command–Vietnam, or MAC-V) drove Sihanouk out and put Lon Nol in: "MAC-V back here in Washington

the American war effort with enthusiasm. Supplied by Washington with T-28 counterinsurgent attack planes and working closely with Pentagon covert operators, the new regime in Phnom Penh visited apocalyptic devastation on the countryside—that is, in addition to what the United States was doing with its B-52 bombs. Lon Nol's stepped-up counterinsurgency had the effect of spreading the insurgency, which now consisted, according to one US embassy staffer, of a broad "anti-fascist" alliance of "non-communists," "Sihanoukists," and "Red Khmers."

Within just weeks of Lon Nol's coup, the argument for escalating the war with a ground assault was hard to refute (at least in Washington). Kissinger, on April 22, 1970, made his case for an invasion to the president and the National Security Council: the spread of the Vietnam War into Cambodia meant the spread of the Vietcong's "sanctuaries," which in turn would "endanger the Vietnamization program, thereby threatening a slowdown in the withdrawal of American troops." As one account, sympathetic to Kissinger, put it, "Kissinger's presentation was meticulous; no one in the room questioned its facts or assumptions. A consensus seemed to emerge: in order to protect American lives in South Vietnam, the United States should take some sort of military action to prevent a Communist victory in Cambodia."[16] In order for de-escalation to proceed, escalation was required. And so Nixon

---

was dickering with Lon Nol to depose Sihanouk." Sihanouk was on a plane flying to China "when MAC-V moved and Lon Nol took over." Pratt makes a point to say that Haig wanted Lon Nol because he came out of the military and the "American military has always wanted to have 'their' man. . . . They do like the military mind, and this, of course, is exactly what Haig thought that he had found in Lon Nol." (See the interview with Pratt in *Cambodia: Country Reader*, compiled by the Foreign Affairs Oral History Collection of the Association for Diplomatic Studies and Training, available at http://www.adst.org/Readers/Cambodia.pdf.) For an in-depth analysis of Lon Nol's coup, see Ben Kienan's chapter, "The Impact on Cambodia of the U.S. Intervention in Vietnam" in Jayne S. Werner and Luu Doan Huynh, eds., *The Vietnam War: Vietnamese and American Perspectives* (1993), which describes the destabilizing effects of Cambodia's enormous customs revenue losses (from contraband rice trade) resulting from Washington's escalation of the war.

ordered a ground invasion of Cambodia, which failed completely in its objective to "clean out" the insurgent refuges but did drive them deeper into the country and further polarize Cambodian society.

The American war's spillover provoked the coup, the coup provoked the invasion, and, in turn, the coup and the invasion provoked, by accelerating the insurgency, escalated bombing. B-52s no longer aimed for just the North Vietnamese and the Vietcong, in a fringe of territory near Cambodia's border with South Vietnam. For the next two years, the bombing raids spread to cover nearly all of Cambodia, targeting the fast-growing rebellion and devastating the country.

We've now passed the fortieth anniversary of Nixon's resignation because of his involvement in the Watergate burglary, which is remembered as nearly an exclusively domestic affair. But, more than any other policy, it was Cambodia—both the 1969–70 secret bombing (which created a siege mentality in the White House) and the spring 1970 invasion (which roused the antiwar movement, compelling Nixon to take steps to contain dissent)—that kicked off the chain of events leading to Nixon's resignation. The crack-up of America's domestic consensus had begun earlier, under Johnson. When Nixon entered the White House, he "inherited near-civil war conditions," wrote Kissinger, referring to "establishment" distrust of the new president but offering a good description of the country's general mood. The actions of Nixon and Kissinger took the crisis to a new level.[17]

If Nixon came into office feeling like he was in a civil war, the Kent and Jackson killings of students were his Fall of Vicksburg. "The expansion of the Indochina war into Cambodia and the shootings at Kent State and Jackson State," the Senate investigation into Watergate concluded, led the White House to push for an illegal expansion of domestic surveillance—that is, the crimes that led to Nixon's ouster. "Kent State marked a turning point for Nixon, a beginning of his downhill slide toward Watergate," Haldeman wrote.

Dissent was felt within the NSC. When a member of his staff, William Watts, a former Rockefeller aide, refused to work up plans for the spring 1970 ground invasion of Cambodia (because it was a neutral nation), Kissinger unloaded: "Your views represent the cowardice of the Eastern establishment." Watts lunged at Kissinger, but Kissinger ducked back behind his desk. Watts resigned. Kissinger told another dissenting staffer, Anthony Lake, that he wasn't "manly enough." Lake resigned too.[18]

The historian Arthur Schlesinger is a good bellwether of that Eastern establishment. Having served in the Kennedy administration, when he backed the decision to deepen US involvement in Southeast Asia, by 1970 he had turned into a moderate critic of the war. Here's his diary entry for May 6, 1970, capturing the desperation of America's political class and intellectual elites:

> Last week Nixon invaded Cambodia. With the evident failure of his Vietnamization policy, he accepted a plan the Joint Chiefs have been hawking around Washington for years and which even Johnson, to his credit, refused. Then he traveled to the Pentagon and denounced protesting students as "bums." When the President of the United States thus creates a national mood, I suppose one cannot be too much surprised if the National Guard of Ohio fails to exercise discrimination. . . . The reaction has been one of gloom and fury—a fury derived from a sense of impotence. . . . What do we tell [young people] now? To wait until 1973, by which time God knows how many Americans and Vietnamese, now alive, will be dead?[19]

It is important to note that Schlesinger's despair concerns *just* the ground invasion of Cambodia. Like most everybody else, he didn't yet know that Nixon and Kissinger had been secretly bombing that country for over a year (and would continue to bomb it for three more).

The "civil war" spiraled out of control. The "credibility gap" widened into a chasm. Dissent begat measures to counter dissent. The bombing of Cambodia turned the White House into a tinderbox of distrust. The ground invasion of Cambodia, announced to the public by Nixon on April 30, 1970, in a rambling, defiant television address, was its spark. Demonstrations spread across the country, with Washington, DC, turning into an "armed camp." On May 4, Kent State. Then, on May 15, Jackson State. Paranoia fueled more paranoia. Crimes led to more crimes. Kissinger was involved in the early plotting, including wiretaps placed on close friends and associates, the surveillances, and the meetings where the nation's highest officers smeared antiwar dissidents as unhinged treasonous elites and discussed blowing up safes and running paramilitary "black bag" operations.

Still the bombing went on, until August 1973. By that time, Cambodia and Laos were destroyed and South Vietnam doomed. But Kissinger was rising. Even at this late date, he was using Cambodia in his ongoing rivalry with Secretary of State William Rogers, who never came around to thinking that the covert devastation of a neutral country was a good idea. Kissinger threatened to resign if Nixon didn't oust Rogers and give him the Department of State. Nixon wavered. He had hoped to rid himself of Kissinger after his landslide November 1972 reelection. "He's going back to Harvard," he told a staffer.[20]

It was Alexander Haig who convinced Nixon to keep Kissinger and give him State. Despite his rivalry with Kissinger, years of planning an illegal and clandestine war had formed a close bond between the two men.* Rogers resigned on August 16, the day after the bombs finally stopped falling on Cambodia. Nixon announced Kissinger's appointment as secretary of state a few days later.

The bombing of Cambodia was illegal in its conception, deceitful in its implementation, and genocidal in its effect. It destroyed the fragile neutrality that Cambodia's leaders had managed to maintain despite the war next door. It committed Washington to a program of escalation, including its 1970 invasion, which hastened the collapse of Cambodian society. And it achieved neither of its two stated objectives. Hanoi never budged on Kissinger's most important demand—that it withdraw troops from South Vietnam—nor was its ability to conduct military operations in South Vietnam seriously damaged. Did Kissinger ever believe these objectives were realistic? Evidence suggests that he couldn't have, since he had concluded by 1965 that the war was hopeless. The question is, in a way, beside the point, for there is an excess surrounding Kissinger's obsession with Cambodia, an intensity that suggests that the bombing escaped its original rationale and took on a momentum, a "cosmic beat," of its own.

Already in the 1950s and 1960s, in his days as a scholar and defense intellectual, Kissinger's circular reasoning (inaction needs to be avoided to show that action is possible; the purpose of Ameri-

---

* In 2007, the historian Douglas Brinkley interviewed Haig. Brinkley: "You called Henry Kissinger a genius, and you get a kind of a twinkle whenever you mention Kissinger. What is it about Henry Kissinger that you found so—" Haig: "You don't think there was something between us, I hope." Brinkley: "I don't know. What is, what is your—what was the relationship with Kissinger? If you're the middleman in between Laird and Rogers, what is your relationship with Kissinger like at this time?" Haig: "My relationship was very good with Kissinger. We seldom differed on a foreign policy issue. I think we came to our solutions through different routes, but we generally felt that we needed far more starch in our foreign affairs."

can power is to create American purpose) and ethical relativism ("what one considers an end, and what one considers a mean, depends essentially on the metaphysics of one's system") often led him to propose what he had warned against: power for power's sake. Now in office, he reiterated his fallacy: we have to escalate in order to prove we aren't impotent, and the more impotent we prove to be, the more we have to escalate. Kissinger helped transform Nixon's madman policy from performance, an act meant to convey insanity, into an actual act of moral insanity: the ravaging of two neutral countries.

Executed on the exclusive authorization of one man, Nixon, on the advice of another, Kissinger, the bombing of Cambodia—and Laos, for largely the same reasons—was among the most brutal military operations ever conducted in US history. According to one study, the United States dropped 790,000 cluster bombs on those two countries (as well as on Vietnam), releasing just under a trillion pieces of shrapnel—either ball bearings or razor-sharp barbed darts.[21] More bombs were dropped separately on Cambodia and Laos than combined on Japan and Germany during World War II.[22] For Cambodia, Ben Kiernan and Taylor Owen provide a definitive tally. They write that it "remains undisputed that in 1969–73 alone, around 500,000 tons of U.S. bombs fell on Cambodia." Moreover, "this figure excludes the additional bomb tonnage dropped on Cambodia by the U.S.-backed air force of the Republic of Viet Nam, which also flew numerous bombing missions there in 1970 and 1971."[23] The amount of bombs that hit Laos is even more stunning: US pilots flew, on average, one sortie every eight minutes and dropped a ton of explosives for each and every Laotian, delivering a total of 2.5 million tons in nearly 600,000 runs. Laos, says the Voice of America, is "the most heavily bombed country in history."[24]

The devastation wasn't caused just by bombs. Defoliation chemicals did their work. Just over a two-week period (April 18 to May 2, 1969) US–dropped Agent Orange caused significant damage. Andrew Wells-Dang, who has long been involved in relief aid to Southeast Asia, writes: "both US Government and independent inspection teams confirmed that 173,000 acres were sprayed (7% of Kompong Cham province), 24,700 of them seriously affected. The rubber plantations totaled approximately one-third of Cambodia's total and represented a loss of 12% of the country's export earnings." Washington agreed to pay over $12 million in reparations, but Kissinger tried to defer the payout to fiscal year 1972, when the money could be paid without a special request that would have revealed US cross-border activity: "Every effort," Kissinger wrote, "should be made to avoid the necessity for a special budgetary request to provide funds to pay this claim."[25]

In his testimony before the Senate on the Cambodia bombing, Creighton Abrams, commander of the US military in Vietnam, said that the "principle limitations [to the air assault] were civilian population." Not so much. According to Kiernan, a professor of history at Yale University, "from 1969 to 1973, the US bombing spread out across Cambodia and killed over 100,000 Khmer civilians."[26] Fewer people were killed in Laos, but only because the country is less populated. It is estimated that 30,000 Laotians died in the campaign. But it is hard to say. In 1972, Nixon asked "how many did we kill in Laos?" Ron Ziegler, White House press secretary, guessed, "Maybe ten thousand—fifteen?" Kissinger concurred: "In the Laotian thing, we killed about ten, fifteen."[27]*

---

* Calculating an accurate number of civilian Cambodian fatalities resulting from the 1969–1973 bombing is, as one might expect, difficult. (Recently, Kissinger claimed that drone attacks carried out during the Barack Obama administration have killed more civilians than his Cambodia campaign. If "one did an honest account," he said, there were fewer civilian casualties in Cambodia than there have been drone attacks.") Kiernan, along with Taylor Owen, bases his count on extensive documentary research and fieldwork, and he pays attention to the intensification and expansion of the bombing into heavily populated regions of the country that took place between 1970 and 1973.

These are ongoing crimes. As many as about 30 percent of the bombs dropped by the United States, the vast majority under Kissinger's tenure, did not detonate. In Laos, there exist an estimated 80 million unexploded cluster bombs, hidden below a thin layer of soil and packed with ball bearings. In addition to the roughly 30,000 Laotians who died under the bombing, these

---

News broadcasts in Cambodia, from the very start of the bombing, reported civilian deaths (these broadcasts were recorded by the United States Foreign Broadcast Information Service). On March 26, 1969, just over a week into Menu, one radio broadcast noted that "the Cambodia population living in the border regions has been bombed and strafed almost daily by U.S. aircraft, and the number of people killed, as well as material destruction, continues to grow;" and this: "They have made many attacks in recent weeks, causing losses to the Cambodian people. The list of victims is getting longer and longer. The aggressors made another murderous attack on the night of 23 March. A plane coming from South Vietnam strafed one of the border villages located about 1,500 meters inside our territory.... This was quite a serious attack. Three children were killed and nine Cambodians were wounded, six of them seriously. This attack is another inhuman and unjustified attack, because the area is densely populated and is not a staging area for the Viet Minh or Viet Cong. The Viet Minh or Viet Cong, as we know, are located in remote and sparsely inhabited areas. However, U.S. airplanes have never attacked them. The Americans and the South Vietnamese prefer to attack the areas inhabited by peaceful Cambodian farmers in order to demoralize the latter" (reprinted in US Senate Hearings, *Bombing in Cambodia*, p. 159). To get a sense of the ferocity of the bombing of Laos, and its escalation across the whole country after Kissinger took office, watch this video made by Jerry Redfern: http://www.motherjones.com/politics/2014/03/laos-vietnam-war-us-bombing-uxo. The time-sequence video shows nearly 600,000 bombing runs—a "planeload of bombs every eight minutes for nine years." For more information on Laos, see Timothy Castle, *At War in the Shadow of Vietnam* (1995). For the full air assault on Southeast Asia, see John Schlight, in *A War Too Long: The USAF in Southeast Asia, 1961–1975* (published by the Air Force History and Museums Program in 1996). Schlight writes: "All told, the Air Force had flown 5.25 million sorties over South Vietnam, North Vietnam, northern and southern Laos, and Cambodia." Michael Clodfelter, *Vietnam in Military Statistics: A History of the Indochina Wars* (1995), p. 225, writes: "The United States Air Force dropped in Indochina, from 1964 to August 15, 1973, a total of 6,162,000 tons of bombs and other ordnance. US Navy and Marine Corps aircraft expended another 1,500,000 tons in Southeast Asia. This tonnage far exceeded that expended in World War II and in the Korean War. The US Air Force consumed 2,150,000 tons of munitions in World War II—1,613,000 tons in the European Theater and 537,000 tons in the Pacific Theater—and 454,000 tons in the Korean War." In April 1972, after bombing North Vietnam's Haiphong port, Kissinger reassured Nixon that his strategy was working: "It's wave after wave of planes. You see, they can't see the B-52 and they dropped a million pounds of bombs.... I bet you we will have had more planes over there in one day than Johnson had in a month.... Each plane can carry about 10 times the load of World War II plane could carry."

devices continue to kill hundreds every year, a total of 20,000 as of 2009. Many more are scarred and maimed. In Cambodia as well, delayed explosions continue to kill.

Some especially targeted areas of fertile land should be off-limits to human traffic. Laotians and Cambodians, though, are poor: to not farm could mean to die. Yet when their plows or feet hit these bombs, many find that to farm is to die. In 2007 in Laos, Por Vandee was rice farming with his wife and three sons when one of his sons hit an unexploded ordnance with his hoe. Vandee was knocked unconscious and when he awoke, he learned that two of his sons were dead and the other had brain injuries. Others die or are wounded trying to collect the bombs to sell as scrap metal.

"There are parts of Laos where there is literally no free space. There are no areas that have not been bombed," one aid worker recently said. "And, when you are in the villages now, you still see the evidence of that. You still see bomb craters. You still see an unbelievable amount of metal and wreckage and unexploded ordnance just lying around in villages and it's still injuring and killing people today." Forty percent of the victims are children.[28]

Long before he and Nixon escalated the Vietnam War into Cambodia and Laos, Henry Kissinger had given a good deal of thought to the problem of democracy, to what, in his 1954 doctoral dissertation, he called the "incommensurability" between domestic politics and foreign policy. In modern democratic societies, politics are founded on principles thought to be absolute and timeless—civil equality, political freedom, and due process—applicable to all people, everywhere, at all times. Diplomacy, however, reveals these ideals to be, by definition, negotiable and their application contingent on political expediency. The interstate system is made up of competing polities, each representing unique cultures and values, each with its own history and interests. Wars, crises, and diplomatic tensions may occur over any given issue. But sustained threats to the international system appear when one nation insists that its parochial "version of justice" is universal and tries to impose it on other nations. "The international experience of a people is a challenge to the universality of its notion of justice," Kissinger wrote, "for the stability of an international order depends on self-limitation, on the reconciliation of different versions of legitimacy."[29]

For Kissinger, the incongruity between domestic absolutism and international relativism was more than a technical problem. It was primal, for it forced nations to confront the fact that there were limits to their "will-to-infinity," that ideals heretofore thought to be in harmony with the heavens were actually just really their own particular thing.

Kissinger dwelled awhile on the danger statesmen face when they point out to their nation's people that they are not, in fact, the world, that their aspirations are not boundless, that other peoples, with different interests and experiences, exist. Unwilling to accept these limits, citizens often stage "an almost hysterical, if subconscious, rebellion against foreign policy." The most common expression of this rebellion, Kissinger argued, is to impose an impossibly high test of purity on diplomats, limiting their ability to compromise with, or even talk to, envoys of nations deemed to be immoral, unnatural, and beyond the pale.

Prevented from performing their duty, foreign policy makers become something like "heroes in classical drama who [have] a vision of the future but who cannot transmit it directly to [their] fellow-men." They often "share the fate of prophets," wrote Kissinger, in that "they are without honor in their own country." This is so because their job is to treat the very thing their citizens cherish most—a sense of themselves as unique and eternal—as a mere "object for negotiation." Trucking and bartering, then, in the international realm becomes a "symbol of imperfection, of impure motives frustrating universal bliss." The ink on any given inter-

national treaty might lay out the protocols of this or that specific
agreement or compromise. The thing itself, though—the very fact
that one has to compromise—is death, smelling of decay, of tran-
sience, of the fleetingness of existence.

Thus the double-bind burden of statesmen. They need to represent the aspirations of their people, yes, and strive to resist the
Spenglerian rot. But they also must gently accommodate citizens
to the fact of mortality. They need to use their art to help their
nation admit its limitations, accepting that its ideals are not timeless, its morals not pristine. "The statesman must therefore be
an educator," Kissinger wrote; "he must bridge the gap between a
people's experience and his vision."

These are subtle observations, the product of a young man's
probing mind methodically building, as he once put it, his "con-
ceptual structure." But what is most remarkable is that they were
written in the early 1950s, a moment of extraordinary trust when
it came to American diplomacy. Maybe Kissinger was thinking of
Woodrow Wilson's inability to sell his League of Nations to the
American people. But that failure, by the time Kissinger composed
his reflections on the relationship between democracy and diplomacy, was decades old. The New Deal, World War II, Allied victory
over Nazism, and then the Cold War had cemented an extraordinary degree of unanimity among the American people.* The White

---

* There was dissent but it was contained through McCarthyism and the House Un-
American Activities Committee. The press supported the Korean War and the Cold
War and, according to Carl Bernstein (who along with Bob Woodward broke Watergate), over four hundred journalists worked at least occasionally for the CIA. Until the
mid-1960s, well into the United States' deepening involvement in Southeast Asia, "the
great heads of the media," David Halberstam, in *The Powers That Be* (1979, p. 446),
writes, "were anxious to be good and loyal citizens, and the working reporters had
almost without question accepted the word of the White House on foreign policy."
University faculty and their presidents were likewise quiet and mostly unquestioning;
the letter Kissinger signed, along with scores of other professors, in support of US
policies in Vietnam in late 1965 was typical academic opinion. Steven Casey, in *Selling
the Korean War: Propaganda, Politics, and Public Opinion, 1950–1953* (2008), argues

House and the foreign policy establishment operated with nearly unquestioned autonomy and legitimacy (Rick Perlstein writes that between 1947 and 1974, around four hundred bills had been introduced in Congress to establish legislative oversight of intelligence agencies; all were voted down).[30]

In other words, the problem Kissinger warned against in 1954 largely didn't exist. Conservative defense analysts like Kissinger complained about the lack of will in the postwar years among citizens to fight small or major wars. But that's not the kind of hysterical filibustering of diplomats that Kissinger is describing in his dissertation. Through to the mid-1960s, voters embraced a robust internationalism; statesmen didn't have a "difficult task in legitimizing their programmes domestically"; the press was decidedly not adversarial, most social scientists saw themselves as facilitators, not opponents, of the Cold War; theologians and intellectuals provided moral and ethical support for containment; and the legislature and judiciary, for the most part, minded their own business when it came to foreign policy. Diplomats, in other words, weren't being cast out of their homeland like dishonored prophets or Greek heroes.

But then came America's war in Southeast Asia. Kissinger, named national security adviser in the middle of that war, isn't singularly responsible for the undoing of America's Cold War consensus. But by executing Nixon's war strategy with such zeal, in Cambodia and elsewhere, he quickened the breakup. He did say that statesmen were prophets, and in a way he fulfilled his own prophecy, helping to bring about the dissensus he had warned about in 1954. It wasn't just the bombing of Cambodia. "Immense damage had been done by 1973–1974," the diplomatic historian Carolyn Eisenberg told me after she generously read this chapter.

---

that the Korean conflict was an unpopular war, enjoying very low public support and backed nearly entirely by institutional elites.

"There were so many lies about so many things," she said. "The biggest lie was that they had wasted thousands of lives and vast sums of money to achieve a peace settlement that they could have obtained four years earlier."*

Kissinger recognizes that his time in public office marked a turning point, complaining that no other American statesman had to face the kind of criticism he faced. Differences of opinion over foreign policy were to be expected, he said. But during his tenure, "a natural critique of decisions that were arguable at various stages became transmuted into a moral issue, first about the moral adequacy of American foreign policy altogether, and then into the moral adequacy of America in conducting any kind of traditional foreign policy."[31]

In trying to account for this turn, Kissinger over the years has occasionally referred back to the argument he made in his 1954 doctoral dissertation regarding the inevitable incongruity between domestic absolutism and international relativism: losing the war in Vietnam, he said in 2010, was "America's first experience with limits in foreign policy, and it was something painful to accept." This is a disingenuous interpretation. It is true, as will shall see, that defeat in Vietnam provoked a conservative reaction against Kissinger. Grassroots activists were suspicious of Kissinger's "foreignness" and "internationalism" (that is, his Jewishness). First-

---

* Forced to confront the fact that their country was capable of the kind of savagery it had visited on Southeast Asia, many in the activist peace movement were pushed to the edge of "existential agony." Norma Becker remembers being "just overwhelmed with this horror, and was feeling powerless—this utter, total, unbelievable horror that human beings could do this." "It was such barbarity, and such dehumanization that was taking place. The whole thing was a horror show." David McReynolds, who came from a two-generation Republican military family, said that learning what the government did in Southeast Asia left him "heartbroken." After visiting Cambodia, Republican representative Paul McCloskey thought that what the United States did "to the country is a greater evil than we have done to any country in the world." See Tom Wells, *The War Within: America's Battle Over Vietnam* (2005), pp. 298, 559; *New York Times*, April 3, 1975.

generation neoconservative intellectuals objected strongly to the idea that there were "limits" to American power. But this isn't the sort of "moral" rebuke Kissinger is talking about, when he complains about the domestic response to his conduct of the war. Rather, the critics who most rankled Kissinger were those—protesters, Congress, and former Harvard colleagues like Thomas Schelling—who told *him* that there were limits to what *he* could do to Cambodia, Laos, and Vietnam. As he complained to a reporter in early 1973, specifically about public oversight of his Cambodia strategy: "I don't see how it is possible to conduct foreign policy when there's a systematic attempt to destroy both your threats and your incentives."[32]

Never has Kissinger acknowledged how his refusal to recognize limits in Southeast Asia accelerated the crisis, the way his war in Cambodia helped to bring about the end of the old "traditional" foreign policy establishment, transforming the early Cold War national security state, based on elite planning, gentlemanly debate, domestic acquiescence, and cross-party consensus, into what came next. Kissinger didn't use his time in office to "instruct" citizens in political realism, as he had earlier defined the responsibility of statesmen. Rather, he helped adapt the imperial presidency to new times, based on an increasingly mobilized and polarized citizenry, more spectacular displays of power, more secrecy, and ever more widening justifications for ever more war.

4

Nixon Style

> Because, because, you've gotta remember that everything is domestic
> politics from now on. And, uh—. Everything's domestic politics.
> Maybe, maybe, maybe, Henry—. To hell with the whole thing. You
> know what I mean?
>
> —Richard Nixon

In recent years, there's been an avalanche of declassified transcripts of phone conversations Kissinger secretly recorded, newly
available Nixon tapes, White House memos, and the papers and
diaries of Haldeman, Haig, and others. In this material it is hard to
find a single foreign policy initiative that was not also conducted for
domestic gain, to quiet dissent, best rivals, or position Nixon for
reelection in 1972. An early push to build an antiballistic missile
system had less to do with Soviet power than with staging a confrontation with Congress to establish Nixon's dominance over foreign policy. The president, with the help of Kissinger, won that fight
by overstating the Soviet threat (something Kissinger had been
doing since the 1950s). The president then gloated in a victory memo
about the "'Nixon style' in dealing with the Congress," without
making even a mention of national defense. In the Middle East, as
the historian Robert Dallek writes in *Nixon and Kissinger: Partners*

in Power, "domestic politics was paramount." Nixon wanted to press Israel to give up its nuclear program but, not wanting to lose pro-Israel votes in Congress, relented. The president also thought he would get "more political than national security value" from SALT talks with Moscow.

"We've got to break the back of this generation of Democratic leaders," Kissinger said, referring to a plan to use the defense budget and an arms control treaty to discredit Nixon's domestic adversaries. Nixon responded: "We've got to destroy the confidence of the people in the American establishment."

"That's right," Kissinger answered.

Nixon: "And we certainly as hell will."[1]

No one country of the globe claimed more of Kissinger's attention than the United States. He became fixated on its domestic politics because his boss, Richard Nixon, was fixated on domestic politics. And Kissinger knew that his position depended entirely on melding himself to Nixon. "I would be losing my only constituency," he once said, about the consequences of displeasing Nixon.[2]

There's more, however, to the subordination of diplomacy to domestic politics than the attachment Kissinger had to Nixon. Vietnam polarized American society. It gave rise, on one side, to a dissenting, skeptical culture and, on the other, to a conservative movement that would eventually coalesce behind Ronald Reagan. As the schism deepened, politicians would increasingly use war— or at least the drumbeat of war—to contain the first and leverage the second to their advantage. Roosevelt, Truman, Eisenhower, Kennedy, and Johnson all played foreign policy for political gain (or loss: consider LBJ and Vietnam). But the Nixon White House raised the stakes.

Startlingly fast after 1968, 1972 came into view. And then, even before 1972 arrived, 1976 loomed. The four-year presidential election cycle has speeded up in recent years, it is often said, but nearly half a century ago, Nixon and Kissinger, in a remarkably short period of time after having landed in office, were running their war in Southeast Asia with an eye on Nixon's reelection.

Here's Kissinger speaking to Senator George McGovern in early 1969 about Vietnam, just after Nixon's inauguration:

> I think that it is clear now that we never should have gone in there, and I don't see how any good can come of it. But we can't do what you recommend and just pull out, because the boss's whole constituency would fall apart; those are his people who support the war effort: the South; the blue-collar Democrats in the North. The Nixon constituency is behind the war effort. If we were to pull out of Vietnam, there would be a disaster, politically, for us here, at home.[3]

The 1968 race for the presidency had been a three-way contest, with Nixon winning 43.4 percent of the vote, Humphrey 42.7, and the segregationist George Wallace 13.5. Nearly ten million voters chose not just Wallace but his running mate, General Curtis LeMay, who made a number of alarming statements during the campaign. "I never said we should bomb them back to the Stone Age," was his response to criticism of his plan for winning the Vietnam War. "I said we had the capability to do it."*

Most of these votes would have gone to Nixon had Wallace and LeMay not run, and Nixon wanted to make sure he got them in 1972. To do so, he intended to implement his famous "southern strategy." That Nixon cultivated racial resentment in order

---

* The North Vietnamese, LeMay wrote in *Mission with LeMay*, have "got to draw in their horns and stop their aggression or we're going to bomb them back to the Stone Age. And we would shove them back into the Stone Age with Air power or Naval power—not with ground forces."

to win the South is well known. Less so is that his strategy had a foreign policy component: maximum air power in Southeast Asia—essentially LeMay's Stone-Age strategy, that is, bomb them into submission. "It was very clear," George McGovern said about his talk with Kissinger, that "they were already starting to chart the so-called Southern Strategy of trying to develop an approach that would pull the South away from Wallace and into the Nixon column. . . . I never again could develop much respect for their Vietnam policy. I thought that they were willing to continue killing Asians and sacrificing the lives of young Americans because of their interpretation of what would play in the United States."[4]

Nixon needed to placate conservatives to forestall another third-party challenge. In this, Kissinger, having established himself as the "hawk of hawks," was a useful emissary. For the next five years, the extreme actions taken by Nixon and Kissinger—the mining of North Vietnam's harbor, the Christmas bombing, Operation Linebacker, the destruction of the Mekong Delta, and, of course, Cambodia and Laos, two countries that were effectively bombed back into the Stone Age—were blood tribute paid to the growing power of the American Right.

Nixon had Kissinger speak with prominent conservatives, including California governor Ronald Reagan, the Reverend Billy Graham, William Buckley, and the comedian Bob Hope: "The president wanted me to give you a brief call to tell you that with all the hysteria on TV and in the news on Laos, we feel we have set up everything we set out to do: Destroyed more supplies than in Cambodia last year. Set them back many months. . . . We achieved what we were after."[5]

They achieved nothing. North Vietnam never wavered, never conceded to Nixon's demand that it remove troops from South Vietnam in exchange for US withdrawal. But that didn't matter, because the bombing was meant to win at home.

Nixon was particularly worried about Reagan, and Kissinger stoked his worry.

"He said that you have a real problem with the conservatives," Kissinger told Nixon in November 1971, about a recent conversation he had had with Reagan.

"Oh, I know," Nixon said.

Kissinger continued: "He says you're going to wind up without any friends because you can't win the liberals anyway."

"Geez," said Nixon.[6]

Kissinger told Nixon that he had counted off the administration's conservative achievements to Reagan, including the deployment, over liberal opposition, of MIRVs, or multiple independently targetable reentry vehicle nuclear missiles. "We wouldn't have had Cambodia," Kissinger said, referring to the 1970 US invasion, "we wouldn't have had Laos . . . And we wouldn't have an $80 billion defense budget."

At one point, Nixon cut in: "We wouldn't have had Amchitka."

"We wouldn't have had Amchitka," Kissinger repeated.

The story of Amchitka, a small island off Alaska, is largely forgotten now, but here Nixon and Kissinger are talking about it as if it were a moment in human events equal to Winston Churchill's "blood, toil, tears, and sweat" speech to the House of Commons in 1940. In the early 1970s, Amchitka was the site of a pitched battle between arms control and environmental groups and the White House over plans to conduct a high-yield, extremely radioactive nuclear test there. The test had no military or scientific benefit but was seen as something of a ritual by the Right, fireworks to celebrate the end of Johnson's presidency, when many hawks (like LeMay) felt the United States had fallen behind on nuclear development. Then, when public opposition to the detonation began to grow, Nixon had a chance to show conservatives that he would stand up to "liberals." He let it be known that, were the Supreme Court to issue an injunction against the test, he would go forward anyway.

The Court didn't block the test, but Haldeman told Kissinger to play it for politics anyway. "Tell Reagan we're taking unmitigated heat in order to keep that thing going. We need all the support of the right." Later, after the test was conducted, Nixon met with Senator Barry Goldwater and mocked the fears of environmentalists. "The seals are still swimming," the president said. "I'm damn proud of you," Goldwater told him.[7]

What would become known as the Reagan Revolution was on the march and Nixon had a conservative majority (as long as it didn't split). Nixon's aides made a calculated decision to play this "positive polarization," as Vice President Spiro Agnew described the breakup of American society, for advantage. "There are twice as many conservatives as Republicans," said Haldeman, and the White House, especially after the Cambodia invasion in the run-up to the 1970s midterms, increasingly turned Vietnam into a "social issue," linking the war to crime and protests at home, tagging dissenters as unpatriotic, blaming the murder of protesters on protesters themselves, on a "radical liberalism," "whimpering isolationism," and "pusillanimous pussyfooting on the critical issue of law and order."[8]

But until conservatives became a dependable voting bloc, Nixon couldn't just govern from the right. Though their moment was passing, he still had to reckon with liberals and the Left, ranging from New Dealers who continued to believe that "Franklin D. Roosevelt was president," as Nixon complained, to the churches, the war protesters, the civil rights movement, antipoverty and environmental groups, and more radical organizations.

To keep this wing of American politics at bay, even as he worked to build his "silent majority" into an electoral coalition,

Nixon could count on the versatile Kissinger. "We knew Henry as the 'hawk of hawks' in the Oval Office," Haldeman recalled. "But in the evenings, a magical transformation took place. Touching glasses at a party with his liberal friends, the belligerent Kissinger would suddenly become a dove. . . . And the press, beguiled by Henry's charm and humor, bought it. They just couldn't believe that the intellectual, smiling, humorous 'Henry the K' was a hawk like 'that bastard' Nixon."[9]

Kissinger was effective with liberal critics. With religious folk, he could invoke his experience in the Holocaust. With reporters, he could flatter and leak and stroke their egos. And with students, he cultivated a compelling mix of irony and candor. One remembers a performance Kissinger gave at MIT, in late January 1971.[10] He started his remarks "with a confidential air," telling the audience that Nixon had not been his "first choice" for president. Then, after a dramatic pause, he confessed "that he had doubts, that he was troubled, yet confident that the Administration had chosen the only sensible path"—gradual withdrawal and "Vietnamization." As to rumors that the administration was considering using nuclear weapons (rumors that turned out to be true), Kissinger "made a disparaging remark about absurd scenarios that might be found in the lower offices of the Pentagon, but the real decision makers would never use those terrible weapons."* Asked by one skeptical student what it would take for him to resign, Kissinger said: when the "whole

---

* Kissinger did in fact plan for the tactical use of nuclear weapons in Vietnam. And he helped execute a plan, code-named "Giant Lance," that put US nuclear forces on extended alert, as part of the mad-Nixon-might-do-anything-to-win-the-war bluff to the Soviets. At times, it didn't seem a bluff: Nixon said to Kissinger in the spring of 1972, in response to a North Vietnamese offensive, "We're going to do it. I'm going to destroy the goddamn country, believe me, I mean destroy it if necessary. And let me say, even the nuclear weapons if necessary. It isn't necessary. But, you know, what I mean is, that shows you the extent to which I'm willing to go. By a nuclear weapon, I mean that we will bomb the living bejeezus out of North Vietnam and then if anybody interferes we will threaten the nuclear weapons." "I just want you to think big, Henry," he said at another point.

trend of the policy became morally reprehensible to me." But, he added, he wouldn't criticize the president publicly "unless gas chambers were set up or some horrendous moral outrage."

Recalling the encounter at a later date, the unconvinced student wondered, "What if . . . there is no need to build ovens? What if . . . the ovens are the infernos created by the napalm and the bombs from the B-52s?"

Kissinger had largely won over the young crowd. "He had sounded so sincere, so sympathetic, so much one of us," said the student. Yet even as Kissinger was lying that the war was winding down, B-52s were pounding southern Laos to prepare for a ground invasion, which took place on the Monday after Kissinger's Saturday MIT speech.

Kissinger was equally good with liberal intellectuals. He pulled them in, letting them think they had an audience. He often lunched with Arthur Schlesinger, and every time he did he let the historian in on a secret: he was thinking about resigning. "I have been thinking a lot about resignation," he said following the invasion of Cambodia. "In fact, I thought about it long before Cambodia." Again, Schlesinger didn't know about the bombing of Cambodia or about Kissinger's deep involvement in planning the invasion. Neither was Schlesinger aware of Kissinger's plotting with the president to "destroy the confidence of the people in the American establishment." So it was possible for him to take Kissinger seriously when he said he stayed on to prevent further damage to "institutions of authority."[11]

And even if Kissinger couldn't convince liberal and left-wing intellectuals about the soundness of Nixon's policy, they were still reassured that someone at ease with concepts such as "bourgeois society," "objective conditions," and "structural crisis" was in the White House. His "soul was conservative," as his mentor Fritz Kraemer once said, meaning he valued hierarchy and order. But his mind was formed by many of the influences that shaped the New

Left, including existential exaltations of individual free will. Kissinger appreciated history's sweep, possessing a dialectical instinct that some compared to Hegel's ("Henry thinks in a constantly theoretical framework. Every time a wave occurs on the east end of the shore, he's got it tied into a relationship with the west bank," said one academic admirer he brought into the NSC as an analyst).[12] "The West," he wrote in his undergraduate thesis, "has produced no political theorist with an ability to reach the souls since Marx."[13] That Kissinger was essentially a New Left mind with Old Right morals wasn't lost on Alexander Haig, who described him to Nixon as someone "cut from that goddamn . . . left wing [cloth] even though he's a hard-line, tough guy."[14]

And when the wit and good wine came up short, Kissinger deftly invoked fear of right-wing revanchism: "If we had done in our first year what our loudest critics called on us to do," Kissinger told the MIT audience, "the 13 percent that voted for Wallace would have grown to 35 or 40 percent; the first thing the president set out to do was to neutralize that faction."[15]

Kissinger, who as a child witnessed the collapse of the Weimar Republic, presented himself as holding the center against the right, telling liberals that if he resigned, Spiro Agnew would be making foreign policy. If there were to be a revolution in America, he warned, it wouldn't be led by Students for a Democratic Society, Tom Hayden, pacifist Quakers, or social-justice Catholics and Jews. When a society truly collapses, Kissinger said, "some real tough guys, . . . the most brutal forces in the society take over."[16] "We are saving you from the right," he told NSC staffers who had resigned in protest over the 1970 invasion of Cambodia. "You are the right," they replied.[17]

The 1971 invasion of Laos—carried out with 17,000 South Vietnamese troops and massive US air strikes—was another catastrophe. It was meant to shut down the so-called Ho Chi Minh trail, over which Hanoi supplied the Vietcong. But the North Vietnamese army routed the South Vietnamese, killing or wounding nearly 8,000 of the attackers. The United States lost over 100 helicopters and 215 soldiers. But Nixon spun the invasion as a success. He told Haldeman: "We should whack the opponents on patriotism, saving American lives, etc."[18] When the press began to report accurately the unfolding disaster, Kissinger took the opportunity to stoke Nixon's anger: the media's reporting on Laos, he said, was "vicious." Never at a loss for a useful historical analogy, Kissinger told Nixon that if "Britain had a press like this in World War II, they would have quit in '42."

Foreign policy was turned inside out, with Nixon and Kissinger keying their actions not to external reality but rather to their need to manipulate domestic opinion. In the real world, the invasion of Laos was a failure. But as Nixon told Kissinger, the real world didn't matter. "The main thing, Henry, on Laos," he said, "I don't care what happens there, it's a win. See?"[19]

"To listen to even a few of the Nixon tapes," write the historians Fredrik Logevall and Andrew Preston, "is to be struck by the degree to which foreign policy options were evaluated in terms of their likely effect on the administration's standing at home."[20] Here are two examples. The first is from March 1971, when Kissinger told Nixon that "we've got to get enough time to get out. We have to make sure that they don't knock the whole place over" (that is, make sure North Vietnam didn't overrun South Vietnam as soon as the United States withdrew its troops). "We can't have it knocked over brutally, to put it brutally, before the election." Then on August 3, 1972, Nixon: "I look at the tide of history out there, South Vietnam probably is never going to survive anyway, I'm just being perfectly candid. . . . We also have to realize, Henry, that winning an election is terribly important. It's terribly important this year, but can we have a viable foreign policy if a year from now

or two years from now, North Vietnam gobbles up South Vietnam? That's the real question." Kissinger replied: "If a year or two
years from now North Vietnam gobbles up South Vietnam, we can
have a viable foreign policy if it looks as if it's the result of South
Vietnamese incompetence." Kissinger then went on to say that
"we've got to find some formula that holds the thing together a year
or two, after which—after a year, Mr. President, Vietnam will be a
backwater." Having helped prolong the war to get Nixon elected,
Kissinger was now working to prolong it—until he could reach a
face-saving agreement—to get him reelected.[21]

Nixon, though, was afraid that Kissinger would be tempted to
strike a deal and bask in the praise he would receive as a peacemaker. He told Haig to keep watch. The president, Haldeman
wrote in his diary, "wants to be sure Haig doesn't let Henry's desire
for a settlement prevail, that's the one way we can lose the election.
We have to stand firm on Vietnam and not get soft."[22] Kissinger
mostly stayed firm. But by early 1972, it was becoming increasingly
apparent that Nixon's and Kissinger's strategy of withdrawing
troops while escalating the bombing wasn't working. Soon, writes
Larry Berman in his detailed history of the Paris negotiations,
the White House would capitulate "on almost every major point"
Hanoi was insisting on, including that "any cease-fire would be a
'cease-fire in place,' that is, North Vietnamese troops would stay
in the South if they were already there."[23]

Fighting, nonetheless, continued. The North launched a major
offensive at the end of March, and Nixon responded with a massive bombing campaign: Haldeman wrote in his diary that Nixon
was massing a huge attack force, still hoping, against all evidence,
that another whack "will give us a fairly good chance of negotiations"
and force concessions out of Hanoi. "Henry has the same view."[24]

At this point, the bombing had as much to do with conciliating
the small group of true believers that had hardened around Nixon
in the White House as it did the broader Right. "I refuse to believe

that a little fourth-rate power like North Vietnam does not have a breaking point," Kissinger had said earlier, amid making plans for one of his savage blows that was supposed to end the war. Kissinger told the Soviet ambassador that Vietnam had become a "major domestic problem." He continued: "We cannot permit our domestic structure to be constantly tormented by this country ten thousand miles away."[25] Confronted with an opponent he could not bend, Kissinger had come to think of the United States as the tormented victim.

By late spring, the negotiating momentum had swung to the North Vietnamese. On May 2, Kissinger sat down in Paris with North Vietnam's main representative, Le Duc Tho, in a meeting he described as "brutal." "Le Duc Tho was not even stalling," Kissinger said. "Our views had become irrelevant; he was laying down terms."[26] "He operated on us like a surgeon with a scalpel with enormous skill," Kissinger remembered years later.[27]

A member of Hanoi's delegation described Kissinger as defeated: he "no longer had the appearance of a university professor making long speeches and continually joking, but a man speaking sparingly, seemingly embarrassed and thoughtful."[28] Le Duc Tho baited Kissinger over and over again with references to a particularly sensitive topic: the rise of domestic dissent in the United States and public opposition to the war. Kissinger tried to say that that subject was off the table, tersely informing the North Vietnamese that he wouldn't discuss domestic politics. But Le Duc Tho kept pressing the point, bringing up Daniel Ellsberg's Pentagon Papers as "evidence of the U.S. process of intervention and aggression" and as an example of how Kissinger was being undercut at home.

"Sadness was apparent on his face," Le Duc Tho later said. "We did not know what he was thinking at that moment, but later he repeatedly wrote that the division of mind in America caused him great pains."[29]

Kissinger quickly regained his rakishness. "We bombed them," he told a number of confidants in private shortly after this meeting, "into letting us accept their terms." It was a remark as callous as it was true.[30]

The only thing left was to spin Le Duc Tho's terms so they didn't hurt Nixon's commanding lead in the polls. "My old friend Henry Kissinger held a press conference the other day explaining his diplomatic triumphs," Arthur Schlesinger wrote in his journal in October 1972, following the announcement that an agreement with Hanoi had been reached. Schlesinger continued: "He was, as usual, subtle, disarming and disingenuous. What is most obvious is the spectacular and unprecedented concessions we have made. But the press, following Henry, has written about it all as if we had made no concessions at all. What is saddest of all is that if Nixonger (as Isaiah Berlin would say) had been willing to make these concessions in 1969, we could have had the settlement then; and 20,000 Americans and God knows how many Vietnamese, now dead, would be alive."[31]

In November, Nixon got his landslide, having managed to win reelection as both a war president and a peace candidate.* The Southeast Asia piece of the "southern strategy," though it did noth-

---

* The settlement reached in October almost broke down in December, as Kissinger made one last effort to push the North Vietnamese on a few matters that might provide domestic political cover for the White House, such as the sensitive issue of prisoners of war (made sensitive largely because of Nixon's effort to use it for domestic political gain; as the investigation into Watergate unfolded, Nixon, who exaggerated the number of American prisoners in North Vietnamese hands, held an increasing number of photo-ops with returned POWs). Kissinger remained frustrated: "Hanoi is almost disdainful of us because we have no effective leverage left." On December 18, Operation Linebacker II—the infamous Christmas Bombing—began, targeting civilian buildings, including hospitals. "The bastards have never been bombed like they're going to be bombed this time," Nixon said. The bombing was indeed vicious, designed to cause "utmost civilian distress." "I want the people of Hanoi to hear the bombs," said one admiral. Over a thousand Vietnamese died in one of the most concentrated bombing campaigns in US history. Again, for no purpose (other than assuring the South Vietnamese that the United States wouldn't abandon them): the treaty finally signed in January was nearly exactly the same as what was on the table at the beginning of December.

ing to move Hanoi, was a success at home. The price of victory, however, was high, and included, as the historian Ken Hughes writes, the lives lost in "the four years it took Nixon to create the illusion of 'peace with honor' and conceal the reality of defeat with deceit."[32]

Later, after Nixon's second inauguration, congressional aides asked William Sullivan, the assistant secretary of state for East Asian and Pacific Affairs, under what constitutional provision could the White House justify its bombing of Cambodia, which by that point had been going on for four years. Sullivan struggled for a response, finally answering: "For now, I'd just say the justification [was] the reelection of President Nixon." "By that theory," the *Washington Post* remarked, "he could level Boston."[33]

The Paris Peace Accords—signed in January 1973—could not hold. Saigon would not allow honest elections and Hanoi, which had been fighting for the independence of *all* Vietnam since the 1940s, would not accept a divided country. The question is, were Nixon and Kissinger hoping for a "decent interval" to pass before Saigon fell, by which time Vietnam might be forgotten as what Kissinger called a "backwater"? Or were they planning to use an inevitable violation of the agreement by Hanoi to legitimate a resumption of the bombing?

Larry Berman argues the latter: Nixon, he writes, "intended for South Vietnam to receive the backing of American airpower through 1976," when his legacy would be secured and his successor elected. "The record shows," Berman writes, "that the United States *expected* that the signed treaty would be immediately violated and that this would trigger a brutal military response. Permanent war (air war, not ground operations) at an acceptable cost was what Nixon and Kissinger anticipated from the so-called peace agreement."[34]

A landslide election and a broken peace agreement would have, in other words, allowed Kissinger to move from the bombing of Cambodia (initially secret because the White House feared the domestic reaction) to a now vindicated and fully justified aerial assault on North Vietnam. Götterdämmerung (as Seymour Hersh described the decisive destruction that Nixon and Kissinger had wanted to visit on North Vietnam since they first entered the White House) would finally have its warrant.* And when North Vietnam began to move against the South, Kissinger did want to retaliate. Told by Nixon's new secretary of defense, Elliot Richardson, that more bombing would have little strategic effect, Kissinger said: "That is not the point. It is a psychological reprisal point we must make."

But domestic politics continued to confound. "Watergate blew up, and we were castrated," Kissinger later said. "We were not permitted to enforce the agreement. . . . I think it's reasonable to assume he [Nixon] would have bombed the hell out of them."

---

* The punishment of North Vietnam was not the only thing derailed by Watergate. Nixon had hoped to leverage his landslide victory to definitively break with the New Deal and the Great Society; he proposed an austerity budget in early 1973 that would have eliminated hundreds of government programs, including the entire bureaucracy of Johnson's War on Poverty, cut funding from education, housing, and health care, and forced significant out-of-pocket expenses on millions of Medicare and Medicaid beneficiaries, as Rick Perlstein points out.

5

Anti-Kissinger

One might well ask: Why bother to play the game at all?
—Daniel Ellsberg, 1956

The ferocity with which Nixon and Kissinger bombed Cambodia, along with the desire to inflict extreme pain on North Vietnam, had a number of motivations, both explicit (to wring concessions out of Hanoi; to disrupt the NLF's supply and command-and-control lines) and implicit (to best bureaucratic rivals; to look tough and prove loyalty; to appease the Right). "Savage was a word that was used again and again" in discussing what needed to be done in Southeast Asia, recalled one of Kissinger's aides, "a savage unremitting blow on North Vietnam to bring them around."[1] But there's another way to think about the savagery, along with the wild, off-the-books way their air assault was carried out.

Everything about the secret operation seemed to be a reaction to the man Henry Kissinger identified as the ultimate technocrat: Kennedy's and Johnson's secretary of defense, Robert

McNamara.* In office from 1961 to 1968, McNamara is famous for imposing on the Pentagon the same integrated system of statistical analysis he had, in the previous decade, used to rescue the Ford Motor Company. "McNamara's revolution" continued reforms that had been underway since World War II, but in a much more intensified and accelerated fashion.[2] McNamara's "whiz kids" sought to subordinate every aspect of defense policy—its lumbering bureaucracy, its cornucopia budget for equipment appropriation, its doctrine, tactics, chains of command, its supply logistics and battlefield maneuvers—to the abstract logic of economic modeling. When Ray Sitton, the Air Force colonel who helped Kissinger come up with the method to cover up the Cambodia bombings, informed the "systems analysts on the third floor [of the Pentagon]" that he didn't "know how to quantify the effectiveness" of bombing by B-52s, they told him he was "dumb."[3] "You can quantify anything," they said. Sitton, known as an expert on B-52s, was charged with graphing out the "cost-effectiveness" of monthly B-52 bombing runs. The idea was to budget only those sorties on the rising

---

* In his memoirs, Kissinger describes McNamara as exactly the kind of rationalist Spengler warned about, who appears during a civilization's mature period, just at the moment it is about to slide into decay. Lost in a thicket of facts and figures, the secretary and his whiz kids were unable to distinguish between information and wisdom, presuming that their mastery over numbers gave them mastery over the world. McNamara, Kissinger wrote, "overemphasized the quantitative aspects of defense planning; by neglecting intangible psychological and political components he aimed for a predictability that was illusory.... His eager young associates hid their moral convictions behind a seemingly objective method of analysis which obscured that their questions too often predetermined the answers." There was something else that disturbed Kissinger about McNamara: the secretary's surplus of facts led to a deficit of conviction, leaving him vulnerable to sentimentality and guilt. Having lost sight of the ends, he had become repulsed by the means. "He had no stomach for an endless war," Kissinger said of him. Late in his life, McNamara made a public act of contrition. "We were wrong, terribly wrong," he said of Kennedy's and Johnson's Vietnam policy. This apology particularly annoyed Kissinger. Speaking with a reporter, Stephen Talbot, who had just interviewed the remorseful former secretary of defense, Kissinger rubbed his eyes, pretending to cry. "Boohoo, boohoo." "He's still beating his breast, right?" he asked Talbot. "Still feeling guilty."

side of the curve. Once "effectiveness" began to decline, funds would be cut off. "I never was successful in explaining to them that if you are a military command in the field, the most important mission they fly may be the one just before they reach zero on the other side of the curve," Sitton said. Intangibles that couldn't be graphed or coded into an economic model—will, ideology, culture, tradition, history—were disregarded (McNamara even tried, without success, to impose a single, standard uniform on all the different branches of the armed services).

As might be expected, such efforts to achieve "cost effectiveness" greatly expanded paperwork. Every operational detail was recorded so that, back in DC, teams of economists and accountants could figure out new opportunities for further rationalization. Finance and budget came under special scrutiny; among McNamara's early major reforms was to "develop some means of presenting" the Pentagon's "costs of operation in mission terms." What this meant for the Strategic Air Command is that every gallon of fuel was accounted for, every flight hour recorded, every spare part used, along with every bomb dropped.

Kissinger's plans to bomb Cambodia—plans worked out with Sitton—weren't quite the antithesis of McNamarian bureaucracy. It was more a shadow version, or perversion, of that bureaucracy. According to Sitton, Kissinger approved a highly elaborate deception to circumvent "the Strategic Air Command's normal command and control system—highly classified in itself—which monitors for budgetary requirements such items as fuel usage and bomb tonnage deployed." A "duel reporting system" was established; briefings of pilots focused exclusively on objectives inside South Vietnam, but once in the air, radar sites would redirect a certain number of planes to their real destination in Cambodia. The mission would be "routinely reported in the Pentagon's secret command and control system as having been in South Vietnam."

Accurate documentation in terms of fuel spent, spare parts used, bombs dropped were put down in the "post-strike" forms. "Clerks and administrators" needed their paperwork, the chairman of the Joint Chiefs of Staff, General Earle Wheeler, told the Senate, after the deception was finally revealed, in order to justify the expenditure. But all documentation—maps, computer printouts, messages, and so on—that might reveal the true targets was burned.

"Every piece of paper, including the scratch paper, the paper that one of our computers might have done some figuring on, every piece of scrap paper was gathered up," Major Hal Knight, who carried out the falsification on the ground in South Vietnam, testified to Congress in 1973: "I would wait until daylight, and as soon as that time came, I would go out and burn that." "I destroyed the papers that had the target coordinates on them. I destroyed the paper that came off the plotting boards that showed the track of the aircraft. . . . I destroyed the computer tape that took the target coordinates, UTM coordinates and translated them into information that the bombing computers could use. Then I also destroyed any scrap paper that went with that, and the brushgraph recording." "A whole special furnace" was set up to dispose of the records of the bombing targets, General Creighton W. Abrams told Congress; "we burned probably 12 hours a day."[4]

"Fire," wrote Spengler, "is for the warrior a weapon, for the craftsmen part of his equipment, for the priest a sign from God, and for the scientist a problem."[5] For Kissinger and the other men who bombed Cambodia for four years, it was a way of subverting the soulless enervation of "systems analysis," of taking war out of the hands of bureaucrats and giving it back to the warriors.*

---

* The bombing of Cambodia was such an extensive campaign that a whole clandestine bureaucracy (an antibureaucracy?) was needed to manage it. Here's General Creighton Abrams, the US military commander in Vietnam, testifying to Congress: "From just a purely administrative viewpoint, you see, the whole thing had become too complicated. I could not keep these things in my mind, so I had to have specialists

I keep coming back to Spengler's influence on Kissinger's critique of the foreign policy bureaucracy not because it reveals something unique to Kissinger, though it does do that. Kissinger, I think, was much more aware of the philosophical foundation of his positions than most other postwar defense intellectuals. Yet, what is more important, at least in terms of understanding the evolution of the national security state, is how his critique reflects a deeper current in American history. The idea that spirit and intuition need to be restored to a society that had become "overcivilized" and "overrationalized," too dependent on logic, instruments, information, and mathematics, has a pedigree reaching back at least to the late 1800s.[6] "Life is painting a picture, not doing a sum," said Oliver Wendell Holmes, in a 1911 Harvard address (quoted by Kissinger in his undergraduate thesis).

Throughout the twentieth century, and into the twenty-first, every generation seemed to throw up a new cohort of "declinists," militarists who warn about the establishment's supposed overreliance on data and expertise, complain about the caution generated by too much bureaucracy, protest the enervation that results from too much information. The solution to such lassitude is, inevitably, more war, or at least more of a willingness to wage war, which often leads to war. Kissinger, in the 1950s and 1960s was part of one such cohort, contributing to the era's right-wing lurch in defense thinking, the idea that we needed to fight little wars in gray areas with resolve. In the mid-1970s, ironically, he himself was a primary target of just such a critique, at the hands of Ronald Reagan and the first generation of neoconservatives.

But before we get to that irony, there's another worth considering:

---

who kept them; and what we had to do for this case and that case and that case. From a purely administrative point of view, efficiency, if you will, I suggested that we go to one common system, more than once. This is just not a good—I am not talking about the things you are talking about, I am talking about just trying to run the thing right. That was my problem. It was too complex."

the role that one of Robert McNamara's left-behinds, the economist
Daniel Ellsberg—a man who liked to do his sums, whose understanding of the way the world worked was so diametrically opposed
to Henry Kissinger's metaphysics that he might be thought of as an
anti-Kissinger—had in bringing down the Nixon White House.

Henry Kissinger and Daniel Ellsberg did their undergraduate and
graduate studies at Harvard around the same time, both young veterans on scholarship and both brilliant and precocious. Ellsberg
handed in his own summa undergraduate thesis two years after
Kissinger. And it was Ellsberg, stationed in the US embassy in Saigon, who briefed Kissinger during his first visit to South Vietnam.

Like Kissinger, Ellsberg was interested in the question of contingency and choice in human affairs. But Ellsberg approached the
subject as an economist, going on in his graduate studies and then
at the RAND Corporation to do groundbreaking work in game
theory and abstract modeling. Focused on atomized individuals
engaged in a series of rational cost-benefit transactions aimed to
maximize their advantage, these methods were far removed from
Kissinger's metaphysical approach to history, ideas, and culture.

Kissinger, in fact, had Ellsberg's kind of methodology in mind
when he criticized, in his undergraduate thesis, the smallness of
American social science and the conceits of "positivism," the idea
that truth or wisdom could be derived from logical postulates or
mathematical formulas. Ellsberg spoke the language of axioms,
theorems, and proofs and believed that sentences like this could
help defense strategists plan for nuclear war: "For any given probability distribution, the probability of outcome a with action III is
$p(A \cup C) = P_A + P_C$. The probability of outcome a with action IV is
$p(B \cup C) = P_B + P_C$. . . . This means there must be a probability
distribution, P_A P_B P_C ($0 \leq p_i \leq p \sum p_i = 1$), such that $P_A > P_B$ and
$P_A + P_C < P_B + P_C$. But there is none."[7]

In contrast, Kissinger the metaphysician, wrote things like: "It does not suffice to show logically deduced theorems, as an absolute test of validity. There must also exist a relation to the pervasiveness of an inward experience which transcends phenomenal reality. For though man is a thinking being, it does not follow that his being exhausts itself in thinking. . . . The microcosm contains tension and polarity, the loneliness of the individual in a world of strange significances, in which the total inner meaning of others remains an eternal riddle. Rhythm and tension, longing and fear, characterize the relationship of the microcosm to the macrocosm."[8]

The clash between these two ways of thinking about human experience would play themselves out in the first few months of Kissinger's tenure as Nixon's national security adviser.*

Shortly before Nixon's inauguration, Ellsberg, in a meeting with Kissinger at the president-elect's headquarters at the Pierre Hotel in Manhattan, offered some advice. He related a story of how Robert McNamara, soon after being named secretary of defense, shook up the bureaucracy by immediately flooding Pentagon officers and staff with written questions. The answers he received weren't important. What mattered was that McNamara,

---

* A qualification: there was more overlap in Kissinger's and Ellsberg's approaches than their methods would suggest. Ellsberg was actually a critic of pure rational choice and game theory, arguing for a degree of irrationality in negotiating and decision making. What became known as "Ellsberg's paradox" holds that people have a strong, irrational aversion to ambiguity, even when to make the ambiguous choice would have a larger beneficial reward than the unambiguous option. Likewise, though Kissinger critiqued "positivism," the influence of game theory calculations is clear in his dissection of Eisenhower's nuclear defense strategy. Ellsberg once lectured in Kissinger's seminar on the "political uses of madness," which argued that irrational behavior could be a useful negotiating tool. "I have learned more from Dan Ellsberg," Kissinger at one point said, "than from any other person about bargaining," and the similarities between Ellsberg's formulations and Nixon and Kissinger's madman theory are clear. See Jeffrey Kimball, "Did Thomas C. Schelling Invent the Madman Theory?" *History News Network*, October 24, 2005. Though Kissinger was philosophically opposed to both the economistic method of systems analysis and the arrogance of many of its practitioners, he strategically used a systems-analysis rationale to reorganize the flow of interagency information so as to increase the power of the NSC.

by demanding detailed responses on an impossibly short deadline, was establishing his dominance. And the questions were designed in such a way as to show that the defense secretary was already familiar with controversies and rivalries, that he had his own informants embedded in the department.

Ellsberg suggested Kissinger do something similar: draft questions on controversial issues and send them out to the whole bureaucracy, to every agency and office. The agency principally responsible for any given subject, Ellsberg predicted, would have one opinion on the matter, and secondary agencies would have another, and the difference between the two opinions would provide a useful map of the ambiguities, doubts, and uncertainties that existed in the bureaucracy. But, Ellsberg said, there was another, more Machiavellian reason to conduct the survey. The "very revelation of controversies and the extremely unconvincing positions of some of the primary agencies," he said, "would be embarrassing to the bureaucracy as a whole. It would put the bureaucrats off-balance and on the defensive relative to the source of the questions—that is, Kissinger."[9]

"Kissinger," Ellsberg remembered, "liked the sound of that." So the new director of national security asked Ellsberg, in early 1969, to compile the questions. According to Marvin and Bernard Kalb, the very first thing Kissinger did when he "arrived at his office in the White House basement on January 20, 1969, was to fire [Ellsberg's] list of fifty questions at a bureaucracy struggling to make the transition from Johnson to Nixon." Kissinger set "impossible deadlines," demanding "detailed answers from the State and Defense departments, the CIA, Commerce and Treasury, and the Bureau of the Budget to such questions as: What is the state of American relations with China? With the Soviet Union? With India, both Vietnams, and Indonesia?" The list went "on and on." The questions, as Ellsberg predicted, prompted a backlash. "Who

the hell does he think he is anyhow?" And soon a counterpro-
posal for reorganizing the NSC around the State Department
began to float around, which allowed Kissinger to identify potential rivals. The proposal was quashed and its authors were sidelined.

That first stage of the exercise worked well for Kissinger. The
next, not so much. Kissinger had asked Ellsberg to collate, analyze, and average the responses to the questions related to the
Vietnam War, over five hundred pages in total. The gloom
revealed by the survey was astounding. Even those hawks "optimistic" about the pacification of Vietnam thought that it would
take, on average, 8.3 years to achieve success. All respondents
agreed that the "enemy's manpower pool and infiltration capa-
bilities can outlast allied attrition efforts indefinitely" and that
nothing short of perpetual troops and bombing could save South
Vietnam.

When the findings were presented to Kissinger, he must have
immediately recognized the trap he had fallen into. For all his
warnings about how the "accumulation of facts" by technocrats like
Ellsberg has the effect of sapping political will, Kissinger had fool-
ishly given him free rein to, in effect, data mine the bureaucracy,
providing him with hard evidence that the majority of the foreign
service thought the war either was unwinnable or could be won
only with actions that were politically impossible: permanent occupation or total obliteration.

The negativity of Ellsberg's survey added to the state of siege
that quickly fell over the Nixon White House, compelling the use,
over and over again, of the word *savage* to describe the violence he
hoped to visit on North Vietnam. Maybe, in the face of ongoing
confirmation that he wouldn't be able to bend Hanoi to his will,
Kissinger thought by repeating the word like an incantation he
could keep Ellsberg's gods of evidence and fact at bay.

Ellsberg proposed a follow-up survey. "We've had enough questions for now," Kissinger said.*

Kissinger was the statesman, Ellsberg the expert. And according to Kissinger's worldview, Ellsberg shouldn't have existed, or at least he shouldn't have done what he did. Midlevel experts and analysts were supposed to be risk-avoiding functionaries, little better than insurance actuaries. Ellsberg was what Kissinger in his undergraduate thesis called a "fact-man." His faith in data, his belief that he could capture the vagaries of human behavior in mathematical codes and then use those codes to make decisions, should have led him to a state of, if not paralysis, then predictability. As Kissinger would later write, "most great statesmen" are "locked in permanent struggle with the experts in their foreign offices, for the scope of the statesman's conception challenges the inclination of the expert toward minimum risk."[10]

But it was Ellsberg who was speaking out against the war and then leaking top-secret documents, taking a tremendous risk, including the possibility of imprisonment. And with this one audacious act, he changed the course of history.

The difference between Ellsberg and Kissinger is illustrated by the Pentagon Papers themselves. The "major lesson" offered by the massive study, Ellsberg thought, "was that each person repeated the same patterns in decision making and pretty much the same policy as his predecessor without even knowing it," thinking that "history had started with his administration, and had nothing to learn from earlier ones." Ellsberg, the economist, believed that breaking down history into discrete pieces and studying the deci-

---

* Ellsberg took the results of the questionnaire back with him to RAND, reinforcing the opinion among its analysts that the war was lost. He also leaked them to Maryland senator Charles Mathias.

sion making process, including the consequences of those decisions, provided a chance to break the destructive pattern.

But when Ellsberg tried, in their last meeting before leaking the documents, to get Kissinger to read the papers, Kissinger brushed him off. Kissinger, when he became national security adviser, was given a copy of the study, so he knew what it was: exactly the kind of history writing he had long warned about, designed to entrap executives into thinking that what was has to be, an endless chain of causes and effects resulting in doubt, guilt, and defeat. That the study was compiled by an amorphous committee of experts, analysts, and functionaries only underscored the danger.* "Research," Kissinger wrote in 1966, "often becomes a means to buy time and to assuage consciences. Studying a problem can turn into an escape from coming to grips with it."[11]

"Do we really have anything to learn from this study?" he asked Ellsberg, wearily. "My heart sank," recalls Ellsberg.[12]

---

* The Pentagon Papers really were something conjured out of Kissinger's worst anti-bureaucratic fever dream. The project was a huge endeavor, written by an anonymous committee staffed by scores of what Robert McNamara called "knowledgeable people" drawn from the midlevel defense bureaucracy, universities, and social science think tanks. Headed by two deductive "experts," Morton Halperin and Leslie Gelb, the committee based its findings on the massive amount of paperwork produced by various departments and agencies over the years—what Kissinger in his undergraduate thesis dismissed as the "surface data" of history. Missing, therefore, from its conclusions was what the young Kissinger would have described as the immanent possibility, the contingency, the intuition, and the "freedom" that went into every decision point. And the whole project was indeed driven by a sense of guilt and doubt. As David Rudenstine writes in *The Day the Presses Stopped: A History of the Pentagon Papers*, McNamara's decision to produce what would become known as the Pentagon Papers was laced with "feelings of responsibility, regret, guilt, and sorrow. At least that is what Nicholas Katzenbach thought: 'I think what happened was that the Vietnam War was one of the worst experiences that McNamara ever had. He saw everything he had done in the Pentagon going down the drain. He spent money on Vietnam and had no way of getting out of Vietnam. . . . He really did not know how this terrible mistake had been made. Where did he go wrong? I think he was assuaging a guilt feeling that he had about Vietnam when he directed the study done.'" As a Harvard professor, Kissinger was aware of the Pentagon Papers project, having spent considerable time discussing them with Gelb and Halperin. Then, after he became national security adviser, he, along with Haig and Laird, was one of the few people in the Nixon administration with access to the files.

On Monday, June 14, 1971, the day after the *New York Times* published its first story on the papers, Kissinger, at a senior staff meeting
that included Nixon, exploded. He waved his arms, stomped his
feet, and pounded his hands on a Chippendale table, shouting: "This
will totally destroy American credibility forever. . . . It will destroy
our ability to conduct foreign policy in confidence. . . . No foreign
government will ever trust us again." "Henry was jumping up and
down," was how Nixon remembered the scene, which according to
one biographer shocked even those used to Kissinger's outbursts. By
this point, Kissinger had become known for his "temper tantrums,
jealous rages, and depressions."[13] "That poor fellow is an emotional
fellow," Nixon remarked in late 1971 to John Ehrlichman. "We just
have to get him some psychotherapy," Ehrlichman responded.[14]

The following days brought more phone calls and meetings,
as Nixon consulted with his inner circle—Kissinger, Haldeman,
Mitchell, and Ehrlichman, and others—on how best to respond.
The Pentagon Papers were a bureaucratic history of America's
involvement in Southeast Asia up until Johnson's presidency. There
was nothing specifically damaging to Nixon. But it was Kissinger's
"fury" that convinced Nixon to take the matter seriously. "Without Henry's stimulus," John Ehrlichman said, "the president and
the rest of us might have concluded that the Papers were Lyndon
Johnson's problem, not ours." Kissinger "fanned Richard Nixon's
flame white hot."[15]

Why? The leak was bad for Kissinger in a number of ways.
He was just then negotiating with China to reestablish relations
and was afraid the scandal might sabotage those talks. He feared
that Ellsberg, working with other dissenters on the NSC staff,
might have breached the closed informational circuit that he had
worked hard to establish, perhaps even acquiring classified memos
on Cambodia.[16]

But Kissinger's rage was also as much about the leaker as about
the leak, obvious in the way he swung between awe and agitation
when describing Ellsberg to his coconspirators, as almost Prome-
thean in his intellect and appetites. "Curse that son of a bitch, I
know him well," he began one Oval Office meeting:

> He's a genius. . . . He was a hardliner. He went—he volunteered for
> service in Vietnam. He was so nuts that he'd drive around all over
> Vietnam with a carbine when it was guerilla-infested, and he'd
> shoot at—he has My Lai cases on his—he'd shoot at peasants
> in the fields on the theory everyone in black—. . . . The man is a
> genius. He's one of the most brilliant men I've ever met.

In other conversations, Kissinger said that Ellsberg had hunted
Vietnamese peasants from helicopters and was a drug-crazed sex
maniac. "A despicable bastard," Kissinger said. "Passionate in his
denunciation of Daniel Ellsberg," was how Ehrlichman remembered Kissinger.[17] Kissinger keyed his performance to stir up
Nixon's varied resentments, depicting Ellsberg as some kind of
liberal and hedonistic superman—smart, subversive, promiscuous,
perverse, and privileged. "He's now married a very rich girl,"
Kissinger told Nixon. "Nixon was fascinated," Ehrlichman said.

"Henry got Nixon cranked up," Haldeman remembered, "and
then they started cranking each other up until they both were in a
frenzy." "Kissinger," he said, "was absolutely infuriated and, in
his inimitable fashion, managed to beat the president into an equal
froth of fury." Haig said that Kissinger "did drive the president's
concern" about the leak.

"It shows you're a weakling, Mr. President," Kissinger warned
Nixon, if he were to let Ellsberg off.

It was in the meeting where Kissinger gave his most detailed
description of Ellsberg (the one where he admitted that he passed
on classified information to Nixon's campaign in the fall of 1968)

that Nixon ordered a series of illegal covert operations. "Blow the safe," he said, hoping to get that bombing-halt file so he could "blackmail" Johnson into speaking out against Ellsberg. "I want it implemented on a thievery basis," the president directed. It was also in this meeting that Nixon ordered the "plumbers" to be established, a clandestine unit headed by Howard Hunt and G. Gordon Liddy that conducted a number of buggings and burglaries, including the one at the Democratic National Committee headquarters at the Watergate Hotel.

The plumbers were also responsible for breaking into Ellsberg's psychiatrist's office in California, an operation that directly stemmed from Kissinger's portrayal of Ellsberg as unhinged. According to Haldeman, "the reason for trying to get Ellsberg's psychiatrist's files is explained by the desire to find evidence to support Kissinger's vivid statement about Ellsberg's weird habits." The information was to be used to "discredit his character."[18]

"He's nuts, isn't he?" Haldeman asked Kissinger in one of their meetings.

"He's nuts," Kissinger answered.

Earlier, in the meeting where he suggested that Kissinger survey the bureaucracy as a way of establishing his dominance over it, Ellsberg, who won the highest of security clearances at a very young age, had warned Kissinger of the danger of too much knowledge. It's a lengthy speech, worth quoting in full:

> Henry, there's something I would like to tell you, for what it's worth, something I wish I had been told years ago. You've been a consultant for a long time, and you've dealt a great deal with top secret information. But you're about to receive a whole slew of special clearances, maybe fifteen or twenty of them, that are higher than top secret.

I've had a number of these myself, and I've known other people who have just acquired them, and I have a pretty good sense of what the effects of receiving these clearances are on a person who didn't previously know they even *existed*. And the effects of reading the information that they will make available to you.

First, you'll be exhilarated by some of this new information, and by having it all—so much! incredible!—suddenly available to you. But second, almost as fast, you will feel like a fool for having studied, written, talked about these subjects, criticized and analyzed decisions made by presidents for years without having known of the existence of all this information, which presidents and others had and you didn't, and which must have influenced their decisions in ways you couldn't even guess. In particular, you'll feel foolish for having literally rubbed shoulders for over a decade with some officials and consultants who did have access to all this information you didn't know about and didn't know they had, and you'll be stunned that they kept that secret from you so well.

You will feel like a fool, and that will last for about two weeks. Then, after you've started reading all this daily intelligence input and become used to using what amounts to whole libraries of hidden information, which is much more closely held than mere top secret data, you will forget there ever was a time when you didn't have it, and you'll be aware only of the fact that you have it now and most others don't . . . and that all those *other* people are fools.

Over a longer period of time—not too long, but a matter of two or three years—you'll eventually become aware of the limitations of this information. There is a great deal that it doesn't tell you, it's often inaccurate, and it can lead you astray just as much as the *New York Times* can. But that takes a while to learn.

In the meantime it will have become very hard for you to *learn* from anybody who doesn't have these clearances. Because you'll be thinking as you listen to them: "What would this man be telling me if he knew what I know? Would he be giving me the same advice, or would it totally change his predictions and recommendations?" And *that* mental exercise is so torturous that after a while you give it up and just stop listening. I've seen this with my superiors, my colleagues . . . and with myself.

You will deal with a person who doesn't have those clearances only from the point of view of what you want him to believe and what impression you want him to go away with, since you'll have to lie carefully to him about what you know. In effect, you will have to manipulate him. You'll give up trying to assess what he has to say. The danger is, you'll become something like a moron. You'll become incapable of learning from most people in the world, no matter how much experience they may have in their particular areas that may be much greater than yours.[19]

Ellsberg says he gave some thought to what he wanted to say before his meeting with Kissinger. The monologue is notable in that it reveals Ellsberg, the deductive rationalist, as the true appreciator of advice that Kissinger to this day likes to give: information isn't wisdom and the truth of facts is found not in the facts themselves but in the questions we ask of them.

Kissinger, at a later date, complained to Ellsberg about his former Harvard colleagues, including Thomas Schelling, who had turned against the war. He was, reports Ellsberg, "contemptuous of their presumption that they could judge a policy when they knew so little about policy making from the inside."

"They never had the clearances," Kissinger said.

For what must have been for him a long year, between mid-1973 and mid-1974, it seemed Henry Kissinger, now holding the position of both national security adviser and secretary of state, was going down with Richard Nixon, along with his top aides: Haldeman,

Ehrlichman, and John Dean, who were all gone by April 1973. Kissinger almost got caught on Cambodia, when Major Hal Knight sent a whistle-blowing letter to Senator William Proxmire informing him of his falsification of records. The Senate Armed Services Committee held hearings through the middle of 1973, and Seymour Hersh came very close to establishing Kissinger's involvement in setting up the dual record reporting system.* Hersh couldn't confirm Kissinger's role (he would at a later date) but that didn't let Kissinger off the hook. In June 1974, Hersh, along with Woodward and Bernstein, had widened the net, filing stories fingering Kissinger for the first round of illegal wiretaps the White House set up, done in the spring of 1969 to keep the Cambodia bombing secret. Reporters, senators, and representatives were circling, asking questions, digging up more information, issuing subpoenas.[20]

Landing in Austria, en route to the Middle East, and finding that the press had run more unflattering stories and editorials, Kissinger took a gamble. He held an impromptu press conference and threatened to resign (this was June 11, less than two months before Nixon's resignation). It was by all accounts a bravura turn. "When the record is written," he said, seemingly on the verge of tears, "one may remember that perhaps some lives were saved and perhaps some mothers can rest more at ease, but I leave that to history. What I will not leave to history is a discussion of my public honor."[21]

The bet worked and the press gushed.† He "seemed totally

---

* To be clear, the White House's off-the-books war making was not limited to Cambodia: Knight decided to write the letter after reading Hersh's earlier stories on other illegal bombings conducted on North Vietnam and Laos.

† Some remained unconvinced. In an essay published in the *Washington Post*, the historian Arthur Schlesinger, perhaps thinking of all those lunches he had with Kissinger where he was told one thing, only to witness the White House do another, wrote that "watching Henry Kissinger babbling about his honor" reminded him of one of Ralph Waldo Emerson's "nonchalant observations: 'The louder he talked of his honor, the

authentic," *New York* magazine wrote. As if in recoil from the unexpected assertiveness they had shown in recent years, reporters and news anchors rallied around. The rest of the White House was being revealed to be little more than a bunch of shady two-bit thugs, but Kissinger was someone America could believe in. "We were half-convinced," Ted Koppel said in a documentary in 1974, just after Kissinger's threatened resignation, "that nothing was beyond the capacity of this remarkable man." The secretary of state was a "legend, the most admired man in America, the magician, the miracle worker." Kissinger, Koppel said, "may be the best thing we've got going for us."[22]

---

faster we counted our spoons.'" When Kissinger complained in a personal letter of the use of the word *babbling*, Schlesinger apologized: "On reflection, I should not have written 'babbling'; 'going on' would have been sufficient. For the rest, I must confess that I still stand with Emerson."

6

The Opposite of Unity

You have a responsibility to recognize that we are living in a revolutionary time.

—Henry Kissinger

Henry Kissinger has long expressed a more than grudging admiration for revolutionaries. Years before he would sit down with Mao to discuss philosophy or sneak away with Soviet ambassador Anatoly Dobrynin to sip scotch and carve out respective spheres of influence, he argued that "most great statesmen have been either representatives of essentially conservative social structures or revolutionaries." The conservative is effective, he said, because as a defender of the status quo he doesn't have to "justify" his "every step along the way." But the revolutionary also has an advantage in that he believes himself liberated from the past. He thus has more freedom to act and more easily "dissolves technical limitations."[1] Kissinger was a conservative, but he was also a dialectician, and he believed that revolutionaries possessed a number of qualities— surety of purpose, a vision for the future, an ability to overcome institutional lethargy—that conservatives would need if they were to best the revolutionary challenge.

Kissinger strived to obtain them. He especially admired the discipline and resolve of his Marxist counterparts. At times, the envy was palpable. North Vietnamese negotiators, he wrote, remained true to their purposes, even as he found himself bowing to political pressure at home: they "changed nothing in their diplomatic objectives and very little in their diplomatic positions." Their "fourth rate" peasant country was being bombed back to the Stone Age, but they "could keep us under constant public pressure."[2] Zhou Enlai was "electric, quick, taut, deft, humorous," Kissinger wrote, and the two men "developed an easy camaraderie not untinged with affection."[3] With the autocratic Mao, he could fantasize about what it was like to conduct foreign policy and not be tormented by the press and Congress. "Why is it in your country," Mao once asked him, "you are always so obsessed with that nonsensical Watergate issue?"

Mao and Kissinger shared a mutual appreciation of German metaphysics. "You are now freer than before," Mao said to Kissinger in November 1973, meaning that with the Vietnam War over and Nixon reelected, he had more room to maneuver. "Much more," Kissinger replied.[4] Mao's mention of freedom here was in a narrow, political sense, now that Nixon had his landslide. But it prompted the Chinese revolutionary to ask Kissinger a question about Hegel. The Chinese leader wanted to know if he was using the correct English translation of Hegel's famous maxim "freedom means the knowledge of necessity."

"Yes," Kissinger replied. The conversation continued:

MAO: Do you pay attention or not to one of the subjects of Hegel's philosophy, that is, the unity of opposites?

KISSINGER: Very much. I was much influenced by Hegel in my philosophic thinking.

MAO: Both Hegel and Feuerbach, who came a little later after him. They were both great thinkers. And Marxism came partially from them. They were predecessors of Marx. If it were not for Hegel and Feuerbach, there would not be Marxism.

KISSINGER: Yes. Marx reversed the tendency of Hegel, but he adopted the basic theory.

MAO: What kind of doctor are you? Are you a doctor of philosophy?

KISSINGER: Yes (laughter).

MAO: Yes, well, then won't you give me a lecture?

Kissinger was familiar with Hegel's "unity of opposites," the notion that ideas, people, political movements, and nations are defined by their contradictions. He believed that effective diplomacy was the managing of those contradictions, that what made great statesmen great was their ability to "restrain contending forces, both domestic and foreign, by manipulating their antagonisms."

By 1975, however, after six years in public office, Kissinger, now Gerald Ford's secretary of state, had achieved the opposite of unity at home and something like perpetual war abroad. Rather than restrain contending forces, he had unleashed them. In the United States, the deceit, cruelty, and corruption of Nixon's inner circle, including Kissinger, were not the only cause of the crack-up taking place at all levels of society, among elites and within the broader population, that, by the early 1970s, had reached crisis proportions. But, as Nixon and Kissinger themselves put it, they used foreign policy to "break the back" of domestic opponents and "destroy the confidence of the people in the American establishment." They had mixed results with the former (Nixon did win a landslide reelection, though he was subsequently driven out of office) but succeeded, stunningly, with the latter. By the end of Kissinger's tenure, all of the institutional pillars of society that previous administrations could rely on to uphold government legitimacy—the press, universities, the movie and music industries, churches, courts, and Congress—seemed to be pushing against it, creating that entrenched adversary culture that so worried conservatives.

In assessing Kissinger's legacy in the realm of diplomacy, one has to, as the *New Yorker* pointed out in late 1973, contend with the foreign policies of "two Henry Kissingers." There was the Kissinger who "established relations with China, improved our relations with Russia, and successfully completed the first phase of SALT—and for these achievements most Americans are grateful." These initiatives were meant to be the pillars of his "grand strategy," stabilizing the post-Vietnam international order and allowing the United States, the Soviet Union, and China to stake out spheres of influence. One might add to this list the shuttle diplomacy that helped end 1973's Arab-Israel War. But then there was the Kissinger who, with Nixon, "planned the undisclosed bombing of Cambodia . . . initiated the unauthorized wiretapping of members of Kissinger's staff and of newsmen in 1969 . . . planned the invasion of Cambodia in 1970 . . . planned the use of American air power to support the invasion of Laos in 1971 . . . planned the mining and blockading of North Vietnamese harbors . . . planned the 'Christmas bombing' of North Vietnam—all this done in secrecy, and without congressional consent. While the President and the men of Watergate were, it now appears, undermining our democratic system of government in domestic affairs, the President and Henry Kissinger were undermining the system in foreign affairs."[5]

If the policies put into place by the first Kissinger were allowed to mature, one could imagine it producing a number of salutary effects.* But they didn't have a chance to mature, and they didn't

---

* In the United States, for instance, Washington could have, in the wake of Vietnam, more thoroughly demilitarized, using funds that would have gone into the military budget to recapitalize domestic infrastructure and nonmilitary research and devel-

because of, at least in part, the actions of the second Kissinger. In the years following the end of the Vietnam War, Kissinger, in one region after another, executed policies that helped doom his own grand strategy. Then, once he was out of office, he threw in with America's new militarists, who were intent on tearing down détente. Remember those "brutal forces in the society," the "real tough guys" he was constantly warning liberals about in 1970 and 1971? By 1980, he was with them, sanctioning their jump-starting of the Cold War and their drive to retake the Third World.

With so much time wasted on a lost war and a failed president, Kissinger, in his last years in office, seemed to have succumbed to something like the same "pattern" of "over-exertion" that diplomatic historian John Lewis Gaddis identifies in the policies of Kissinger's Soviet and Chinese counterparts during this period: "The efforts of old revolutionaries," Gaddis writes, "for reasons more sentimental than rational, to rediscover their roots, to convince themselves that the purposes for which they had sacrificed so much in seizing power had not been totally overwhelmed by the compromises they had had to make in actually wielding power."[6] Struggling to come up with a coherent post-Vietnam policy, Kissinger responded to crises in an ad hoc manner, playing this one off of that, shoring up Washington's position with sundry dictators and giving the green light to invasions, coups, and assassinations.[7]

The initiatives he did put into place (especially after 1973 in the Middle East) not only overshadowed détente but canceled out whatever steadying effect it might have provided the planet. That the policies Kissinger would hand off to his successors were

---

opment, making possible a different kind of response to the 1973–75 economic crisis, a good-paying, mass industrial public policy rather than the "free trade" race-to-the-bottom that was put into place.

morally indefensible is a matter of opinion. Less contestable is the claim that he left the world polarized and, in the long run, volatile, despite the short-term stability of the jackboot.

In a way, Kissinger did to the larger Third World what he did to Cambodia: he institutionalized a self-fulfilling logic of intervention. Action led to reaction, reaction demanded more action. Just as his secret bombing so roiled Cambodia's borders that, by early 1970, it made a major land invasion using US troops seem like a good idea, Kissinger's global post-Vietnam War diplomacy so inflamed the international order that it made the neocon's radical vision of perpetual war look like a reasonable option for many of the world's problems.

ASIA

The Khmer Rouge had taken Phnom Penh on April 17, 1975, and Saigon fell to North Vietnamese troops shortly thereafter. Having lost Southeast Asia, Kissinger reinforced the White House's commitment to neighboring dictators, including Ferdinand Marcos in the Philippines and Suharto in Indonesia. Nixon and Kissinger had given Marcos permission to impose martial law, and under Kissinger, US military and economic funding to the Philippines had soared. Kissinger, in exchange for a deal on US military bases in the Philippines, offered Marcos a significant increase in aid. Marcos held out for more. "We offered them $1 billion," Kissinger reported to Ford, "and they asked for $2 billion."[8]

Indonesia, with its vast natural resources, including significant oil reserves, was even more important. On December 6, 1975, on a layover in Jakarta on the way back to Washington from a state visit to China, Kissinger and President Gerald Ford had given the country's president, Suharto, the go-ahead to invade East Timor, a former Portuguese colony seeking independence. Would it be a "long guerilla war"? Kissinger wanted to know. "A small guerilla war,"

Suharto replied. "It is important that whatever you do succeeds quickly," Kissinger said, asking only that Suharto wait until he and Ford had returned to the United States before launching the operations. The conversation then turned to Indonesian petroleum production, with Kissinger advising Suharto to "not create a climate that discourages investment."[9]

Suharto was in even more of a hurry than Kissinger. He had been planning the invasion for some time but fear of diplomatic isolation led him to hold off. Now that he had his green light, he began the assault on East Timor the next day. At least 102,800 Timorese were killed in the invasion and during the twenty-four-year Indonesian occupation, either in combat or by starvation and illness, according to a United Nations truth commission. Other sources estimate an even higher number of victims, including hundreds of thousands put in Indonesian concentration camps. This out of a population of less than 700,000. Throughout it all, Suharto continued to receive thousands of M-16s and other small arms, armored cars, and aircraft, including Bronco planes, specially designed during the Vietnam War for counterinsurgent operations, able to fly low over rugged terrain like that found in East Timor. Major fighting went on for three years, followed by a low-intensity counterinsurgency that continued until 1999.

Kissinger left his mark in South Asia as well, having, in 1971, condoned West Pakistan's invasion of East Pakistan (now Bangladesh). Nixon and Kissinger knew that "selective genocide," as the US envoy to Dhaka described the brutality of the invasion, was taking place. But they silently extended military aid to Pakistan. The result was half a million dead, hundreds of thousands of women raped, and millions of refugees pouring into India. At one point, Nixon compared the slaughter to the Holocaust, indicating that he realized the immorality of remaining quiet. Kissinger told him not to worry. Kissinger wanted to appease Pakistan's ally, China.

And Pakistan itself was an important Cold War friend. He also hated India's prime minister, Indira Gandhi ("a bitch," he called her), and didn't think highly of Indians in general ("bastards," he thought). Besides, he told Nixon that if Bangladesh were to break from Pakistan, the new country would "go left anyway." Bengalis "are by nature left." And indeed, a left-wing government did emerge to rule what eventually, after India intervened to stop the killing, became an independent Bangladesh. But in August 1975, that government was overthrown in a bloody coup that Kissinger almost certainly knew about in advance and supported, bringing to power an Islamic, pro-American, and anti-Indian military regime.[10]

AFRICA

Focused as he was on Southeast Asia, Kissinger often treated Africa as little more than an object of ridicule. He was known to make racist jokes ("I wonder what the dining room is going to smell like?" he asked Arkansas senator William Fulbright on the way to a dinner for African ambassadors) and referred to at least one African head of state as an "ape."[11] Bigotry might have been yet another way to ingratiate himself with arch-racists in the White House like Haig, Nixon, and Haldeman.

As far as policy was concerned, early in Nixon's administration, Kissinger implemented what became known as the "tar baby option" for southern Africa, which included strengthening ties with the white supremacist nations of South Africa and Rhodesia, expanding arms sales to their militaries, and establishing clandestine networks to conduct covert operations to counter liberation movements. And just as a hard line in Southeast Asia had its domestic component, carried out with an eye toward Nixon's 1972 reelection, support for Pretoria and Salisbury was meant to advance the "southern strategy." The "tar baby option" played well in the

US South, as did Kissinger's and Nixon's insistence that the internal affairs of apartheid regimes were not any business of the United Nations—a clear echo of the segregationist defense of "states' rights."[12]

But southern Africa was fast becoming a major battleground, convulsed by movements demanding an end to racial oppression and colonialism. Portuguese rule in Angola and Mozambique had collapsed, giving rise to civil wars between broadly popular liberation movements and "freedom fighters" backed by Washington, South Africa, and Rhodesia.

Kissinger came into open conflict with area experts, in the CIA and State Department, who actually knew something about southern Africa. For example, both Washington's consul general to Angola and the CIA's station chief felt that the country's largest insurgent organization, the left-leaning Movimento Popular de Libertação de Angola, or MPLA, composed of engineers, agronomists, teachers, doctors, and economists from the colony's educated middle class, "was the best qualified movement to govern Angola."[13] Kissinger disagreed, dismissing those soft on the MPLA as "missionaries," "anti-white," "obsessively liberal," and "bleeding hearts." Kissinger, who believed these experts were underestimating Soviet influence in the region, also clashed with his assistant secretaries of state for Africa. One he fired, and the other resigned in protest over policy.[14]

Kissinger would later write that "nuance" had to guide statesmen and that diplomats needed to avoid applying a "mechanical blueprint" to "day-to-day foreign policy." But Kissinger looked at southern Africa in the 1970s and all he could see was Southeast Asia in the 1960s. The United States, Kissinger argued in a planning meeting in mid-1975 would have to take "an active role" in Angola's conflict in order to "demonstrate that events in Southeast Asia have not lessened our determination to protect our interests." What was going on in Angola was more than a civil war, he said. Ever on the lookout for that crisis when spontaneous action could create order out of chaos, Kissinger said that Angola was an "opportunity." During a moment of "great uncertainty," America had a chance to prove "our will and determination to remain the preeminent leader and defender of freedom in the West."[15] Angola barely figured.

Again, we have the demonstrative effect as both means and ends: specific objectives are left unstated, aside from an implied circularity; we need to demonstrate resolve in order to protect our interests and defend freedom, with "interests" and "freedom" defined entirely as our ability to demonstrate our resolve.

For once, though, Kissinger wasn't the most casually cruel person in the room. "We might wish," Ford's secretary of defense, James Schlesinger, said during one strategy session, "to encourage the disintegration of Angola."[16] In July, Kissinger stepped up covert aid to a pro-American insurgency in Angola that he had already been running. He also urged South African mercenaries and the apartheid regimes' regular forces to invade. Conducting these operations through the CIA and proxy white supremacists in Rhodesia and South Africa was useful, since it allowed Kissinger to avoid all those cumbersome restrictions placed on him by the "McGovernite Congress." In fact, at the *very* moment Kissinger was apologizing to a congressional commission for having used the CIA in Laos, he was doing the exact same thing in southern Africa.*

In his memoir, John Stockwell, the CIA agent in charge of operations during the early stages of Kissinger's covert war in Angola, wrote that "coordination was effected at all CIA levels and

---

* On November 21, 1975, Kissinger testified to Congress: "I do not believe in retrospect that it was good national policy to have the CIA conduct the war in Laos. I think we should have found some other way of doing it. And to use the CIA simply because it is less accountable for very visible major operations is poor national policy." The CIA, he said, shouldn't be deployed "simply for the convenience of the executive branch and its accountability." Even as he was doing just that.

the South Africans escalated their involvement in step with our own." This was done, Stockwell said, "without any memos being written at CIA headquarters saying 'Let's coordinate with the South Africans.'" "There was close collaboration and encouragement between the CIA and the South Africans," Stockwell testified to Congress, and Kissinger, along with the CIA director, was in charge of the operation.[17] Similar coordination in fact took place throughout the region, in Angola as well as in Mozambique, Zaire, and Namibia.[18]

Kissinger's wars in southern Africa were catastrophic. In Angola, the MPLA was proving formidable, and South Africa's incursion prompted Cuba to enter the war, with Fidel Castro's army routing the US-backed invaders. Kissinger began to waver. "Maybe we should let Angola go," he said to Brent Scowcroft, the national security adviser, in early 1976. "This is going to turn into a worse disaster."

It did. The civil wars spun out of control. Panicked white-minority governments in Pretoria and Salisbury were striking first this way, then that. In response, Havana made it known that it would increase its support for freedom struggles. Castro's remarkable victory in Angola had already raised his prestige. If the war were to escalate and if Cuban troops were to vanquish white supremacy elsewhere, in Rhodesia, for example, that prestige would increase many fold.

Adding to Kissinger's worries was a series of critical articles, starting in 1974, in the US and international press on his "tar baby tilt." Morally defending anti-Communism, even if it meant relying on murderous dictators, was one thing. Justifying his support for white supremacy and racism was quite another. Kissinger was forced to reverse course and play the peacemaker. In April 1976, he took a tour of Africa, meeting with left-leaning leaders, talking about universal and "common" values, and affirming African "aspirations." He visited Victoria Falls, toured a game park in a Land Rover, donned a dashiki, and referred to Rhodesia as Zimbabwe. "Africa for Africans," Kissinger told *Jet* magazine upon his return, saying that Washington shouldn't force the diversity of the region into a Cold War template.

Then, in order to preempt another triumph for Castro, Kissinger helped negotiate the surrender of Rhodesia's white supremacist government. "I have a basic sympathy with the white Rhodesians," Kissinger, the refugee from Weimar Germany, said, "but black Africa is absolutely united on this issue, and if we don't grab the initiative we will be faced with the Soviets, and Cuban troops."[19]

This about-face notwithstanding, the damage was done. Kissinger left behind him a terrorist infrastructure that would be rebooted by the New Right. Hard-liners in the Reagan White House, as part of their revival of the Cold War, continued to support apartheid in South Africa and, even more tragically, murderous pro-Washington insurgents in Mozambique and Angola.* In Mozambique, RENAMO, or Resistência Nacional Moçambicana, was brutal, known for cutting off limbs and mutilating the faces of civilians. "There can be no ambiguity as to the terrorist activities of RENAMO," wrote the US embassy in Maputo; its "insurgents have engaged in increasingly cruel and senseless acts of armed terrorism."[20] In Angola, Washington-backed rebels were led by Jonas Savimbi, described by the British ambassador to Angola as a "monster" whose "lust for power had brought appalling misery to his people."[21]

Savimbi was first cultivated by Kissinger, who spent millions on him. Now, he was taken up by Reagan, who in 1986 hosted him in the White House and praised him at the annual dinner of the Conservative Political Action Conference. After hailing "the rise of the

---

* George Shultz, as secretary of state, tried with some success to moderate Reagan's stance on Angola, Mozambique, and South Africa, but he was often undercut by CIA director William Casey, who, along with the same group of hard-liners who ran the Contras in Nicaragua, activated the covert network Kissinger had left behind.

New Right and the religious revival of the mid-seventies and the final, triumphant march to Washington in 1980," Reagan turned to the revolution abroad, toasting Savimbi. The "revolutionary" struggle of Angola's "freedom fighters," led by Savimbi, "electrifies the world." "Their hopes," Reagan said, "reside in us, as ours do in them."[22] Two months later, the administration provided Savimbi's rebels with a $25 million aid package, including surface-to-air missiles.

Scholars estimate Savimbi's insurgency cost 400,000 lives. All told, historians guess that these wars killed as many as two million Angolans and Mozambicans. Neither country "disintegrated." But they were devastated, their infrastructure ruined, their governments militarized and bankrupted, their hospitals and morgues filled beyond capacity. Mozambique's civil war ended in 1992, while fighting in Angola dragged on for yet another decade.*

---

* In his January 1976 testimony to the Senate subcommittee regarding Angola, Kissinger insisted that the U.S. needed to show resolve, to be "determined to use its strength" in "Black Africa." "If the United States is seen to emasculate itself in the face of massive, unprecedented Soviet and Cuban intervention," Kissinger asked, "what will be the perception of leaders around the world?" Kissinger cited the Monroe Doctrine, claiming that that 1823 presidential statement—which declared the Western Hemisphere off limits to European powers—granted the president the "unusual discretion" to act in Africa without congressional oversight (Senator Joe Biden accused him of trying to implement a "global Monroe Doctrine"). But Kissinger's intrigues came first, provoking the Soviet intervention that Kissinger then said the U.S. had to answer so as not to emasculate itself. In his May 1978 congressional testimony, Stockwell, the CIA agent who ran the agency's southern African operations, is unambiguous that the Soviets and the Cubans entered the Angola conflict only *after* Kissinger and CIA director William Colby began their covert operation. The CIA and Kissinger's proxy, China, began providing training and weapons to anti-MPLA rebels in May 1974. The Soviets *subsequently* began to arm the MPLA, in September 1974. The Cubans became involved the *following* year. Stockwell described Kissinger's 1976 testimony as a complete fabrication: "The CIA director and Mr. Kissinger were surely acutely aware that the American public would not tolerate such an operation 3 months after the humiliation of our evacuation of South Vietnam, so they lied about it. Even in secret briefings to Congress they dissembled. Director [William] Colby and Secretary Kissinger testified to the Congress that no Americans were involved in the Angola conflict, that no American arms were being sent directly into Angola, that the CIA had no involvement with South Africa, and that the CIA was not involved in the recruitment of mercenaries. Their testimony was misleading on all of these points." For Kissinger's testimony, see US Senate, *Hearings before the Subcommittee on African Affairs of the Committee on Foreign Relations . . . on U.S. Involvement in Civil War in Angola,*

THE MIDDLE EAST

December 1975 was a busy month in a busy year for Kissinger. Just about ten days after okaying Suharto's assault on East Timor, Kissinger met with Iraq's foreign minister, Sa'dun Hammadi. Hoping to turn Baghdad against Moscow, Kissinger promised Hammadi that in exchange for toning down Iraq's Baathist radicalism and moving away from the Soviet Union, Ford would bring Israel to heel and force it to give up its occupied territories. "Israel does us more harm than good in the Arab world," Kissinger said to Iraq's foreign minister. "We can't negotiate about the existence of Israel, but we can reduce its size to historical proportions."[23]

Kissinger had no intention of doing anything of the kind. Over the course of the previous two years, since his "shuttle diplomacy" helped end the 1973 Arab-Israel War, Kissinger had been working out the contours of what political scientist Stephen Walt describes as the "ascendency of the United States" in the region.

This ascendance involved many different elements. But its essence entailed the combustible combination of creating inseparable alliances with *both* Israel and oil-producing Arab nations, telling each what they wanted to hear. To Arab states, he was promising (as he told Hammadi) that Washington would press Israel to give back its occupied territory. But to Israel, he pledged something else entirely. In September 1975, for example, he signed a secret agreement with Israel that committed the United States to neither "recognize" nor "negotiate" with the PLO until the PLO

January 29, February 3, 4, and 6, 1976 (1976); for Stockwell's, see *United States-Angolan Relations: Hearing Before the Subcommittee on Africa of the Committee on International Relations* (1978). The effects of Kissinger's and then Reagan's covert wars spread north of Angola, into Central Africa. Human Rights Watch, in its 2004 *World Report*, p. 313, linked the ongoing resource-war crisis in the Congo to US covert operations in Angola in the 1970s, particularly to the support, weapons, and encouragement the United States gave to Zaire's anti-MPLA leader, Mobutu Sese Seko.

acknowledged "Israel's right to exist" (while exempting Israel from having to reciprocate and recognize Palestine's "right to exist"). Kissinger's guarantees to Israel had the effect of locking in the crisis, proving a method to manage the impasse, not to resolve it. As the historian Salim Yaqub writes, Kissinger "*deliberately* designed the step-by-step approach to be a mechanism for Israel's indefinite occupation of Arab land, a function it continued to serve in later decades, whatever the intentions of his successors."[24]

Notwithstanding what he had told Hammadi, Kissinger was not going to reduce Israel to "historical proportions." But he did have a more expendable people he could offer up and keep his word: the Kurds. Just three years earlier, he had schemed with Iran to destabilize Baathist Iraq by supporting the Kurds, providing them with weapons (supplied by Israel so as not to alert the State Department) to wage an insurgent war for independence in northern Iraq. Kissinger didn't expect the Kurds to triumph. He often complained about the unworkable size of the United Nations and the last thing he wanted was yet another member state (Bangladesh was bad enough). He just needed the Kurdish insurgency to provide enough pressure on Baghdad to give him leverage.

But now in 1975, believing he had worked out a lasting pro-American balance of power between Iran and Iraq, Kissinger withdrew US support from the Kurds. Baghdad moved quickly, launching an assault that killed thousands and implementing a program of ethnic cleansing. Arabs were moved into the region and hundreds of thousands of Kurds were rounded up and forcibly relocated. According to a congressional committee that later investigated Kissinger's policy, Kissinger and Iran "hoped that our clients"—the Kurds—"would not prevail." Rather, they wanted that "the insurgents simply continue a level of hostilities sufficient to sap the resources" of Iraq. The prose of such committee reports is often bland, but the next two sentences convey a cutting mordancy: "This policy was not imparted to our clients, who were encouraged to continue fighting. . . . Even in the context of covert action ours was a cynical enterprise."[25]*

Also in the Middle East, it was Kissinger who, in 1972, began the "policy of unconditional support" for the shah of Iran, as a way to steady American power in the Gulf as the United States tried to extricate itself from Southeast Asia.[26] And as James Schlesinger, who served as Nixon's CIA director and secretary of defense, noted, if "we were going to make the Shah the Guardian of the Gulf, we've got to give him what he needs." Which, Schlesinger went on, really meant "giving him what he wants."[27] And what the shah wanted most of all were weapons—and American military trainers, and a navy, and an air force. "Arms dealers joked," writes the historian Ervand Abrahamian, "that the shah devoured their manuals in much the same way as other men read *Playboy*." Kissinger overrode objections by State and Defense to give the shah what no other country in the world had: the ability to buy whatever it wanted from US military contractors. "We are looking for a navy," the shah told Kissinger. "We have a large shopping list." Kissinger let him buy a navy. By 1977, Abrahamian notes, "the shah had the largest navy in the Persian Gulf, the largest air force in Western Asia, and the fifth largest army in the whole world": thousands of modern tanks, 400 helicopters, 28 hovercraft, 100 long-range artillery pieces, thousands of Maverick missiles, 173 F4 fighter jets, 141 F5s, and so on. The next year, the shah bought another $12 billion worth of equipment.

---

* Kissinger sacrificed the Kurds for nothing; the shah would be gone by 1979 and all that military hardware Washington made available to Iran would be inherited by the ayatollahs. A year later, Iraq and Iran would begin a pointlessly tragic war that would consume hundreds of thousands of lives, with the Reagan administration "tilting" toward Baghdad (which included giving Hussein the material needed to produce sarin gas and the intelligence needed to deploy the gas on the Kurds) while at the same time selling high-tech weapons to Revolutionary Iran [in what became known as Iran–Contra].

The shah's military buildup was about more than protecting the gulf. It was part of a larger transformation of the global political economy, in which the West grew increasingly dependent on recycled petrodollars.* That dependency further increased in 1975, when

---

* *The Los Angeles Times* (February 14, 1974) says that the word *petrodollar* was coined in late 1973, introduced into English by New York investment bankers who courted oil-producing countries of the Middle East. Already by June 1973—with the worst of that year's many crises still in the future (October's Arab-Israeli War, the oil embargo, and November's recession, which lasted for two years), Nixon's Treasury Secretary George Shultz gave a speech saying that rising oil prices could result in a "highly advantageous mutual bargain" between the United States and petroleum-producing countries in the Middle East. Indeed, many began to argue that such a "bargain" might solve a number of problems: create demand for the US dollar (to compensate for Nixon's 1971 withdrawal from the Bretton-Woods system); inject needed money into a flagging defense industry, which was hit hard by the Vietnam wind-down (Secretary of Defense Schlesinger said that Iranian weapons sales helped pay for military research and development); and cover mounting deficits, through the petrodollar purchase of Treasury bonds. Petrodollars were not a quick fix; high energy prices remained a drag on the US economy, with inflation and high interest rates a problem for nearly a decade. Nor was petrodollar dependence part of a preconceived plan. Rather, that dependence grew fitfully, in response to an array of global events, as illustrated by Kissinger's evolving relationship to the Middle East. Between 1969 and 1971, Nixon and Kissinger accommodated Arab and Iranian economic nationalism, working, for instance, with Muammar al-Qaddafi after he seized power in Libya in 1969 and forced new terms on Occidental Oil. During these years, "Washington," the historian Daniel Sargent writes, "had tolerated—and even encouraged—price increases that enhanced Iran's and Saudi Arabia's capacities to serve as guarantors of Cold War security interests." But the Arab-Israeli War, followed by the embargo, forced a reckoning: "The United States," as Kissinger would later sum up the problem, "has an interest in the survival of Israel, but we of course have an interest in the 130 million Arabs that sit athwart the world's oil supplies." What to do? Washington's two gulf "guarantors"—Iran and Saudi Arabia—were proving recalcitrant (the spiraling cost of oil made the shah giddy: "of course it is going to rise. Certainly!" he told an interviewer at the end of 1973; the Saudis, meanwhile, begged Kissinger to understand that they were under pressure from radicals: they had no choice but to send troops to fight Israel and cut oil production, including oil it supplied to the US Seventh Fleet in the Pacific). Kissinger tried saber rattling, working up various military options with Secretary of Defense James Schlesinger, including the possible occupation of Abu Dhabi. "Let's work out a plan for grabbing some Middle East oil if we want," Kissinger said. "Can't we overthrow one of the sheikhs just to show that we can do it?" he asked. But on November 28, the Saudis blinked and backed down. Within less than a year, Saudi Arabia helped end the embargo and agreed to increase production by a million barrels a day, to be sold to the United States. For his part, Kissinger began to promote the idea of a so-called oil floor price policy, below which the cost per barrel wouldn't fall, which, among other things, was meant to protect the shah and the Saudis from a sudden drop in demand and provide US petroleum corporations a guaranteed profit margin. At the same time, Nixon and Kissinger began to increase US military aid and weapons sales to

Kissinger worked out an arrangement with Saudi Arabia that was similar to the one he had with Iran, which included a $750 million contract for the sale of 60 F-5E/F fighters to the sheiks. By this time, the United States already had over a trillion dollars' worth of military agreements with Riyadh. Only Iran had more.[28]

The shah also wanted to be treated as a serious statesman, and he expected Iran to be treated with the same respect Washington showed West Germany and Great Britain. It was Kissinger's job to pump up the shah's airs, to make the shah feel like he truly was the "king of kings." The only person Kissinger flattered more than Mohammad Reza Pahlavi was Richard Nixon.

Reading the diplomatic record, one comes away with an impression that Kissinger must have felt an enormous weariness preparing for meetings with the shah, as he considered the precise gestures and words he would need to make it clear that his majesty mattered, that he was valued. "Let's see," an aide who was helping Kissinger get ready for one such meeting said, "the Shah will want to talk about Pakistan, Afghanistan, Saudi Arabia, the Gulf, the Kurds, and Brezhnev."[29] During another prep Kissinger was told that "the Shah wants to ride in an F-14."[30] A lengthy discussion resulted in the conclusion that this might not be advisable, and it fell on Kissinger to try to dissuade him. "We can say," Kissinger supposed, "that if he has his heart set on it, okay, but the President would feel easier if he didn't have that one worry in 10,000. The Shah will be flattered." Once, Nixon asked Kissinger to book the singer Danny Kaye for a private performance for the shah and his wife.

After neighboring Afghanistan's July 1973 coup brought to power a moderate, secular, but Soviet-leaning republican govern-

---

Saudi Arabia. Throughout 1974 and 1975, Kissinger continued to fantasize occasionally about a decisive strike: "We may have to take some oil fields." "I'm not saying we have to take over Saudi Arabia," he said at a later date, "how about Abu Dhabi, or Libya?" But the foundation for what has become the rock-solid alliance between the House of Saud and Washington's political class was already in place.

ment, the shah pressed his advantage, asking for even more military assistance. Now, he said, he "must cover the East with fighter aircraft."[31] Teheran began to meddle in Afghan politics, offering Kabul billions of dollars for development and security, in exchange for loosening "its ties with the Soviet Union."[32] This might have seemed a reasonably peaceful way of increasing US influence, via Iran, over Kabul. Except that it was paired with the explosive initiative of running, via the shah's secret police, SAVAK, and Pakistan's Inter-Services Intelligence agency (ISI), Islamic insurgents into Afghanistan to destabilize Kabul's republican government.

Pakistan had its own reasons for wanting to destabilize Afghanistan, having to do with border disputes and its ongoing rivalry with India. And Kissinger had long appreciated Pakistan's strategic importance. "The defense of Afghanistan," he wrote in 1955, in the essay where he urged Washington to fight "little wars" in the world's gray areas, "depends on the strength of Pakistan." And so in 1975, Kissinger, hoping to put Afghanistan back in play, pushed to restore military aid to Islamabad, which had been cut off since its 1971 rampage in Bangladesh (which Kissinger sanctioned with his silence).[33]

As national security adviser and then secretary of state, Kissinger, we know, was involved in planning and executing covert activity elsewhere, in Cambodia and Chile (discussed in the next chapter), for example. No information is available that indicates his direct involvement in encouraging Pakistan's ISI or Iran's SAVAK to destabilize Afghanistan.[34] But we don't need a smoking gun to appreciate the larger context, to consider the negative consequences of his initiatives. In their 1995 book, *Out of Afghanistan*, foreign policy analysts Diego Cordovez and Selig Harrison, based on research in Soviet archives, provide a good description of how many of the policies Kissinger put into place—the empowerment of Iran, the restoration of military relations with Pakistan, and weapon sales—came together to spark jihadism:

It was in the early 1970s, with oil prices rising, that Shah Moham-
med Reza Pahlavi of Iran embarked on his ambitious effort to
roll back Soviet influence in neighboring countries and create a
modern version of the ancient Persian empire. . . . Beginning in
1974, the Shah launched a determined effort to draw Kabul into a
Western-tilted, Teheran-centered regional economic and security
sphere embracing India, Pakistan and the Persian Gulf states. . . .
The United States actively encouraged this roll-back policy as
part of its broad partnership with the Shah. . . . Savak and the
CIA worked hand in hand, sometimes in loose collaboration
with underground Afghan Islamic fundamentalist groups that
shared their anti-Soviet objectives but had their own agendas as
well. . . . As oil profits skyrocketed, emissaries from these newly
affluent Arab fundamentalist groups arrived on the Afghan scene
with bulging bankrolls.[35]

Harrison also writes that "Savak, the CIA, and Pakistani agents"
were all involved in failed "fundamentalist coup attempts" in
Afghanistan in 1973 and 1974, along with an attempted Islamic
insurrection in the Panjshir Valley in 1975, laying the groundwork
for the jihad of the 1980s (and beyond).[36]

Much has been made of Jimmy Carter's decision, on the advice of
his national security adviser, Zbigniew Brzezinski, to authorize
"nonlethal" aid to the Afghan mujahideen in July 1979, six
months *before* Moscow sent troops to help the Afghan government
fight against the spreading Islamic insurgency.* But lethal aid had

* The rivalry between the two Harvard immigrant grand strategists, Kissinger and
Brzezinski, is well known. But Brzezinski by 1979 was absolutely Kissingerian in his
advice to Carter. In fact, a number of Kissinger's allies who continued on in the Carter
administration, including Walter Slocombe and David Newsom, influenced the July
decision to politically support the jihad. Newsom, Carter's undersecretary of state for

already been flowing to the jihadists via two key Washington allies: Pakistan and Iran (until its revolution in 1979). This provision of support to radical Islamists, initiated under Kissinger's tenure and continuing on through Carter and Reagan, had a number of unfortunate consequences. It put unsustainable pressure on Afghanistan's fragile secular modernist government. It laid the early infrastructure for today's transnational radical Islam. And, of course, destabilizing Afghanistan provoked the Soviet invasion.

Some celebrate Carter's and Reagan's decision as hastening the demise of the Soviet Union, since it had the effect of pulling Moscow, in December 1979, into its own quagmire. "What is most important to the history of the world?" Brzezinski once asked. "The Taliban or the collapse of the Soviet empire? Some stirred-up Moslems or the liberation of Central Europe and the end of the cold war?" But Moscow's occupation of Afghanistan was a disaster, and not just for the Soviet Union. When Soviet troops pulled out in 1989, they left behind a shattered Afghanistan to face a shadowy network of insurgent fundamentalists, who for years worked closely with the CIA (in what was the agency's longest counterinsurgent operation) and a bulked-up, unaccountable Pakistani ISI.[37] And few serious scholars believe that the Soviet Union would have proved any more durable had it not invaded Afghanistan. Nor did the allegiance of Afghanistan—whether it tilted toward Washington,

political affairs, stated in a March 30, 1979, meeting that "it was U.S. policy to reverse the current Soviet trend and presence in Afghanistan, and to demonstrate to the Pakistanis our interest and concern about Soviet involvement, to demonstrate to the Pakistanis, Saudis, and others our resolve to stop the extension of Soviet influence in the Third World." Newsom had earlier been Kissinger's man in Africa and the "leading public advocate" of Kissinger's "tar baby tilt"—that is, the set of policy recommendations that led to civil wars in Angola and Mozambique and renewed support for white supremacist governments in South Africa and Rhodesia. Slocombe, Carter's undersecretary of defense, asked at that meeting if there might not be "value" in continuing to support the Afghan insurgency, "sucking the Soviets into a Vietnam quagmire."

Moscow, or Tehran—make any difference to the outcome of the Cold War, any more than did, say, that of Cuba, Iraq, Angola, or Vietnam.

What is certain is that individually each of Kissinger's Middle East initiatives—banking on despots, inflating the shah, providing massive amounts of aid to security forces that tortured and terrorized citizens, pumping up the US defense industry with recycled petrodollars, which in turn spurred a Middle East arms race financed by high gas prices, emboldening Pakistan's intelligence service, nurturing embryonic Islamist fundamentalism, playing Iran and the Kurds off Iraq, and then Iraq and Iran off the Kurds, and committing Washington to defending Israel's occupation of Arab lands—has been disastrous in the long run.

Combined, they've helped work the modern Middle East into a knot that even Alexander's sword can't cut.

7

Secrecy and Spectacle

Let's look ferocious!
—Henry Kissinger

In his last years in office, Henry Kissinger helped inaugurate a new kind of public spectacle: the congressional inquest into matters of national security and covert action.[1] As national security adviser, Kissinger could invoke executive privilege to rebuff Senate requests that he come testify. But when Nixon named him secretary of state in mid-1973, he had no choice. Confirmation hearings took place in September, exactly at the moment the coup that ousted Allende was unfolding. Senators asked Kissinger about that operation. "We have absolutely stayed away from any coups," he said. As to the four-year air assault against Cambodia, Kissinger denied that he had anything to do with the "double bookkeeping" that kept Congress in the dark about the bombing. But he insisted that he "believed then, and must say in all honesty that I believe now, that the action itself was correct." He hedged on his involvement in the first round of wiretaps, which the FBI had placed on journalists and members of his NSC, and he insisted that he had no knowledge of Nixon's black-bag plumbers unit, which conducted the break-in of the Democratic headquarters at the Watergate and of Daniel Ellsberg's psychiatrist's office.*

These hearings really weren't confrontational.[2] The senators questioned Kissinger with a "mixture of admiration, respect, and bewilderment," as one magazine noted, unable to reconcile the fact that the man before them *both* orchestrated the secret bombing of Cambodia *and* negotiated rapprochement with China, *both* encouraged the wiretapping of his own staff *and* normalized relations with the Soviet Union, *both* tilted toward Pakistan even as Pakistan was slaughtering Bengalis *and* laid the groundwork for strategic arms talks with Moscow. In any case, Nixon was in freefall due to Watergate, and Kissinger wasn't just nearly the last man in the administration standing; he was the *only* man associated with that administration who seemed "intelligent, articulate, talented, witty, captivating," who possessed "style . . . intellectual finesse" and "warmth and humor." Compared to the preverbal thuggery of the rest of Nixon's inner circle, he at least "speaks the English language." His confirmation as secretary of state was never in doubt.

Kissinger did, though, complain about these and other hearings. "A merciless Congressional onslaught," is how he later described legislative efforts to supervise his execution of the war, and he resisted subsequent requests for more testimony or more documentation concerning this or that policy, the bombing of hospitals in North Vietnam, say, or CIA raids into Laos. Kissinger bristled at the very principle of oversight.[3] Having approved Suharto's invasion of East Timor, for example, Kissinger wanted to continue

---

* David Young, who served as an assistant to both Kissinger at the NSC and to Kissinger's wife, Nancy Maginnes, when she worked at the Rockefeller brothers' office, helped run the plumbers. Young received immunity in exchange for testifying against John Ehrlichman.

to supply arms to the Indonesian army. To do so, however, would have violated US law, which prohibited weapon transfers to aggressor armies. Kissinger thought he could get around the ban by suspending shipments for a few weeks and then, after public attention had turned away, quietly resuming them. But someone on his staff wrote up a cable listing the legal questions related to the matter. "It will go to congress," Kissinger complained, "and then we'll have hearings on it." Kissinger learned there was yet a second cable on the subject. "Two cables!" he cried. "That means twenty guys have seen it. . . . That will leak in three months and it will come out that Kissinger overruled his pristine bureaucrats and violated the law."[4]

Kissinger wasn't alone in thinking that the new era of congressional oversight would cripple the national security state. In 1976, James Angleton, the CIA's former chief of counterintelligence, likened Congress to a pillaging "foreign power," with the agency suffering the indignity of having "our files rifled, our officials humiliated and our agents exposed." Far from being "imperial," the presidency, Angleton said, was "impotent."[5]

Such fears were misplaced, and not just because many of the post-Vietnam and post-Watergate reforms have since been repealed or gutted (especially after 9/11). Over the last four decades, since Kissinger has left office, the very nature of the relationship between secrecy and spectacle has changed. Those two qualities—secrecy and spectacle, the covert and the overt—might seem antithetical but they have come to comprise a unified form of modern imperial power. Secrecy is fine and well when possible to achieve. But secrecy no longer is really required for the national security state to function. What is needed is political forgetfulness, or amnesia, and that amnesia is created not in the shadows but on the stage.

The Senate Church Committee, which Angleton complained about, previewed what has turned out to be a perpetual pageant: from the Pike Committee to the Rockefeller Commission, from William Fulbright's many inquiries to the Walsh Report on

Iran-Contra and Senator John Kerry's hearings on the CIA's use of drug runners to support its illegal activities in Nicaragua, and now to Senator Dianne Feinstein's torture report, and the too-many-to-count investigations between: the safe has been thrown open and the family jewels of clandestine activity have been cast to the public. WikiLeaks, Chelsea Manning, the nongovernmental National Security Archive, Edward Snowden, and tell-all books by apostate agents like Philip Agee add to the mountain of information. Fact upon top-secret fact, witness upon witness, and document after declassified document—the Pentagon Papers ad infinitum: assassinations, coups, Cambodia, Cointelpro, Iran-Contra, support for jihadists to counter the Soviets; torture; endless surveillance; psychological operations run against US citizens; manipulation of intelligence and the press; Blackwater; Abu Ghraib; war profiteering; the torture memos; drones. And yet today the national security state—its endless war, its all-pervasive system of domestic spying, and the ability of its agents to defend any action, no matter how illegal or immoral, from indefinite detention and targeted assassinations of individuals not charged with any crime to unregulated drone warfare and torture—is stronger than ever.

Much of the information gathered on these topics remains secret, including the bulk of Senator Feinstein's torture report and apparently the "worst" of the Abu Ghraib images, including videotapes of young children being raped by US soldiers.[6] But, really, what don't we know? Certainly the fact that we had been torturing people—and training our allies to torture people—long before 9/11 was known to anyone who wanted to know. Kissinger was right: information alone is not knowledge; too much data can overwhelm wisdom; the "truth" revealed by "facts" is not self-evident.

There are a number of ways that the spectacle of congressional hearings, and similar public investigations, produces political amnesia, or at least political indifference.[7] There's the vicarious enjoyment of the theater of the hearings, which can have the effect of turning citizens into spectators, with its endless regression of witnesses and inquisitors embodying the soft pleasures of contemporary visual entertainment. Think of the crisp Oliver North squaring off against his shaggy Democratic questioners in the Iran-Contra hearings.

Amnesia, or paralysis, is also created by the fact that the two parties in our two-party system basically share a common set of assumptions regarding national defense and the righteousness of American power in the world. Consider Cambodia. The bombing of that country conducted under Operation Menu (1969–70) stayed secret for longer than anyone had believed possible, mostly because the North Vietnamese made a decision not to issue a complaint. It wasn't until mid-1973 that the Senate held an inquiry, prompted by the letter from Major Hal Knight informing Congress that it was his job to burn all the paperwork related to the raids. For a brief moment during the hearings, politicians and journalists, a few anyway, made the connection between Watergate and the bombing. "Some members" of Congress, Seymour Hersh wrote in July 1973, "are convinced that the secret bombing of Cambodia will emerge as another, perhaps more dangerous, facet of the Watergate scandal." And in July 1973, the very first impeachment resolution against Nixon, introduced in the House by Massachusetts representative Robert Drinan, focused not on the Watergate break-in but on the illegal war on Cambodia. But Drinan's colleagues didn't take up the resolution and the Senate never did establish it was Kissinger who had, along with Haig and Sitton, created the double bookkeeping system for the destruction and falsification of flight data.

Rather than expose Menu as a crime, the Senate's inquiry came close to justifying the deception. "Some members" of Congress might have taken the bombing seriously, but by the final days of the public hearings held by the Committee on Armed Services (which ran July 16 to August 9, 1973), only three of its fourteen members bothered to attend: Stuart Symington and Harold Hughes, Democrats from Missouri and Iowa, and South Carolina

Republican Strom Thurmond. Symington summed up the "dove" position: "What I do not like about this is that we did not know about it," he complained to one witness, General Creighton Abrams, "we put the money up for one thing and it was used for another." Symington was the only senator who questioned the consequences of the secret bombing, and he did so only once: "As an experienced military man, would you not think this pressure [from bombing] made it almost inevitable that they would have to expand their area of control or operations, thus bringing them into increasing conflict with the Cambodian authorities?" General Abrams's answer was succinct: "Yes, I think that is a fair statement."[8]

The hawks (Thurmond, mostly, but also Senators Barry Goldwater, Sam Nunn, and John Tower the few times they showed up) dominated the proceedings. They not only insisted that the bombing was an effective and legitimate policy, but argued that the burning of documents was really just an extension of secrecy protocols, and secrecy was an accepted practice of war. "I do think that we have to endorse the idea of a degree of covertness, cover, deception and secretiveness," said Tower, "particularly in an open society like ours, which is already in a difficult position in time of war when confronted by a closed society as it was in the case of Nazi Germany and Soviet Russia." "How about the Normandy invasion?" Nunn asked, wanting to know if the committee's main witness, the whistle-blower Major Knight, would have felt compelled to reveal that operation. Others took the argument further, maintaining that there was no inherent "intent to deceive" in falsifying information if that falsification was conducted in response to "genuine and legal orders." One senator suggested that the code Knight used when he called Saigon to indicate that he had successfully burned all evidence ("the ballgame is over") was itself accurate reporting. Hence, no deception had taken place.

The committee's hawks kept repeating, over and over again, that the bombing was necessary to "save American lives," with doves all but conceding that, had the White House come to them in 1969 with that argument, they would have both approved the operation and kept it secret. What, then, was the issue?

The public's attention soon turned to the break-in at the Watergate Hotel, which was largely treated as a domestic crime; and the destruction of Cambodia receded into memory. In July 1974, the House Judiciary Committee finally approved three articles of impeachment against Nixon, all related to the domestic obstruction of justice. The committee declined, by a vote of 26 to 12, to pursue a fourth charge of not seeking Congress's approval to wage war on Cambodia. Committee member John Conyers dissented, thinking it the worst of Nixon's impeachable offenses. But a bipartisan majority disagreed. "We might as well resurrect President Johnson and impeach him posthumously for Vietnam and Laos," the Democrat Walter Flowers said, or Kennedy for the Bay of Pigs and Truman for Korea.[9]

Political forgetfulness is also created through the transformation of the crime into a procedural question or a domestic drama between two political parties: one party executes, the other explicates. Framing whatever the controversial policy is—be it the bombing of a neutral country, domestic wiretapping, the support of coups, torture—as a technical matter, as an argument over the legality of the means in which the policy was carried out creates an implied affirmation that the objective of the action is agreed upon by all. Kissinger was a master at this kind of re-framing. In 1975, for instance, he consented to be questioned by Congress, appearing before the Pike Committee, which was chaired by New York representative Otis Pike and charged with investigating the covert activities of the CIA, the FBI, and the National Security Agency. Kissinger was grilled extensively by Representative Ron Dellums on various clandestine matters. "Frankly, Mr. Secretary," said Dellums, thinking he had cornered Kissinger, "and I mean this very sincerely, I am concerned with your power, and the method of your operation, and I am afraid of the result on American policy. . . . Would you please comment, sir?"

Kissinger gave a pitch-perfect response, delivered with just a hint of borscht-belt syntax: "Except for that," he asked, "there is nothing wrong with my operation?"[10] The room laughed and the evening TV news had its clip, which for millions of viewers summed up the hearings: a pushy congressman getting pushed back by a rapier wit.* Over a decade later, in Senate hearings into the illegal sale of high-tech missiles to Iran and the diversion of funds to support the Nicaraguan Contras, Colonel North and his coconspirators would say it more solemnly but they said pretty much the same thing: if you agree with our ends, then why question our means?

The symbiotic relationship between spectacle and secrecy is pronounced in Henry Kissinger's post-Vietnam diplomacy. Kissinger felt that public displays of resolve would help America restore its damaged credibility and legitimacy. "The United States must carry out some act somewhere in the world," he said to reporters shortly after the 1975 fall of Saigon, "which shows its determination to continue to be a world power."[11] Some act. Somewhere. In the future, he wrote in a "Lessons of Vietnam" memo to Gerald Ford, who had become president just a few months earlier, Washington will have to take "tougher stands" in the international arena "in order to make others believe in us again."[12] Inaction needs to be avoided to show that action is possible.

The opportunities were limited as to where the United States might put on such a show. Take, for instance, Kissinger's and Ford's "rescue" of the crew of the US container ship *Mayaguez*.

---

* The final report of the Pike Committee was never officially released, although it was leaked to the *Village Voice*, which published a large excerpt. See "The CIA Report the President Doesn't Want You to Read," February 16, 1976.

On May 12, 1975, Khmer Rouge forces seized the *Mayaguez*, along with thirty-nine merchant seamen. Cambodia was then in chaos, the genocide under way at home. The crew and ship were taken to a nearby, heavily fortified island named Koh Tang in the Gulf of Thailand, near the coast of Cambodia.

Nearly all involved in the series of White House meetings called to deal with the crisis seized on the incident to take that "tougher stand" (though historian Rick Perlstein points out that calling it a crisis is a stretch since it is quite common for US merchant ships to be taken and then released by foreign navies). Kissinger was forceful. His biographer, Walter Isaacson, describes him in one of these meetings as "leaning over the Cabinet Room table and speaking with emotion," saying "the U.S. must draw the line. . . . We must act upon it now, and act firmly." And not just Kissinger. "I think a violent response is in order," said Kissinger's old boss, vice president Nelson Rockefeller. "The world should know that we will act and that we will act quickly."[13]

Kissinger advised that the United States "do something that will impress the Koreans and the Chinese." Ford's speechwriter, Bob Hartmann, said a tough response might contribute to Ford's popularity at home: "We should not just think of what is the right thing to do, but of what the public perceives."[14]

"This crisis, like the Cuban missile crisis, is the first real test of your leadership," Hartmann told Ford. Kennedy had responded to that crisis methodically, opening up back channels of communication with the Soviets, considering his every move, and offering key concessions to resolve the crisis. But Kissinger, in 1975, couldn't wait. He didn't even try to contact Phnom Penh to make a deal. Instead, he urged Ford to launch a military rescue, let the B-52s loose on Cambodia one last time, and sink Cambodian ships at will. And not gradually but all at once. "I'm afraid that if we do a few little steps every few hours," Kissinger said, "we are in trouble. I think we should go ahead with the island . . . and the ship all at once. I think people should have the impression that we are potentially trigger-happy." The incident also gave Kissinger a chance to tutor the new president in the madman theory of international relations. "This is your first crisis," he said, "you should establish a reputation for being too tough to tackle."[15]

There was no need for any of it. Even before the assault on the island began, the Cambodians had signaled they would give the ship back. And the crew had been released, put aboard a fishing ship, and returned to the US Navy. But the military operation went forward anyway. Eighteen Americans were killed trying to take the island, and another twenty-three died when their helicopter went down preparing for the raid. Nobody knows how many Cambodians were killed in the attack, but B-52s hit the mainland, destroying a railroad yard, port, oil refinery, and over three hundred buildings. Nine Cambodian ships were sunk.

"Let's look ferocious!" Kissinger said, urging Ford not to waver.[16] Ford later said the *Mayaguez* rescue was one of his most important foreign policy decisions. "It convinced some of our adversaries we were not a paper tiger." "It was wonderful," Barry Goldwater agreed. "It shows we've still got balls in this country."[17]

Kissinger didn't want a crisis "like" the Cuban crisis. He wanted the real thing. And a few years before the *Mayaguez* incident, during Richard Nixon's first term, he almost had one. In September 1970, Kissinger rushed into Bob Haldeman's office with reconnaissance photographs taken of an area around the port city of Cienfuegos, on Cuba's southern coast. "These pictures show the Cubans are building soccer fields," he said. "These soccer fields could mean war, Bob." Haldeman seemed confused, until Kissinger told him, "Cubans play *baseball*. Russians play *soccer*."[18] Kissinger insisted that Moscow was building a permanent naval base to house nuclear submarines. More photographs were taken, high-level meetings were held where Kissinger lectured on the lessons of Kennedy's bold actions eight years earlier, and contingency plans to blockade Cuba were drawn up.

The submarine base seems to have been a fantasy.[19] The Soviets didn't back down, because they were doing nothing to back down from (or at least no evidence was ever produced that they were doing anything to back down from). Of course Cubans play soccer, they had been since the 1920s, and the Cuban Revolution even brought a renewed interest in the sport. Reconnaissance flights photographed every inch of Cienfuegos and couldn't find one piece of heavy equipment that could be put to building such a port. There were no cranes, no dredges, no deep-water docks. They couldn't find a Soviet submarine in the harbor. No matter. This "crisis," taking place just after the 1970 invasion of Cambodia, gave Kissinger yet another opportunity to impress Nixon with his toughness, using his perceived victory over the Soviets in his ongoing rivalry with Secretary of State Rogers, who, "baffled by Kissinger's warning," seemed indecisive and weak.[20]

To this day, in memoirs and other published writings, Kissinger presents his charge that the Soviets were building a sophisticated deep-water nuclear submarine port at Cienfuegos as a fact. It is hard, however, to find anything other than befuddlement in official documents recording the Soviet response to Kissinger's charges.*

---

* Compare Kissinger's memorandum of a conversation he had with Dobrynin (which took place before his meeting with Haig) with Dobrynin's diary entry of the same meeting. Kissinger describes Dobrynin as "ashen" and "clearly" worried about the "Cuban problem." He says he dressed the Soviet envoy down, threatened "drastic action," and warned of the "grave" situation, cutting him off when he tried to change the topic. But Dobrynin's diary records no such confrontation. They simply matter-of-factly record that the point of the meeting was for Kissinger to pass on Nixon's "concerns." "Kissinger," Dobrynin wrote, "said that the President requests that this message not be regarded as some kind of official representation or protest, but rather as his strictly confidential and important appeal to the Soviet leaders in the hope that it will receive the attention it deserves" (both found in Douglas Selvage et al., *Soviet-American Relations* [2007], pp. 193, 197). One study noted that Kissinger's reported "language [was] uncannily reminiscent of the ultimatums of the original Cuban missile crisis."

———

Kissinger wasn't yet finished with Cuba, and his subsequent dealings with the island, along with the rest of Latin America, help reveal the dependent relationship between the overt and the covert, the spectacular and the secret, the way very real limits on what the United States could do in the world in the wake of being driven out of Indochina led to a reliance on clandestine "black-bag" work.

In February 1976, Kissinger, after engaging in some effort to normalize relations between Havana and Washington, suddenly found himself in a geopolitical standoff with Fidel Castro, when Castro sent Cuban troops to southern Africa to defend Angola against US-backed South African mercenaries. The Cuban intervention—an audacious stroke on Castro's part, saving the Angolan capital of Luanda for the left-wing Movimento Popular de Libertação de Angola and routing Washington's allies—was the kind of action Kissinger might have appreciated if it hadn't been directed at undermining his foreign policy.

In one move, Castro had exposed the unviability of Kissinger's "tar baby" tilt in southern Africa—that is, his efforts to uphold white supremacy there—to the whole world: the Iranians, Pakistanis, and Latin American allies all remarked on Cuba's action, expressing admiration for its success but fear as to what Castro would do next. Egypt said that Washington's "association with South Africa is anathema in African eyes," making an "impassioned plea" that the United States be more "understanding and tolerant of emerging African movements," even if they were left-leaning.[21]

Kissinger pushed for a harder line. "If the Cubans destroy Rhodesia then Namibia is next and then there is South Africa," he said at a high-level crisis meeting on March 24, 1976. "I think we have to humiliate them," Kissinger said at an earlier meeting, instructing his aides to draw up contingency plans that included political and economic sanctions, air and naval blockades, the mining of Cuba's ports, punitive strikes, and even an invasion. "There should be no halfway measures," Kissinger instructed; whatever they did, it needed to be "ruthless and rapid and efficient." As with the *Mayaguez* a year earlier, Kissinger insisted that what was at stake with Cuba in Angola was a matter of appearance. "If there is a perception overseas that we are so weakened by our internal debate [over Vietnam] so that it looks like we can't do anything about a country of 8 million people, then in three or four years we are going to have a real crisis."

It is true that, with the broadcast images of the April 1975 fall of Saigon and the chaotic evacuation of remaining US troops and embassy staff fresh in the public's mind, there was little enthusiasm for military operations abroad. But it wasn't America's "internal debate" that "weakened" Kissinger in southern Africa. Rather, Castro had revealed the paralyzing contradiction that lay at the heart of Kissinger's "little war" thesis. On the one hand, Kissinger argued that little wars in areas of marginal importance could remain *limited* in scope. On the other hand, he demanded that *no limits* be placed on the force statesmen and military leaders could use to fight those wars (including the tactical use of nuclear weapons). Diplomacy, Kissinger had consistently argued, needed to be backed up by credible threats, and threats could only be credible if they were limitless.

In small places of true insignificance, such a paradox could be contained. Brutalizing a small island in the Gulf of Thailand and killing an unknown number of Cambodians to "rescue" the *Mayaguez* was one thing. Unleashing a war on Cuba, allied with the Soviet Union, was another. But his advisers told him that, unlike Kennedy's success in 1962, "a new Cuban crisis would not necessarily lead to a Soviet retreat." The crisis could "escalate in areas that would maximize US casualties and thus provoke stronger response." "Serious business," Kissinger admitted. There was no way to imagine a "little war" against Cuba that might not lead to what Kissinger's advisers called a "general war" between the United States and the Soviet Union.

Kissinger knew he was backed into a corner. There was nothing Washington could do that wouldn't seem like it was playing catch-up to Havana. Ignore Cuba, and the United States appears weak. Hit Cuba, and it seems reactive, dramatizing that the world's greatest power had been played by a small island nation, a giant swatting at a fly. Kissinger admitted as much: "The problem is that no matter how we build our policy in southern Africa anything that happens will appear to have resulted from Cuban pressure." Just so. Castro had checkmated Kissinger.

"I think we are going to have to smash Castro," Kissinger told Ford, but, he conceded, "we probably can't do it before the elections," referring to the presidential vote in November 1976.[22] "I agree," Ford responded. And that was that. Afterward, Kissinger reversed his "tar baby" tilt, implementing what some commentators called an African détente.

In Latin America, Kissinger, having been denied a public triumph, continued private plotting. In 1969, when he first took office, only Paraguay and Brazil in South America were ruled by right-wing dictatorships. Nearly every other country was experiencing a revolutionary upheaval, inspired, to some degree, by Cuba. That would soon change. Bolivia was the first Latin American democracy to fall to a military coup on Kissinger's watch. "We are having a major problem in Bolivia," said Kissinger on June 11, 1971, telling the CIA to "crank up an operation, post-haste."[23] On August 21, a military coup installed a right-wing dictator promptly recognized by Washington (according to the State Department, the CIA moved in "response to a White House request for a political action program to arrest the leftward trend" of the Bolivian government). A few months later, Brazil, acting as Nixon and Kissinger's deputy, "helped rig the Uruguayan elections," as Nixon put it, making sure a popular left coalition could not take power.[24] The turmoil that ensued fed directly into a June 1973 coup led by Juan María Bordaberry, who turned Uruguay into a police state. Shortly after the coup, Kissinger sent Bordaberry a note wishing him "best wishes on this happy occasion."[25] The dictator's wife had just given birth to their second child.*

Then came Chile, on September 11, 1973. It was Kissinger who had pushed Nixon to take "a harder line," as he himself put it, against the country's democratically elected socialist president, Salvador Allende, who died in the coup.[26] Chile was followed by coups in Peru and Ecuador. Then on March 23, 1976, the Argentine military took over the government. This putsch corresponded with Kissinger's renewed obsession with Cuba in Southern Africa. And as it became clear that Castro was going to win the day in Angola—and then possibly send his troops into Rhodesia—Kissinger moved closer toward Latin America's new praetorians.

Over the last decade, more and more government documents have been declassified revealing Kissinger's involvement in and cover-up of human rights abuses in Latin America. He's tried to

---

* Central America was not a high priority for Kissinger, but he continued giving steadfast support to right-wing dictatorships and death-squad states already in power when he took office. In 1970 in Guatemala, for example, Kissinger and Alexander Haig were involved in passing the names and addresses of "Guatemalan terrorists" to security forces, even though Washington was well aware that the government was using its US-funded counterterror program to eliminate not just armed insurgents but *all* political opposition and that the great majority of political prisoners taken were summarily executed. Indeed, in 1971, the CIA reported that Guatemala's president at the time, Carlos Arana, was directly involved "in drawing up death lists." Repression in Guatemala got so out of hand that a member of Kissinger's NSC staff urged that the so-called 40 Committee—the committee chaired by Kissinger that brought together various arms of the national security state that helped organize the campaign to overthrow Allende in Chile—reconsider US support for the Guatemalan government. Kissinger, as chair, didn't think it was an issue worth taking up and robust military support continued through to the Carter administration. The mass slaughter of Guatemalan Maya peasants between 1978 and 1983 is often not included in the genocides Kissinger is associated with since it took place after his public service. But throughout his tenure, aid provided by Washington (which strengthened the security forces that carried out the genocide) steadily increased. See note 24 for sources for this discussion.

defend himself. "Just to take a sentence out of a telephone conversation when you have 50 other conversations, it's just not the way to analyze it," he said, after a particularly unflattering recording of him plumping for Pinochet was released. "I've been telling people to read a month's worth of conversations, so you know what else went on."[27] But now that more information is available, a month's worth of conversations reads like one of Shakespeare's bloodiest plays. Perhaps *Macbeth*, with its description of what today is called blowback: "We but teach bloody instructions, which, being taught, return."

There's Kissinger's support of Pinochet's dictatorship in Chile. In August 1975, Kissinger had received Chile's foreign minister, Vice Admiral Patricio Carvajal, in Washington. By this point, Chilean security forces had killed or disappeared thousands, tortured even more, turning Santiago's soccer stadium into a concentration camp. Kissinger had pushed back hard on Congress's attempt to impose sanctions on the country for these violations. And so he opened his meeting with Carvajal with a joke, making fun of the fretting, by some of his staffers, over human rights: "The State Department is made up of people who have a vocation for the ministry. Because there were not enough churches for them, they went into the Department of State." The discussion then took a cryptic turn. Carvajal told Kissinger that Chile was having trouble with about two hundred people it had just released from prison. "They are creating problems," the minister said, and he couldn't find a country that would take them as exiles. Kissinger responded: "You will know what to do. We cannot go beyond what we have said. What other problem do we have to discuss?"

The Pinochet regime did know what to do; torture, murder, and disappearances in Chile continued.

There's his support for the Argentine junta. Shortly after the coup, one of Kissinger's aides advised him not to "rush out and embrace this new regime." "We've got to expect a fair amount of repression," the aide said, "probably a good deal of blood, in Argentina before too long. I think they're going to have to come down very hard not only on the terrorists but on the dissidents of trade unions and their parties." Kissinger disagreed with the suggestion that he keep his distance. "Whatever chance they have, they will need a little encouragement," he replied to his cautious aide, "because I do want to encourage them." The next day, on March 27, 1976, the International Monetary Fund extended $127 million line of credit to the junta, with many millions more to come from both public and private loans.[28]

There's also Kissinger's visit to Santiago, Chile, in early June 1976, to attend a session of the Organization of American States. There, he had a one-on-one with Pinochet and assured him that whatever mild criticism he might hear in his remarks to the OAS shouldn't be taken seriously. Just a month later, Kissinger's assistant secretary for Latin America, Harry Shlaudeman, urged Kissinger to help tone down the "rhetorical exaggerations of the 'Third-World-War' type." Shlaudeman meant those conservative militants who thought they were on the front line of an international crusade against global Marxism. Chile was the worst of the lot. "Perhaps," Shlaudeman said, offering understated advice, "we can convince them that a Third World War is undesirable."

But in his meeting with Pinochet, Kissinger stoked the fire: they commiserated about Vietnam and agreed that the Spanish Civil War was but the first battle in the current "world war." The general, Kissinger said, is "a victim of all left-wing groups around the world" and that his "greatest sin" was that he "overthrew a government that was going Communist." Kissinger told Pinochet that he would have to include a few words about human rights in his upcoming remarks to the General Assembly but that Pinochet could safely ignore them: "The speech is not aimed at Chile."*

---

* The speech was titled "Human Rights and the Western Hemisphere" and began like this: "One of the most compelling issues of our time, and one which calls for the con-

In Santiago, Kissinger also met with Admiral César Augusto Guzzetti, of the newly installed Argentine military junta. He gave Guzzetti the same advice he gave to Suharto a year earlier: "If there are things that have to be done, you should do them quickly. But you should get back quickly to normal procedures." As he did with Pinochet, Kissinger encouraged the idea that Argentina was a frontline state in a global war, telling the admiral that the United States "will do what we can to help it succeed. . . . We understand you must establish authority." As in the earlier meeting with Pinochet's foreign minister, the problem of displaced peoples came up; these included a number of exiles from the neighboring countries fleeing right-wing repression. Again Kissinger was cryptic: "I understand the problem." They are creating "unrest," Guzzetti said. "We wish you success," Kissinger, himself a refugee, answered.

At the end of the meeting, Kissinger and Guzzetti left the room for "a word alone," according to the note taker. It was a brief four-minute conversation.[29] What was said? Judging from the incriminatory comments Kissinger allowed to stay on the public record, we can assume he wasn't urging Guzzetti to act with restraint.

The next day, June 11, a death squad abducted and tortured twenty-four Chilean and Uruguayan refugees living in Argentina. There were many other operations that day, including the executions of Raúl Albert Ramat, a twenty-seven-year-old student activist at the Catholic University, in Buenos Aires, and fifty-nine-year-old Santiago Bruschtein, the last of seven members of his family to be either killed or disappeared. The junta was in no rush to get "back quickly to normal procedures." The admirals and generals stayed in power for seven years and the murders and disappearances continued. Surviving military documents suggest that the dead or disappeared numbered 22,000 by July 1978.[30]

---

certed action of all responsible peoples and nations, is the necessity to protect and extend the fundamental rights of humanity."

Then there's Kissinger's involvement in the establishment of Operation Condor, an international death-squad consortium that carried out operations in Latin America, the United States, and Europe. J. Patrice McSherry, one of the foremost researchers into Condor activities, argues that the available State Department documentation was actually designed to mislead. That may well be the case. Kissinger himself has noted that the sheer volume of foreign policy paperwork makes it impossible to determine "which documents were produced to provide an alibi and which genuinely guided decisions." "Kissinger rarely put anything on the record in normal diplomatic channels if he could devise a more secretive back channel instead," writes Walter Isaacson.[31]

What does exist is damning. Condor was formally established on November 26, 1975, in Santiago, Chile (just after Castro decided to send combat troops to Angola) at a meeting attended by intelligence and military officers, as well as a few heads of state, representing nearly all of South America. It is clear that they had Washington's help. The US ambassador to Paraguay confirmed that the different franchises of Condor kept "in touch with one another through a U.S. communications installation in the Panama Canal Zone which covers all of Latin America." It was an "encrypted system within U.S. communications net" that allowed Condor countries (Bolivia, Paraguay, Uruguay, Argentina, Brazil, and Chile) to "maintain the confidentiality of their communication." And it was after Kissinger's visit to Santiago, and his conversations with Pinochet and Guzzetti, that Operation Condor got fully under way, including so-called phase III operations—the carrying out of executions outside of Latin America.

The most famous of these took place on September 21, 1976, in Washington, DC's Sheridan Circle, near Embassy Row, when a car bomb killed Orlando Letelier and his assistant, Ronni Moffitt. Letelier held a number of high-level positions in Allende's government and after the coup had established himself in Washington, where he lobbied Congress to impose sanctions on Chile. In his meeting with Kissinger, Pinochet had complained twice about Letelier.

Kissinger had been briefed repeatedly about Condor by the CIA and the State Department. He knew it was conducting operations in Latin America, Europe, and the United States. And he knew that it was targeting, as Assistant Secretary Shlaudeman told him, "nonviolent" leftists and center leftists living abroad, like Letelier. "What we are trying to head off is a series of international murders," Shlaudeman would subsequently write, just before Letelier's killing.

On August 23, Kissinger did approve a "stand down" cable, instructing his ambassadors to approach "the highest appropriate official" in their respective countries and tell that person that the "assassination of subversives, politicians and prominent figures . . . abroad . . . would create a most serious moral and political problem." But then Kissinger reversed himself. On September 16, told by an aide that such an order might offend Pinochet, he rescinded his démarche. He was in Africa, in the middle of his goodwill tour to reverse the damage of his "tar baby" policy and the disastrous Angolan civil war, and he sent a note to Shlaudeman instructing that "no further action be taken on this matter." Shlaudeman, in turn, told Kissinger's ambassadors to "take no further action."

Five days later, Letelier and Moffitt were dead. Condor continued on.

All told, the allies that Kissinger "encouraged" in Latin America murdered tens of thousands of civilians and tortured an equal number.* Among those abducted and brutalized by Kissinger's

---

* The use of torture by US security agents in Latin America—and the training provided by Washington to Latin Americans on how best to torture—took place both before and after Kissinger's time in public office. But some of the most famous US torturers plied their trade while Kissinger was presiding, as chair of the 40 Committee, over covert activities in the region. Dan Mitrione, for instance, was sent in 1969 to Uruguay, where he taught the police how to torture. "Before all else, you must be efficient," Mitrione instructed. "You must cause only the damage that is strictly necessary, not a bit more." Mitrione taught by demonstration, reportedly torturing to death a number of

proxies include the current presidents of Chile and Brazil and a former president of Uruguay. Brazil's Dilma Rousseff was captured in 1970 and "spent three years behind bars, where interrogators repeatedly tortured her with electric shocks to her feet and ears, and forced her into the pau de arara, or parrot's perch, in which victims are suspended upside down naked, from a stick, with bound wrists and ankles."[32] A recent Brazilian truth commission investigation found that over three hundred Brazilian soldiers were trained by the United States in the "theory and practice of torture."[33] Uruguay's former president, José Mujica, was also tortured. Kidnapped in 1971, Mujica spent fourteen years in prison, including extended periods at the bottom of a well. The father of Michelle Bachelet, Chile's president, was kidnapped and tortured, dying in Pinochet's prison. President Bachelet and her mother were also captured and tortured but were eventually released, upon which they went into exile.[34]

The silent nod, the public gesture. A four-minute "word alone" with a key player in an international death-squad consortium, an impassioned speech on human rights. Secrecy and spectacle. Modern statecraft has long operated between these two poles, as diplomats have moved back and forth between the dark corner and the

---

homeless people kidnapped off the streets of Montevideo. "We must control our tempers in any case," he said. "You have to act with the efficiency and cleanliness of a surgeon and with the perfection of an artist." Many of the techniques practiced and taught by Mitrione were codified in the Pentagon's infamous "torture manuals" in the 1980s and subsequently influenced the practices described in Senator Dianne Feinstein's 2014 "torture report." According to journalist Marcy Wheeler, after the Pentagon destroyed copies of its infamous torture instruction manuals it had used to train Latin American allies, Dick Cheney, then secretary of defense, and his legal counsel, David Addington "saved the only known copies" for their personal files. Also, one of the CIA agents, Jose Rodriguez, who ran the CIA's post 9/11 torture program had spent thirty years working in Latin America. See Wheeler, "The Thirteen People Who Made Torture Possible," *Salon,* May 18, 2009; for Rodriguez, see the links in my "Misery Made Me a Fiend: Latin America and the Torture Report," *Nation,* December 11, 2014.

limelight. Do it quickly, Kissinger told his foreign allies. Do it theat-
rically, he told Ford: "Let's look ferocious!"

As Kissinger's experience in Latin America and southern
Africa suggests, the post-Vietnam and post-Watergate revival of the
national security state came to depend, to a greater extent than it
had in the past, on a dynamic coupling of secrecy and spectacle.
On one level, the relationship of the overt to the covert is sequen-
tial. Kissinger wanted to go big after Vietnam, to take "tougher
stands" someplace around the world over some issue. But he
couldn't. Checked by Castro and worried about a post-Vietnam
public and Congress with no appetite for further war, he had to go
dark and throw in with the men of Condor. On another level,
though, secrecy and spectacle coexist simultaneously, feeding off
each other. The death-squad disappearance regime put in place in
Latin America during Kissinger's tenure was a clandestine network of undisclosed prisons and torture rooms, hidden graves,
and shadowy paramilitary units. But its effectiveness in spreading
terror resided in public knowledge, publicizing death lists, adopting brand names for the death squads—"The White Hand," "Eye
for an Eye," and so on—and snatching people off the street in
broad daylight, never to be seen again. The message was clear.

In southern Africa, Kissinger wanted to teach Cuba a public lesson for all the rest of the Third World, allies and adversaries, to
see. But even as he was drawing up plans to do so, he was running
a covert war in multiple countries. In the United States, he didn't
just lie to the public about that war. He ran domestic propaganda
campaigns to build support for a harder line in southern Africa.
John Stockwell, a CIA operative in Angola, testified before the
House's Subcommittee on Africa in May 1978. What he described
sounded like a dress rehearsal for the clandestine Iran-Contra network the Reagan administration would put into place to execute
its secret, illegal wars. According to Stockwell (and other sources),
Kissinger and the CIA director, William Colby, used proxy nations

(Israel and South Africa) to stage military operations and deliver weapons to rebel allies. They also conducted a covert publicity campaign to influence the opinion of American citizens. "Mr. Kissinger and the CIA," Stockwell testified, "lied to the American people through public statements and false propaganda activities in the United States. The CIA funded and directed the activities of two teams of propagandists inside the United States and fed them false information to be used to influence the United Nations and the American people. It also placed false stories in American newspapers."[35] Later, after 9/11, neoconservatives would hope to confront, and uproot, America's "adversary culture." Here, though, not long out of Vietnam, Kissinger was just looking to work around it.

This coupling of secrecy and spectacle would evolve over the years, finding innovative expression especially during the Reagan and George W. Bush administrations. Even as covert operators were reactivating Kissinger's clandestine wars in Angola and Mozambique, building on Kissinger's ties with the ISI in Pakistan to destabilize Afghanistan, and starting new operations in Central America and elsewhere, the Pentagon was, as we shall see, testing public displays of military power, sending troops into Grenada, bombing Libya, and invading Panama.

But it was after 9/11 when the lords of spectacle and secrecy would come fully into their own. And when they did, they would have Henry Kissinger to advise them.

8

Inconceivable

But the spirits once called forth refused to be banished.
—Henry Kissinger

In November 1971, Richard Nixon asked Henry Kissinger, who had just returned from one of his California missions to shore up the right flank, what he thought of the state's governor, Ronald Reagan. Kissinger is known for the "lapidary precision" of his character analysis, his ability to capture a person's essence in a few exact words.* But Reagan left him at a loss.

He was a decent enough man, Kissinger said. But "he's shallow. He's got no ... ur, ur ... he's, he's an actor. He ... When he gets a line he does it very well." Reagan had apparently told Kissinger, "Hell, people are remembered not for what they do, but for what they say. Can't you find a few good lines?" Kissinger laughed

---

* "His movements were slightly vague," Kissinger said of Nixon about their first extended meeting, "and unrelated to what he was saying, as if two different impulses were behind speech and gesture" (Isaacson, *Kissinger*, p. 77).

nervously when he related this to Nixon. "That's really an actor's approach," he told the president, "to foreign policy—to substantive—"[1]

Nixon knew what he meant. "The fellow really is a decent guy, a decent guy. But there isn't—there's no, in other words, everything is. . . ."

You want to finish Nixon's sentence: there's no there there, everything is surface. As to Kissinger, he seemed to intend to dismiss Reagan as a mere actor but hesitated, trailing off when he realized that wasn't quite what he wanted to say. Acting implies calculation. Nixon and Kissinger were calculated: they manipulated events and choreographed gestures, creating the atmospherics that served their purposes. And even the existentialist Kissinger believed that reality existed. He wasn't a solipsist. Individuals might not have unmediated access to that reality beyond their relative, subjective perspective, but he did think that that reality set limits and imposed restraints, or "necessities."

Reagan was a rung further up the metaphysical ladder, a politician who managed to abolish the distinction between appearance and reality. "There are not two Ronald Reagans," Nancy Reagan once said, responding to the idea that her husband was a cynic, that his homespun was disingenuous. "You look in back of a statement for what the man really means," Nancy continued, "but it takes people a while to realize that with Ronnie you don't have to look in back of anything."[2]

Actors know they are acting, and Kissinger had a sense that Reagan didn't. At one point in their conversation, he complained to the governor about Nixon's "disloyal bureaucracy." Kissinger, of course, had done more than any of his predecessors to tame that bureaucracy, to neuter its ability to restrain his actions. But he never once doubted that he needed a bureaucracy. Reagan, though, offered a solution to his complaint one better. "Well then," he said, "why don't you fire the bureaucracy?" One wonders if at this

moment Kissinger saw Reagan as an extension of his policies or
their perversion.*

Nixon asked Kissinger if he could imagine Reagan, who had
done surprisingly well in the 1968 Republican primaries considering that he never actually entered them, sitting in the Oval Office.

"Inconceivable," Kissinger replied.

They then wondered what Reagan would do next, and if he
might accept the ambassadorship to the United Kingdom. "I'm
sure he won't go," said Nixon. "We've offered it to him. He doesn't
want it." "But what does he want?" Kissinger asked.

It was against Kissinger that Ronald Reagan broke his so-called
Eleventh Commandment: Thou shall not speak ill of any fellow
Republican. The breach came in March 1976, after Reagan lost the
first four primaries in his bid to snatch the Republican nomination
from Gerald Ford. Up until this point, Reagan had kept his criticisms vague, complaining about an aimless foreign policy but not
blaming any one person in particular. But having come close to taking New Hampshire and in striking distance of winning Florida,
he began to name names, accusing Henry Kissinger and, almost as

---

* Kissinger never lost his sense of bewilderment about Reagan, the idea that there was
no difference between substance and surface, no interiority, that he was a mirror or a
recording device repeating the world back to itself. In 1981: "I don't have the impression
that he ever ingests anything you tell him. I used to brief him for Nixon when he was
governor. I find that years later he could tell me almost verbatim something I told him
back then. He remembers exactly, but I have the feeling that the item has lain unused
in his mind all those years." Again in 1981: "He is a nice man, a decent man. One odd
thing, though. When he talks, all his illustrations are drawn from the movie business."
In 1982: "I have known a number of Presidents and of presidential candidates. With all
the rest, when you talk to them, you can feel them translating what you are telling
them into 'What can I do about this?' With Reagan, you feel him translating it into
'What can I say about this?' Words are the reality for him. . . . He is the only president
with whom I would rather have someone else in the room when I see him. If you talk
to him alone, you can be sure that nothing will ever happen." In 1986: "He has a kind
of instinct that I cannot explain."

a second thought, Ford of presiding over a dangerous decline in American global power.

In speech after speech, TV ads, and a nationally broadcast address, Reagan placed Kissinger's name ahead of Ford's. Sometimes he'd refer to them collectively with the vaguely French and somewhat archaic "Messrs.": "Under Messrs. Kissinger and Ford," he said in one TV spot, "this nation has become number two in military power in a world where it is dangerous and—if not fatal—to be second best."[3] The heart of that ad hammered "Dr. Kissinger" on his Middle East policy, on oil prices, on negotiations with Panama over the canal, on Vietnam—which Reagan called "the worst humiliation" in US history—on Cuba, and on Angola. Maybe there was some "great strategy" in place, said Reagan, but he was at a loss to see it: "Henry Kissinger's recent stewardship of US foreign policy has coincided precisely with the loss of US military supremacy."

Having teed off on Kissinger, Reagan landed squarely on Ford: "I believe in the peace of which Mr. Ford speaks—as much as any man. But, in places such as Angola, Cambodia and Vietnam, the peace they have come to know is the peace of the grave."[4]

Reagan in 1976 was using Kissinger to boost himself into the final phase of a remarkable transformation of the Republican Party. Not the party's takeover by the forces of the New Right but rather its conversion into the primary political vessel of a weaponized version of American exceptionalism. Previously, at least since World War I, it had been mostly Democrats who started and ran the nation's wars, doing so (whatever their actual causes) in the name of spreading democracy. Republicans had long been the party of the hard line, but their hard line tended to be chauvinist, isolationist, and know-nothing, devoid of the democratic evangelicalism associated with the Wilsonian tradition of the Democratic Party. That would change with Reagan.

Earlier, during his 1968 feint for the Republican nomination,

Reagan focused on national security, arguing that the Soviet Union was overtaking the United States in the arms race. With all the other candidates focused on getting the country out of Vietnam, Reagan had trouble gaining traction. He pledged that he wouldn't "be ashamed to talk out in the open about morality."[5] Other than standing up to the Soviets—for instance, later in the year calling on Washington to place what we today call "sanctions" on the USSR for having invaded Czechoslovakia to end the Prague Spring—it was unclear what he meant by that pledge.

Eight years of Henry Kissinger allowed Reagan to focus his criticisms.* When Reagan talked about "moralism" in 1976, every-

---

* Kissinger escaped association with the Watergate scandal, but starting in 1974 he became a primary target of right-wing anger, in the tabloids and alternative conservative press, over having lost Vietnam. In March 1974, for example, the *Review of the News* published a lengthy essay by Frank Capell called "The Kissinger Caper," which made the case that Kissinger, while in Europe in Army intelligence during World War II, had been recruited by Soviet intelligence and given the code name "Bor." Capell was a vehemently anti-Communist gossipmonger who published the newsletter *Herald of Freedom*. He tied his allegation that Kissinger was a Soviet agent to the 1974 fall of West German chancellor Willy Brandt, who resigned when it was revealed that one of his top aides, Günter Guillaume, was an East German Stasi spy. Capell, best known for reporting on the relationship between Robert F. Kennedy and Marilyn Monroe, expanded his essay into a short book, *Henry Kissinger, Soviet Spy*, which he self-published in 1974. Also supposedly involved in the conspiracy was Frank Wisner, a retired CIA agent who killed himself in 1965, and Kim Philby, who was a KGB spy in British intelligence. Wisner had a long-standing connection with William Y. Elliott, Kissinger's Harvard mentor. The idea that Kissinger was a Soviet agent was embraced and repeated by the rank-and-file New Right. Beyond accusations of treason, Kissinger was subject to an increasing number of unflattering profiles in the populist press, including an August 12, 1975, profile in the *National Enquirer*. "The Real Kissinger" alleged that he enjoyed humiliating his first wife in public. It quoted Maury Feld, an old Harvard associate from the International Seminar days, saying that he was often "repelled" by Kissinger's "calculating approach with people." The article also quoted a former housekeeper who reported that Kissinger was a "restless sleeper," ripping the sheets off the bed every evening. Many of these reports reflect the xenophobia and anti-Semitism that mark the American Right. On July 8, 1974, William Loeb, the editor of New Hampshire's *Manchester Union*, raised the (extremely unlikely due to constitutional prohibition) prospect of Kissinger's running for president: "An educated man who can't even speak the English language without a heavy accent is disgusting." Interestingly, grassroots conservatives in the 1970s saw themselves as opposed to the corporate interests of the fossil fuel industry and were particularly angry at Kissinger's "oil floor price" (discussed in chapter 6) which one conservative identified as a plan "to sell

one knew what he meant: the opposite of what was presented as Kissinger's amoral realpolitik, of Kissinger's willingness to treat Leonid Brezhnev, Mao, and Mao's successors as ethical equals. The standard bearer of the rising American Right had a rolling list of complaints: Angola, Vietnam, Cuba, the Panama Canal, Israel. But behind all these issues lay the main target: détente.

Kissinger didn't introduce that word into America's political lexicon; it had long been part of the diplomatic vernacular. Nor was Kissinger primarily responsible for easing tensions between Moscow and Washington. The dynamics of normalization were under way for over a decade, traced back to, among other events, Stalin's death in 1953, JFK's willingness to negotiate with Moscow during the Cuban missile crisis, and Willy Brandt's "Ostpolitik," which improved relations between West and East Germany. But by the mid-1970s, détente had become associated with Kissinger, particularly with the ratification of a series of treaties between the United States and the USSR meant to slow the arms race, including SALT in 1972 and the Helsinki Accords in 1975.[6]

Reagan in 1976 pronounced the word "détente" as if it were M. Kissinger's middle name. He'd include in his speeches a litany of crises in which Washington apparently lost the upper hand to Moscow—Angola, Vietnam, Cuba, the Middle East—repeating, after the mention of each, the same refrain: "Doctor Kissinger said 'we must not allow this to interfere with détente.'" For the rising Right, the word became synonymous with decline, defeat, appeasement, and surrender. Détente, Reagan and his supporters charged, was Kissinger's way of managing decline.

a large chunk of America" to "the major oil producers to convince them to formalize their support for the 'new world order.'" The writer continued: "It is sort of a perpetual hijacking plan whereby we pay tribute continually to the major petroleum interests." See William Hoar, "Henry Kissinger: This Man Is on the Other Side," *American Opinion*, June 1975. Some of these clippings are found in box 47 of the Nathaniel Weyl Papers, found at the Hoover Institution Archives.

Kissinger didn't respond to these attacks during the 1976 primaries; to do so would have hurt Ford, since Kissinger was so unpopular with rank-and-file Republicans. But later, out of office, he would defend détente, saying it was a framework not for managing decline but for ensuring that Washington didn't waste its resources in pointless crises as it steadily worked to "wear down the Soviet system." Ford judged the "challenge to be in the nature of a marathon race," Kissinger said, and he was concerned to not dissipate the nation's "strength in a series of sprints designed for the gallery." The goal of détente was "to prove to the American people that crisis and confrontation were a last resort, not an everyday means of conducting foreign policy."[7]

In reality, détente was much more than suggested either by Reagan's criticism or by Kissinger's defense.[8] Nixon entered the White House in 1969, as the golden years of America's postwar economic boom were coming to an end. Public debt was increasing, trade balances were tightening, energy costs were mounting, the dollar was devaluing, Third World markets were closing (thanks to nationalization and high tariffs and subsidies), and economic rivals in Europe and Asia were expanding. In this context, détente became as much an economic strategy as a political one, a lifeline for the corporate base of the fraying New Deal coalition (which included Kissinger's first patron with real power, Nelson Rockefeller). Military deescalation would free up public revenue for productive investment and tamp down the inflationary pressures that scared the big banking houses, while the normalization of international relations would open the USSR, Eastern Europe, and China for trade and investment.

If détente had restored the American economy to global primacy, criticisms of the policy by Reagan and the other tribunes of the New Right might have missed their mark. But normalization failed to solve the economic crisis, which by 1975 seemed intractable: China, coming out of the Cultural Revolution, was a basket case, while the economies of Eastern Europe and the USSR were too anemic to absorb sufficient amounts of US capital and too poor to serve as profitable trading partners. So when Reagan, in his TV spots, looked at the camera and said (a tad angrily, not with the "happy warrior" demeanor he would perfect in his 1980 run) that "we've given the Soviets our trade and technology" and have gotten nothing in return, the complaint registered. "Well, the time has come," Reagan said, "to tell us, the American people, what we are getting out of détente." He continued: "What has the United States gotten in return, other than Soviet belligerence in the Middle East, Soviet duplicity in Southeast Asia, and Soviet imperialism in south-central Africa?"

Kissinger, muzzled for the duration of the election season, couldn't respond (he had become such a target for the Right that Ford asked him to cancel a series of planned addresses in California; Kissinger spent much of 1976's spring and early summer primary season traveling abroad, including to Latin America, Europe, and Africa). But given the poor state of the US economy, the ongoing effects of both inflation and stagnation, what could he have said?

Kissinger in 1976 must have felt a little bit like the sorcerer's apprentice. In the 1950s and 1960s, he used fear of the "missile gap," which he knew to be nonexistent, to establish his credentials as a serious defense intellectual raising hard questions and suggesting hard alternatives. Now he had to listen in silence as Reagan used a similar set of lies, accusing him of letting the United States fall behind Moscow: "The Soviet army is twice the size of ours. . . . We are outgunned three to one in artillery pieces, four to one in tanks. Soviet strategic missiles are larger, more numerous and powerful than those of the United States."[9]

During the primaries, a story circulated about Kissinger, told by Admiral Elmo Zumwalt, that electrified Reagan's base. The admiral, in his memoirs published in early 1976, said that Kissinger had confessed to him that he thought America's best years were behind him. The two men were traveling in a train from Washington to Philadelphia, and Kissinger, according to notes Zumwalt claimed he wrote down immediately following their conversation, said that he:

> feels that U.S. has passed its historic high point like so many earlier civilizations. He believes U.S. is on downhill and cannot be roused by political challenge. He states that his job is to persuade the Russians to give us the best deal we can get, recognizing that the historical forces favor them. He says that he realizes that in light of history he will be recognized as one of those who negotiated terms favorable to the Soviets, but that the American people have only themselves to blame because they lack stamina to stay the course against the Russians who are "Sparta to our Athens."[10]

Zumwalt's memoir was published in May but Reagan was already quoting from it in April. In a half-hour television ad, he said that according to an "unpublished book"—Zumwalt's—Kissinger thought his job was "to negotiate the most acceptable second-best position available" behind the Soviet Union. Reagan here was sounding a lot like Kissinger in the 1950s, drawing on Oswald Spengler's diagnosis of the threat of decline but insisting that decline wasn't inevitable: "I don't believe the people I've met in almost every State of the Union are ready to consign this, the last island of freedom, to the dustbin of history, along with the bones of dead civilizations of the past."[11]

From Spengler, Kissinger also developed, as we have seen, his critique of sterile rationalism and his appreciation of the importance of "spontaneity," "instinct," and "intuition" in conducting statecraft, of knowing one's "purpose." Where Spengler and Kissinger believed there existed a realm of experience not subject to the laws of reason but rather governed by these intangible values. Now listen to Reagan, continuing his brief against Kissinger. "Call it mysticism, if you will, but I believe God had a divine purpose" for the United States. And while Kissinger in the past had drawn from Spengler to warn of the bureaucrats who insist that things are so complicated that nothing can be done about anything, in 1976 it was Kissinger who was tagged by Reagan as the bureaucrat.[12] Clearly referring to Kissinger, Reagan lambasted the "self-anointed elite in our nation's capital" who spend their time "telling us" that governance is "too complex for our understanding."*

Kissinger, the Spenglerian, had been out-Spenglered.

Reagan lost his 1976 bid against Ford, and Ford went on to lose to Jimmy Carter. Yet before he exited Foggy Bottom, Kissinger, who had outlasted all his original rivals from the first Nixon administration, had to suffer the ignominy of watching Donald Rumsfeld, Dick Cheney, and Paul Wolfowitz—the men who would later lead the United States into Iraq and Afghanistan—outmaneuver and undercut him.

Wolfowitz, who would serve George W. Bush as assistant secretary of defense, was part of the CIA's infamous "Team B," an

---

* Earlier, in 1968, Reagan sounded indistinguishable from Kissinger when he assailed the "fetish of complexity, the trick of making hard decisions harder to make—the art, finally, of rationalizing the nondecision." Such a bureaucratic mind-set, Reagan said, had "made a ruin of American foreign policy."

ad hoc intelligence review that Ford set up to appease conservatives who insisted that the CIA was underplaying its estimates of Soviet power. In the White House, Cheney and Rumsfeld pushed the idea. "They wanted to toughen up the agency's estimates," Melvin Goodman, a former CIA analyst, said. "Cheney wanted to drive [the CIA] so far to the right it would never say no to the generals."[13]

Weak on facts, hard evidence, and verifiable numbers, Team B was strong on rhetoric, depicting the Soviets as an expansionist threat gathering its forces and preparing to strike. Its fifty-five-page report, finished in December 1976, was the Right's answer to the Pentagon Papers, a nearly perfect negation of the document Daniel Ellsberg had leaked three years earlier. The scholars and policy makers who composed the Pentagon Papers represented the kind of men Kissinger disdained: experts enthralled to facts. In contrast, the members of Team B were admitted ideologues. "Its members," as J. Peter Scoblic notes, "saw the Soviet threat not as an empirical problem but as a matter of faith."[14]

Where the Pentagon Paper authors pored over raw data and produced a dense, empirical exposition of the cause and effect leading to deeper, disastrous involvement in Vietnam, Team B-ers barely considered any actual intelligence. They knew the CIA had underestimated Soviet strength even before they saw the CIA's estimates. Previewing what would become known as Dick Cheney's "one percent doctrine," Team B interpreted threats with the smallest probability of occurring as likely to occur. Absence of proof of Russian superiority was taken as proof of superiority: "Team B's failure to find a Soviet non-acoustic anti-submarine system was evidence that there could well be one," noted one summary of the findings.[15]

Like the Pentagon Papers, Team B's findings were secretly passed on to the press to influence public debate. Ellsberg leaked to try to end a war. Team B-ers leaked to restart one: the Cold War. In December 1977, the *New York Times* published a front-page story legitimizing the "intelligence" findings of Team B, shaping subsequent public discussion of the defense budget. It would take some time to have its effect, but Team B's assessment would provide the justification for Reagan's massive arms buildup.

And just as the Pentagon Papers continued to be a point of reference for opponents of intervention, the success of Team B continued to inspire the neoconservative Right, especially the policy makers and intellectuals who drove the United States to war in 2003 by politicizing official intelligence or manufacturing false intel on Iraqi efforts to obtain weapons of mass destruction.* At the Pentagon, for instance, Donald Rumsfeld after 9/11 "was reprising Team B by creating his own intelligence shop," based on false reports on Saddam Hussein's nuclear weapons. "That's why they set up an intelligence unit in [Undersecretary of Defense Douglas] Feith's office," said James Bamford, who writes on matters related to national security. "The whole purpose was to get that kind of information and send it to Cheney."[16]

The philosophy of history that motivated most members of Team B (as it did most of those involved in pushing for war in 2003) was Kissinger's philosophy of history. They swore on the validity of intuition in assessing threats and on the importance of will in rendering material power effective. They assailed the "objectivity" of previous CIA estimates, the misguided insistence of intelligence experts on focusing only on what the Soviets were actually doing

---

* The CIA's estimate of Soviet power was wrong. In 1989, the agency reviewed its threat assessments from 1974 to 1986 and found that in each year Soviet strength had been "substantially overestimated." Many of the neocons who resurfaced in the 2000s had worked on Team B or were instrumental in its establishment, including Rumsfeld, Wolfowitz, Cheney, and Richard Pipes. Others not directly connected to Team B, such as Fox pundit William Kristol, made the argument that since Team B won the Cold War its assumptions on how to read intelligence should be resurrected to confront Al Qaeda. Frank Gaffney, ever present on cable news making the case for war and warning about Islam, has joined other militarists, including Lieutenant General William Boykin, who served as the deputy undersecretary of defense for intelligence in the Pentagon during the Iraq War, in what they call "Team B II."

and not on what, based on their material power, they were capable of doing. Team B-ers maintained that one had to look at the material power (which, in any case, they greatly exaggerated) of the Soviet arsenal and assume the worst—that is, take as a baseline that Moscow *would* do what it *could* do. Sounding a little bit like the young metaphysician Henry Kissinger, who insisted that truth was a matter of interpretation, Leo Cherne, a member of the President's Foreign Intelligence Advisory Board who helped set up Team B, said, "We are in the midst of a crisis of belief, and a crisis of belief can only be resolved by belief."[17] The irony, of course, is that members of Team B used the intuitive philosophy of history to derail Kissinger the philosopher of intuitive history.* Their objective was, as historian Anne Hessing Cahn writes, to "belittle, besmirch, and tarnish Henry Kissinger."[18] Rumsfeld, as Ford's secretary of defense, and Dick Cheney, the White House chief of staff, for instance, used Team B to isolate Kissinger in his last months in office and sabotage the possibility of a new SALT treaty with Russia.[19]

Even before Team B issued its final report, Cheney had worked with the Reaganite insurgents to insert a "morality plank" into the 1976 Republican platform (a better name of which might have been an "anti-Kissinger plank"), repudiating the "undue concessions" made in "secret agreements" with the Soviets. The formerly isolationist and chauvinist Republicans were now calling for a foreign policy motivated not just by defense of national interests but by a "belief in the rights of man, the rule of law, and guidance by

---

* In an October 1986 *Commentary* essay defending the work of Team B, neoconservative historian Richard Pipes charged Kissinger with embracing "positivism." Echoing the Kissinger of 1950, Pipes complained about the "growing influence of scientific modes of thinking on all aspects of life," reflected in the White House's insistence that intelligence agencies, when considering Soviet strength, "concentrate exclusively on the technical data or hardware, avoiding what Kissinger called 'talmudic' estimates. This had the same effect because by eliminating informed, conscious, and overt political judgment from the estimates, it led to the injection of surreptitious political judgments disguised as hardware analyses."

the hand of God." This appeared to repudiate everything that Kissinger—who as much as said that God died in the Nazi death camps and Soviet gulags—stood for.[20]

Team B and its ongoing consequences were a stunning defeat for Kissinger, who started the Ford presidency supreme: his former patron Nelson Rockefeller was vice president and he held, simultaneously, the position of secretary of state and national security adviser. Kissinger even considered Rumsfeld, Ford's chief of staff, an ally, conspiring with him during some post-Nixon bureaucratic infighting. But soon, the liberal Rockefeller became a liability with the gathering forces of the New Right. In early 1975, representatives of the conservative movement met with Rumsfeld and said they would hold Ford personally responsible "for any leftward drift" led by Rockefeller.[21] Perhaps Rumsfeld, at that moment himself considered a "liberal," sensed that the future belonged to the conservatives. In any case, he soon sided with the militarists against Kissinger. Kissinger later complained about Rumsfeld's "ambitions." He was, Kissinger said, "the rottenest person he had known in government."[22]

There were, without doubt, dissimilarities between Kissinger's diplomatic philosophy and the "ideological élan" of the Reaganites, which Kissinger himself pointed out. Neoconservatives disdain history, Kissinger said in 1999: "Tactics bored them; they discerned no worthy goals for American foreign policy short of total victory. . . . Even after the neoconservatives had achieved major influence within the Reagan ascendancy, they continued their assault by insisting on a version of history that lures the United States away from the need to face complexity."[23]

It might appear on first read that Kissinger, considering his foreign policy metaphysics, is drawing a distinction without a difference. After all, he had long insisted that statesmen not be paralyzed by the past, that they act with resolution to bend history to their will. "We create our own reality," said a Bush staffer to justify the invasion of Iraq. The West needs men who can "create their own reality," Kissinger said four decades earlier.

But there was a difference. Kissinger burdened his own action-oriented philosophy of history with the weight, or "element," of tragedy, with the awareness that in the end human ambitions are always frustrated and happiness always stymied. "Life is suffering," he wrote in 1950, "birth involves death." And for all his insistence that human interpretation of reality could never be anything other than relative and subjective, Kissinger did think (or at least he said he thought) that reality imposed restraints and limits; however important it was for great leaders to act on hunches and demonstrate resolve, it was equally important to pay attention to those restraints and limits (if only so as not to get bogged down in a series of energy-, resource-, and will-sapping crises that divert from larger goals). This, above all, is what drove both the intellectuals and the rank-and-file of the New Right crazy, why the Zumwalt story resonated so deeply with movement conservatives. Kissinger, having lost Vietnam and reversed course in southern Africa, reminded them of mortality and vulnerability, that their will-to-infinity was constrained by social reality—not to mention what Kissinger called the tragic element of human affairs. The secretary of state had a "predilection," as one conservative columnist, syndicated in small-town, heartland newspapers, summed up why the Right disliked Kissinger, for "walking with tragedy." "Subconsciously, he thinks the U.S. is destined to lose."[24]

Then there was Kissinger's habit, which by 1975 had become marked in his public speeches, of referring to the "fact" or the "reality" of "interdependence"—a word that provoked conservatives almost as much as did détente. We live, Kissinger said, in "a new international environment—a world of multiple centers of power, of ideological differences both old and new, clouded by nuclear

peril and marked by the new imperatives of interdependence."
"American policy" is based not on "confrontation" but on the "consciousness of global interdependence as the basis of the ultimate
fulfillment of national objectives." "A world of interdependence."
"The structure of global interdependence." "The big problem is to
bring the nations of the world together in recognition of the fact of
interdependence." "The awareness of our interdependence." "Today's
interdependent world." "Increasing interdependence." "Interdependence impels international co-operation." "Interdependence
imposes," Kissinger said, obligations.

Reporter: "Mr. Secretary, you spoke a great deal about interdependence in your speech." Secretary Kissinger: "Yes."[25]

In a recent book, *The Age of Fracture*, the Princeton intellectual
historian Daniel Rodgers echoes Kissinger's sense that the Reagan White House represented a new kind of presidency, a qualitative leap into a different realm of public symbolism. "No president
before Reagan had invested belief itself with such extravagant
power and possibilities. In Reagan's urgency-filled speeches of the
1960s and early 1970s the enemies were institutionally and socio-
logically palpable: the Kremlin and its 'anti-heap of totalitarianism,' the planners and welfare-state advocates, the forces of
'anarchy and insurrection' on the Berkeley campus."[26] I would add
Henry Kissinger to this list of tangible enemies to be vanquished.

Yet however much they disliked him and what he stood for, the
New Right couldn't dispose of Kissinger so easily. His intellectual
defense of war at a moment, the late 1960s and early 1970s, when
the idea of war was most vulnerable was too important. Over the
course of his long career he articulated a powerful set of assumptions and arguments that would continue to justify bold action in
the world, up to and beyond the 2003 invasion of Iraq.

What Reagan and his followers did, then, was to keep Kissingerism by splitting it in two. They claimed as their own the half that
emphasized that the human condition was radical freedom, that

decline was not inevitable, that the course of history could be swayed by the will of purposeful men. Rodgers writes that "by the time Reagan entered the White House, freedom's nemesis had migrated into the psyche. Freedom's deepest enemy was pessimism: the mental undertow of doubt, the paralyzing specter of limits, the 'cynic who's trying to tell us we're not going to get any better.'" Into Reagan's speeches slipped an "enchanted, disembedded, psychically involute sense of freedom" celebrating the "limitless possibilities of self and change."[27]

As to the rest of Kissingerism—the part that said that history was tragedy, that life was suffering, birth death, that existence was, at the end of the day, meaningless, and that individuals come into the world trapped in a web of wants, necessities, demands, and obligations—that half was for the world's other peoples, those who would be sacrificed in a revived Cold War. For those peoples, in Angola, Mozambique, Chile, Nicaragua, El Salvador, Guatemala, Iraq, Afghanistan, and Iran and other frontline states, the Reaganites would recommend an ever-increasing degree of violence so they could have freedom, like us. "America's not just a word," Ronald Reagan said in his July 4, 1984, address, "it is a hope, a torch shedding light to all the hopeless of the world. . . . You know, throughout the world, the persecuted hear the word 'America,' and in that sound they hear the sunrise, hear the rivers push, hear the cold, swift air at the top of the peak. Yes, you can hear freedom."[28]

9

Cause and Effect

Values are, at best, a mode of causality. The mystery of life is limited
by classifiable data; it exhausts itself in the riddle of the first cause. . . .
Resignation as to the purposes of the universe serves as the first step
toward ethical activity and the realization ensues that the meaning
of history is not confined to its mere manifestations and that no
causal analysis can absolve Man from giving his own content to his
own existence.

—Henry Kissinger

On April 15, 1998, Pol Pot, the former leader of the Khmer Rouge,
died in Cambodia, an old man with no remorse. A few months
earlier, a journalist had asked him if he felt regret for the crimes
committed against the Cambodian people—over a million people
died after he took power in 1975. No, he answered. "My conscience
is clear." "We had to defend ourselves," Pol Pot said, referring to
the revolution's enemies.[1]

Henry Kissinger has faced similar questions about his role in
Cambodia. Did he have "any pangs of conscience," *Die Zeit* asked
him in 1976, about a year after the fall of Phnom Penh to Pol Pot's
rebels. No, Kissinger said. North Vietnamese troops had invaded
first and they were using Cambodian sanctuaries to kill American soldiers. "I may have a lack of imagination," Kissinger told the
German magazine, "but I fail to see the moral issue involved."
America, Kissinger said elsewhere, had to "defend itself."[2]

In 1979, not long after Kissinger left office, a British journalist, William Shawcross, published a best-selling book called *Sideshow: Kissinger, Nixon, and the Destruction of Cambodia*, which called him to account not just for his illegal war but for its subsequent effects: by polarizing Cambodia with a massive bombing campaign, Shawcross argued, Kissinger created the conditions for the triumph of the Khmer Rouge. "The Khmer Rouge were born out of the inferno that American policy did much to create."[3] The accusation gnawed at Kissinger. He devoted a considerable number of pages in each of his three memoirs, and in almost every other book he wrote, defending himself against the accusation that he was to blame for the rise of Pol Pot. Finally, by 1998, with the Cold War over and Kissinger well settled in his role as America's statesman emeritus, the matter seemed to be behind him.

But then Pol Pot died, and Kissinger once again found himself rehearsing arguments that he first started making in 1969: North Vietnam had violated Cambodia's sovereignty first; the neutral country had become a haven for enemies of the United States; and America took care not to target civilians, just Vietcong and North Vietnamese. Interviewed by the BBC about Pol Pot's legacy, Kissinger used the phrase "the so-called bombing of Cambodia." The *Guardian* quipped the next day that this was "presumably . . . distinct from a proper bombing which would have destroyed the entire Cambodian infrastructure and traumatized the entire Cambodian people—not just a large proportion of both."[4]

The BBC interviewer also asked Kissinger the question "Do you feel responsible?" "Absolutely," Kissinger replied. "I feel just as responsible as you should feel for the Holocaust because you bombed Hamburg."

It's a fatuous answer. The Nazis, of course, had come to power *before* the British air assault on Hamburg in 1943, and they initiated the Holocaust *before* the Allies targeted that German city. The Khmer Rouge came to power *after* the carpet bombing of Cambodia. They launched their campaign of mass terror *after* Kissinger's bombing campaign.

The flimsiness of Kissinger's comparison is instructive. Foreign policy makers often invoke analogies—usually ones involving Nazis, Hitler, or Munich—for two reasons. The first is to provide a simple framing mechanism to justify action in the present. Saddam is Hitler—three words that concisely convey a world of moral and historical meaning. The second is to deflect away from methods of historical inquiry, such as cause-and-effect analysis, that might place responsibility for current crises on past policies. Kissinger has said, over and over again, that one of the worst conditions that can befall a political leader is to become "prisoner of the past," to be overly worried about repeating mistakes.[5] Statesmen must refuse, as Kissinger has refused, to accept the proposition that the consequences of any previous action, no matter how horrific, should restrict their room to maneuver in the future. Kissinger's analogy, though, is so unpersuasive it actually achieves the opposite of its intent, forcing us to look at the relationship of cause to effect, action to reaction, and the moral responsibility that attaches to that relationship.

The bombing of Cambodia is distinct from Kissinger's other transgressions, and not just because of its magnitude of cruelty or its body count. Most of Kissinger's policies that draw censure can be justified by reason of state. Read Machiavelli—with his counsel to statesmen to act according to how the world really works as opposed to how it ideally should work—and you'll have your defense for Kissinger's support for Pinochet and the shah, his sanctioning of Suharto's invasion of East Timor, and even his military aid to Pakistan while it perpetuated genocide against Bangladesh.* One

---

* Machiavelli: "There's such a difference between the way we really live and the way we ought to live that the man who neglects the real to study the ideal will learn how to accomplish his ruin, not his salvation."

might support or condemn any one of these actions, but the terms of the debate would have to do with questions of national interest, political effectiveness, and whether order is a higher value than justice or vice versa. The effect of most of these policies—the blowback—is two or three steps removed from Kissinger: one could argue, as Kissinger and his supporters have argued on different occasions, that backing allied strongmen is not the same thing as sanctioning the acts they do. As to the U.S. armed slaughter of hundreds of thousands in East Timor and Bangladesh, that, Kissinger has said, would have happened no matter what he did.

In Cambodia, however, the relationship of cause and effect is much more direct—if only because it was the United States, and not a US-armed proxy, that executed the cause, or at least one of the causes (the four-year air assault), that led to the effect (Pol Pot's genocide). And one can't justify the bombing by reason of state for it was driven by motives that were the opposite of Machiavellian realism: it was executed to try to bring about a world Nixon and Kissinger believed they *ought* to live in—one in which they could, by the force of their material power, bend peasant-poor countries like Cambodia (and Laos and North Vietnam) to their will—rather than reflect the real world they did live in, one in which, try as they might, they had been unable to terrorize weaker nations into submission.[6]

That Kissinger, along with Nixon, presided over the bombing of Cambodia, and had done so since March of 1969, is now well known. Less so is that the worst of his bombing started in February 1973, a month *after* Washington, Hanoi, and Saigon signed the Paris Peace Accords. In 1972, the United States dropped, in total, 53,000 tons of bombs on Cambodia. Between February 8 and August 15, 1973, that number increased nearly fivefold and targeted not just Vietnamese "sanctuaries" in the country's east but most of the entire country.

In other words, Washington dropped almost the same amount of explosives on Cambodia in these six months as it had in the entire previous four years. Think of it as an accelerando climax to Nixon and Kissinger's epic bombing opera. "We would rather err on the side of doing too much," Kissinger said to his envoy in Cambodia the day after the escalation began, referring to the bombing, than too little.[7] "I see no reason not to really whack the hell out of them in Cambodia," Nixon said to Kissinger a few days later.[8]

The nominal reason for this intensified bombing was the same as it ever was: to save face. The initial secret bombing—Operation Menu—helped create an untenable situation in Cambodia, which led to a 1970 coup that broadened the social base of the insurgency to include not just Khmer Rouge but royalist "Sihanoukists" (supporters of deposed Prince Sihanouk) and other non-Communists. Nixon's and Kissinger's solution to this crisis aggravated by their bombing was more bombing, including phosphorous explosives and cluster bombs that each released thousands of either ball bearings or darts. The redoubled carpet bombing of 1973 was meant to force the Khmer Rouge insurgency to the bargaining table, or at least force North Vietnam (which was withdrawing from Cambodia) or China (which had no presence there) to force the Cambodian insurgents to the table. And, as always, there were domestic calculations: bombing Cambodia might distract from the Watergate scandal (the escalation started a week after the Watergate burglary trial ended in the convictions of Gordon Liddy and James W. McCord).

It didn't. Congress mandated that the assault end on August 15. Enough, it said. The war in Southeast Asia was over.

The historian Ben Kiernan calls this intensified phase of the bombing a "watershed" in Cambodian history.[9] Kiernan is now a professor of history at Yale University and founding director of its

Genocide Studies Program. In the 1970s, he learned the Khmer language and interviewed hundreds of Cambodian refugees, including victims and former members of the Khmer Rouge. Kiernan believes, as he told me, that the "cause of the genocide was the decision of Pol Pot's leadership to conduct it." As an historian, though, he places that decision within a broader context, a set of necessary conditions that made possible the execution of the decision. The U.S. bombing of Cambodia was a major cause (among others) of, if not the genocide directly, then the massive growth of the Khmer Rouge movement, which when in power conducted the genocide. In the period of the Nixon-Kissinger bombardment, the Khmer Rouge forces increased from about 5,000 in 1969 to more than 200,000 troops and militia in 1973. There were certainly other reasons for this rapid recruitment, including the support received from Sihanouk (itself a result of the U.S.-backed coup against him) and the Vietnamese Communists. But it is hard to deny that one major political effect of the 1969–73 bombing was the rapid spread of the Khmer Rouge insurgency and the increased control of that insurgency by its most radical, paranoid, and murderous faction.

Based on his interviews, as well as extensive documentary research, including declassified CIA reports and air force bombing data, Kiernan drew the following three conclusions.

First: The bombing caused "enormous losses" of Cambodian "life and property" on an almost unimaginable scale, across the country. The campaign was indiscriminate, with rural civilians the primary victims. Besides the more than 100,000 Cambodians killed, as many as two million people were forced out of their homes during the war, one-quarter of the country's population. It's impossible to read the testimonies taken by Kiernan and others and not be stunned: twenty people killed in one raid, thirty in another, entire families obliterated, hundreds of acres of crops scorched, whole villages destroyed. "They hit houses in Samrong," one survivor recalls, "and thirty people were killed." Another said that the "bombing was massive and devastating, and they just kept bombing more and more massively, so massively you couldn't believe it, so that it engulfed the forests, engulfed the forests with bombs, with devastation."[10]

Second: The bombing was an effective recruitment tool for the Khmer Rouge. Propaganda doesn't seem like quite the right word, since it implies some form of deception or manipulation. Object lesson might be a better description of the service Kissinger provided to Pol Pot. Here's a former Khmer Rouge cadre describing the effect of the bombing:

> The ordinary people . . . sometimes literally shit in their pants when the big bombs and shells came. . . . Their minds just froze up and they would wander around mute for three or four days. Terrified and half-crazy, the people were ready to believe what they were told. . . . It was because of their dissatisfaction with the bombing that they kept on cooperating with the Khmer Rouge, joining up with the Khmer Rouge, sending their children off to go with them. . . . Sometimes the bombs fell and hit little children, and their fathers would be all for the Khmer Rouge.

Another told a journalist that his village had been destroyed by US bombs, as Kiernan reports, "killing 200 of its 350 inhabitants and propelling him into a career of violence and absolute loyalty" to the Khmer Rouge. One elderly woman said she had never met a Khmer Rouge until her village was destroyed. The propaganda was strategic but the fury and confusion real: "The people were angry with the US, and that is why so many of them joined the Khmer communists," reported one witness. Another said that after the bombs destroyed a number of monasteries, "people in our village were furious with the Americans; they did not know why the Americans had bombed them."[11]

Third: The bombing that took place between February and August 1973 had two consequences, delaying a Communist victory while at the same time radically transforming the nature of that victory when it did come two years later. Had Lon Nol fallen in early or mid-1973, the insurgent victors would have been comprised of diverse factions, including moderates and Sihanouk loyalists. By the time Lon Nol did fall in early 1975, not only had the Khmer Rouge come to dominate the insurgency but the most radical faction had come to dominate the Khmer Rouge.

Nixon and Kissinger's intensification of the bombing killed or scattered much of the anti–Lon Nol opposition, driving the insurgency into siege mode and giving the upper hand to a hardened corps of extremists circling around Pol Pot. The bombing sanctioned their extremism: when political-education cadres pointed to charred corpses and limbless children and said this was a "manifestation of simple American barbarism," who could disagree? And the bombing provoked even greater extremism: in the villages, "people were made angry by the bombing and went to join the revolution," and so it followed that those who didn't join the revolution were accused of being "CIA agents" and targeted for reprisal. The destruction of the countryside also prompted a "revival of national chauvinism," which included anger toward the Vietnamese for abandoning the struggle even as Cambodia was being devastated. Sihanouk supporters, Vietnamese-trained Communists, and other moderates were purged from the opposition forces.

At the same time, the strain of living under constant bombardment forced those areas under Khmer Rouge rule into suffering the Khmer Rouge imposition of an accelerated program of peasant collectivization, justified by the demands of having to survive during wartime. Emerging from the carnage was fury directed not just at United States imperialism but at the capital, Phnom Penh, the city as a symbol of decadent, urban, and industrial modernity.

On April 17, 1975, the Khmer Rouge took Phnom Penh."* Pol Pot's victorious cadre immediately began to empty out the capital and other cities, deporting millions of urban dwellers mostly to the country's northwest. Cambodia's new rulers targeted for persecution Buddhist monks, ethnic minorities, former government loyalists, intellectuals, moderate Communists, and anyone who would stand in the way of establishing their agrarian utopia. Nearly the entire population of Cambodia was forced into rural labor camps. By the time a now unified Vietnam invaded the country in 1979, overthrew the Khmer Rouge, and put an end to the genocidal madness, as many as two million people had been murdered or had died—of starvation, exhaustion, disease, and denial of medical care.

Kissinger doesn't believe that the British, by bombing Hamburg, were responsible for the Holocaust. But implied in his comparison of the Nazis to the Khmer Rouge are three assumptions worth considering.

The first is that genocidal intent was inherent in the ideology of the Khmer Rouge since its inception, much as eliminationist anti-Semitism was inherent in the Nazi movement since it was founded. Over the years, Kissinger has offered variations of this position, including in a 1994 book titled *Diplomacy*: "All evidence shows that the Khmer Rouge had been fanatical ideologues as early as their student days in Paris in the 1950s. They were determined to uproot and destroy the existing Cambodian society

---

* Kissinger's State Department arranged safe transit for Lon Nol out of the country and gave him half a million dollars in compensation: "We helped to arrange the transfer of $500,000," said one State official, though "Nol wanted one million." (See interview with Robert Keeley, in *Cambodia: Country Reader*, compiled by the Foreign Affairs Oral History Collection of the Association for Diplomatic Studies and Training; available at http://www.adst.org/Readers/Cambodia.pdf.)

and to impose a sort of mad utopia by exterminating everybody with the slightest 'bourgeois' education. To allege that they had been turned into killers by American actions has the same moral stature as would be the argument that the Holocaust had been caused by American strategic bombing of Germany."[12]

I asked Ben Kiernan about this argument, and his response was succinct and convincing: "This is irrelevant. The impact of the US bombing of rural Cambodia was not to create a genocidal ideology or political faction but to facilitate its mass recruitment and rise to power over the alternatives." Kiernan continues: "A similar outcome didn't happen in Vietnam despite the very intensive bombing there because no comparable extremist or genocidal faction existed in Vietnam. It did in Cambodia but would not have come to power without the US bombing."

Kissinger's second assumption is that the Khmer Rouge would have come to power even without US bombing. To make this argument, Kissinger usually blames North Vietnam for intervening in Cambodian affairs and for providing aid to the Khmer Rouge. He writes in his memoir *The White House Years*: "It was Hanoi—animated by an insatiable drive to dominate Indochina—that organized the Khmer Rouge long before *any* American bombs fell on Cambodian soil; it was North Vietnamese troops who were trying to strangle Cambodia in the months before our limited attack. . . . Had we not invaded the sanctuaries Cambodia would have been engulfed in 1970 instead of 1975." Then he neatly shifts blame from Hanoi to "doves" in the United States: "If anything doomed the free Cambodians, it was war weariness in the United States," which prevented Kissinger from continuing the bombing beyond August 1973.[13] "The effect of congressional restrictions was to impose an unbearable, almost vindictive constraint," he wrote in yet another book, on "the scale of American assistance to impoverished Cambodia." His hands tied by Congress, there was "nothing left" for Kissinger "to do other than to watch in anguish" as Cambodia eventually fell to the Khmer Rouge.[14]

There are a number of problems with these statements. To begin with, Kissinger knew the Khmer Rouge were not controlled by Hanoi (nor by Peking for that matter). In fact, declassified documents reveal that Kissinger had spent the months of the bombing escalation looking to find a way to take advantage of the tensions and animosity that existed between China, North Vietnam, and the Khmer Rouge to press a deal, to, in the words of his ambassador to Cambodia, "drive a wedge" between Washington's adversaries.[15]

Likewise, Kissinger in mid-1973 wasn't waging a heroic Churchillian war to keep the Nazi-like Khmer Rouge from taking power and implementing their genocide. Quite the opposite. His goal with the intensified bombing was not specifically to keep the Khmer Rouge *out*, but rather help bring them *into* power— as part of an acceptable coalition government. "We would be prepared," Kissinger told the Soviet foreign minister, Andrei Gromyko, on May 8 "for a solution analogous to Laos."[16] By this, Kissinger was referring to the Laotian government that included the Laotian Communist insurgency, Pathet Lao (which, before the 1975–79 Cambodian genocide, was seen as roughly equivalent to the Khmer Rouge). Kissinger said that if a ceasefire could be reached, he would be willing to accept "some coalition structure in Phnom Penh in which all factions are included," including the Khmer Rouge.*

If we accept Kissinger's analogy—associating the Khmer Rouge

---

* Eight months after their takeover of Phnom Penh, as late as November 1975, by which time he had been fully briefed on the extent of Khmer Rouge atrocities, Kissinger asked Thailand's foreign minister to relay them a message: "You should tell the Cambodians [i.e., the Khmer Rouge regime] that we will be friends with them. They are murderous thugs, but we won't let that stand in the way. We are prepared to improve relations with them."

to the Nazis—then he wasn't Churchill in 1940 but Neville Chamberlain in 1938.[17]

Kissinger didn't, in 1970 or 1973, think the Khmer Rouge were the Nazis. And the notion that he would have, were it not for Congress, bombed indefinitely to save Cambodia is a myth he has conjured retroactively. That Kissinger didn't want Congress to stop him from bombing had more to do with his relationship with Congress than it did with anything he hoped to achieve in Cambodia. It was the principle of the matter, the need to be able to conduct diplomacy unhampered in his ability to deliver on threats and offer incentives. Cambodia, as Shawcross wrote, was just a sideshow to this struggle; Kissinger planned to continue the bombing just long enough to cut a deal, including with the Khmer Rouge, and get out.*

But it is the third assumption of Kissinger's Nazi comparison that goes to the heart of the matter, revealing the usefulness of historical analogies in sanctioning military action: it doesn't matter if the United States, with its bombs, created the causal conditions for the radicalization and victory of the Khmer Rouge. Even if true, his reasoning goes, that fact should have no bearing on future US policy. Think of it this way: let's say for argument's sake that British policy was somehow responsible for the Nazi Holocaust; does it then follow that London would be unjustified in waging war on the Nazis once the nature of their threat became evident? Of course not.

Kissinger is in effect saying: let investigative journalists like William Shawcross and historians like Ben Kiernan establish a credible cause-and-effect relationship between his bombs and Pol

---

* On this point, Kissinger is unrepentant: he argues that "Cambodia was taken over by a homicidal clique primarily because Americans subordinated the country's survival to their own domestic drama." Only with this term, *Americans,* he means the domestic political pressure to stop the bombing—not his own instrumentalization of the terror to demonstrate his loyalty to Nixon and his toughness to Haig.

Pot's genocide. The United States has a moral responsibility to act, to refuse to be paralyzed either by the fact or the fear of blowback.

Kissinger got most of his critique of "cause and effect" history from Oswald Spengler, a "historian" in only the wobbliest sense of the word. Spengler played fast and loose with facts, making some up and distorting others. The British historian Hugh Trevor-Roper accused him of fabricating a "civilization"—the Magian—from the whole cloth of his imagination. It was "entirely invented by him," Trevor-Roper said, flabbergasted.[18] Over the years, critics have spent a considerable amount of time pointing out passages where Spengler is wrong on the facts.

Why should Spengler care? After all, he rejected the whole idea of logical analysis, saying that his metaphysics represented a more profound truth than the material realities of the world. "Once we grasp this distinction," says Stuart Hughes, his intellectual biographer, then we can stop wasting our efforts trying to prove him wrong or right. "He is not writing the sort of history that most of us have been trained to think of as the only possible kind. Hence three-fourths of our objections simply fall to the ground," missing their mark.[19] "Fired by the discovery of some factual error, they have dashed off to meet him on a field of battle where he never had the slightest intention of putting in an appearance."*

Kissinger learned well from Spengler. Confronted with literal-minded critics bearing facts, he responded with emotional analo-

---

* Kissinger agreed, writing in 1950 that "purely analytical criticism of Spengler will, however, never discover the profounder levels of his philosophy. These reside in the evocation of those elements of life that will ever be the subject of an inner experience, in his intuition of a mystic relationship to the infinite that expresses personality. Spengler's vision encompassed an approach to history which—whatever our opinion of his conclusions—transcended the mere causal analysis of data and the shallow dogmatisms of many progress theories." Spengler's "poetry in life" is immune, Kissinger insisted, to criticism based on reason.

gies. Of course, at this point Kissinger doesn't have to answer anyone's questions. No one is going to force him to account for his many errors and inconsistencies, for the faultiness of his facts and logic, for the way he deduces justification for his actions based on his own theories and legitimates the hardest response based on the most fragmentary of evidence.

But sometimes he does get to first principles. Like when he used his experience bombing Cambodia to make a case for why, in 1998, we needed to bomb Iraq.

10

Onward to the Gulf

For if the trumpet gives forth an uncertain sound, who shall prepare himself for battle?
—Henry Kissinger at the 1980 Republican National Convention

Just as he did with Nixon in 1968, Kissinger in 1980 quickly became comfortable with the inconceivable. In April, with the Republican primaries under way, Kissinger was actively lobbying for a spot with any of the main Republican candidates vying to challenge Carter. And as Reagan began to take the lead, he keyed his public remarks to the front-runner's foreign policy statements. Through the primaries, though, the Reagan campaign wouldn't return his calls. "Many people have asked me if I would want to go through it all again," he told a group of newspaper editors, referring to his time as secretary of state. "The problem is nobody has really asked me to." "I'm not totally discouraged," he joked. "There's still some hope."[1]

When Reagan did secure the nomination, Kissinger was asked to speak at the Republican National Convention. "We all now turn to Ronald Reagan as the trustee of our hopes," he told the crowd of delegates who had gathered in Detroit and who held him in only slightly less contempt than they did Jimmy Carter.[2] Under Reagan's leadership, Kissinger said, "we will overcome the storms ahead; we will hold our heads high and we will build that better world at peace that fulfills the dreams of mankind and the high ideals of our people."*

It gives a sense of just how much our standards have shifted that what Thomas Schelling and his Harvard colleagues considered a commonsensical wrong nearly fifty years ago—that the United States had no right to use the potential threat of terrorism to justify military action against a sovereign country it wasn't at war with—has now become a self-evident moral right. Today, exactly such reasoning is used to sanction the US military's involvement in, by some estimates, seventy-four global conflicts. The journalist Nick Turse doubles that number, reporting that elite US forces are operating in 134 countries (a more than 123 percent increase since Obama became president).[3]

Kissinger played a key role in shifting those standards. His

---

* All political speeches, especially ones given at presidential nominating conventions, are partisan, but Kissinger's remarks at the 1980 Republican Convention are notable for two reasons. First, they mimic nearly perfectly Reagan's attacks on him four years earlier. Kissinger sounds like a movement-conservative critic of Kissinger, excoriating policies that have made America "impotent," saying that the Soviets can't be trusted, and denouncing a "philosophy of abdication." Once again, Kissinger, as he did in the 1950s (and Reagan and Team B did in 1976), invoked a nonexistent missile gap. "We are falling behind," he said, endorsing Reagan's proposal to dramatically increase defense spending. Secondly, Kissinger's litany of complaints against the Carter administration read like a roll call of the consequences of *his* policies: revolution in Iran, Cuban troops in Africa, high oil prices and America's "dependence" on Gulf producers, the Soviet invasion of Afghanistan were all problems that were, if not created, then certainly worsened by Kissinger's initiatives. Just as in the 1950s Kissinger urged Washington not to flinch in fighting little wars in the world's gray areas, here he was again telling America to "prepare" itself "for battle" in what Kissinger called the "developing world." This time he was more frank about the motive. Perhaps wanting to hold on to some distinction between his worldview and the heavy-handed moralism on display at the convention, he said: "to guarantee our access to vital minerals and raw materials."

circumvention of the bureaucracy, neutralizing overly cautious area experts and sidestepping congressional oversight—by, for instance, waging secret wars, relying on proxy nations like Iran, South Africa, Brazil, and Israel to conduct covert operations, and cutting deals with dictators like Suharto in Indonesia and Pinochet in Chile—would be replicated by his successors in the Reagan (and, later, George W. Bush) administrations.* We know some of

---

* The Iran-Contra scandal, which became public in 1986 and nearly brought down the Reagan administration, was an important step in the reformation of the national security state. The scandal was about many things, centering on the illegal triangle trade by which the United States sold high-tech missiles to Iran's ayatollahs and then used the money to fund anti-Communist Contra rebels in Nicaragua. But its overarching motivation was to figure out how to counteract the cynicism and antimilitarism that had infected America's political institutions. Based in the National Security Council, Oliver North ran a shadow foreign policy, establishing unaccountable sources of funding, bypassing the State Department, dodging Congress, and running domestic psych-ops to neutralize the press and skeptical public opinion. But before there was Oliver North, there was Henry Kissinger. His reorganization of the NSC in 1969 entailed transforming it from an office whose responsibility was primarily to advise the president into a body that made and executed decisions. Jimmy Carter reversed much of this, returning authority back to the Department of State. But, as Harold Koh argues, Kissinger's precedent was crucial. Koh, a professor of law at Yale University and a former State Department official, writes that Kissinger's NSC provided the blueprint for Reagan's militarists: Iran-Contra, Koh argues, "only brought full circle an inversion of institutional responsibility" that Kissinger orchestrated in the late 1960s. And Kissinger's covert war in Angola rehearsed many of the tactics that would be deployed in Iran-Contra, including the use of proxy countries and the running of propaganda campaigns within the United States to neutralize the post-Vietnam "adversary culture." As Koh's remark suggests, it is important not to isolate Iran-Contra as its own isolated conspiracy. To do so, would be to miss two of its key elements. The first is the way it really was just one phase in the evolution of the national security state. The second is how Iran-Contra was part of Reagan's broader push to restart the Cold War in the Third World. In 1993, for instance, a yearlong Senate inquiry turned up what one investigator called a "precursor to Iran-Contra, an illegal, off-the-shelf operation involving the NSC and private funds just like Iran-Contra"—a covert plan, drawn up as early as March 1981, to "roll back communism worldwide by aiding resistance forces in Afghanistan, Cuba, Grenada, Iran, Libya, Nicaragua, Cambodia and Laos." Laos in particular was an early focus; there, a "Reagan administration official secretly used donations from POW-MIA groups to arm and supply Laotian rebels in the early 1980s. It "sounds like a dry run" for Iran-Contra, said Jack Blum, a former investigator for the Senate Foreign Relations Committee ("Report Says Reagan Aide Sent POW Funds to Rebels," *Washington Post*, January 14, 1993; "Probe Links 'Reagan Doctrine' to Covert Aid to Laos Rebels," *Los Angeles Times*, January 23, 1993). The report is published as United States Senate, *Select Committee on POW/MIA Affairs. POW/MIA's. Special Report 103-1* (1993).

what Kissinger did in Cambodia, Chile, and Angola.[4] But we have only the shadow outlines of other operations that were running while he was in office, the extent of his support for Operation Condor or his involvement in Bangladesh's 1975 coup, for instance, or what he was doing with Pakistan running jihadists into Afghanistan. This last has had consequences that we are still living with.

Likewise, as domestic politics became increasingly polarized, Kissinger's (and Nixon's) use of foreign policy to deflect dissent and mobilize supporters was continued in subsequent administrations. Kissinger was especially good at throwing red meat, in the form of bomb tonnage dropped and Southeast Asians killed, to a rising New Right. "We must escalate or P is lost," he advised in 1970. P being the president, Nixon. Kissinger was worried about upcoming elections. And when even Nixon began to doubt the efficacy of bombing, Kissinger kept insisting that a good "jolt" might, if not break Hanoi, then end the domestic political stalemate in his favor.

But covert ops and political opportunism were not Kissinger's chief contribution to American militarism. Rather, it is his philosophy of history that was key in restoring the imperial presidency at the moment of its greatest vulnerability. As we saw earlier, the "realism" he is famous for is profoundly elastic, anticipating the extreme subjectivism of the neoconservatives. Kissinger taught that there was no such thing as stasis in international affairs: great states are always either gaining or losing influence, which means that the balance of power has to be constantly tested through gesture and deed. He warned policy makers and defense intellectuals to watch out for the "causal principle." Let antiquarians concern themselves with why the current crisis has come about. Statesmen have to respond to the crisis and not obsess over its root causes. Their responsibility is to the future, not to the past.

Neoconservatism, however, is just the highly self-conscious core of a broader consensus that reaches out well beyond the Republican Party to capture ideologue and pragmatist alike, pretty much any politician with any chance at winning higher office. And Kissinger's contribution to this larger worldview can be found in the arguments used by successive administrations to legitimate ongoing interventionism. From Central America to Grenada, Panama to the first Gulf War and beyond, one can plot the crescendo, the way each military action represented a bit more—more commitment, more confidence regained, more troops deployed, more spectacular displays of firepower, more lives lost.

From the broadcasting studios of ABC, CBS, NBC, and PBS, on the opinion pages of leading newspapers, and, no doubt, in the private counsel he's given to his allies in public office, Kissinger supported each and every one of these military operations, with rationales drawn from his own experience in office reworked to fit new times.

CENTRAL AMERICA AND GRENADA

Henry Kissinger started out as a lightning rod for the rank-and-file Right. Phyllis Schlafly forced Reagan to pledge that he would never "reappoint Henry Kissinger or give him any role in making our policy toward the Soviet Union."[5] But by 1983, Kissinger had inched closer to the administration, leading Reagan to break part of his promise. The president kept Kissinger away from the Soviet Union but named him the head of the National Bipartisan Commission on Central America.

By this point, Central America was in the throes of war. The repressive status quo that the United States had long imposed on the poverty-stricken region—ever-increasing military aid to ever more murderous governments—had collapsed. The left-wing Sandinistas had triumphed in Nicaragua in 1979, and similar insurgencies were on the upswing in Guatemala and El Salvador. Reagan's hawks were

already assembling and arming the Contras in Nicaragua and reinforcing death-squad states in El Salvador and Guatemala. But setting
up a bipartisan commission to investigate the "crisis" was a smart
move, since it would help to establish broad-based legitimacy for a
hard line already in place. More importantly, at least for Kissinger,
it gave him a chance to prove his worth to the White House.

Kissinger's commission issued its findings in early 1984. The
conservative grassroots might have wanted Reagan to keep the former secretary of state as far away from the Soviet Union as possible.
This, though, was hard, since Reagan conservatives believed that
Moscow's hand was everywhere, including in Central America. It
was a belief that Kissinger was more than willing to affirm. His
commission warned of a grave situation, invoking the threat of
Russian-interdicted shipping lanes, of torpedoed oil tankers, and
of Soviet missile bases. Applying Southeast Asia's domino theory, the commission said that Nicaragua might topple El Salvador,
El Salvador Guatemala, and Guatemala Mexico. The commission's
report stressed the need for Washington to maintain "credibility
worldwide." In the case of Nicaragua, "the triumph of hostile forces
in what the Soviets call the 'strategic rear' of the United States
would be read as a sign of U.S. impotence."[6]

Even New York senator Daniel Patrick Moynihan, a hawk when
it came to Third World radicalism, called the Kissinger commission's
findings a "doctrinal position." "Facts please," Moynihan pleaded.[7]

Facts weren't the point. The wars in Central America raged on,
costing hundreds and hundreds of thousands of lives, the vast
majority at the hands of US-backed allies. But the commission had
served its purpose, for both the White House and Kissinger. For the
Reagan administration, it provided cover.[8] For Kissinger, the commission gave him a chance to establish his credibility and reconcile
with the Right. Kissinger used the commission not just to appease
those like Schlafly who saw Moscow behind every world event but
to rehearse an important argument justifying intervention.

"There might be an argument for doing nothing to help the government of El Salvador," the commission's final report concluded. "There might be an argument for doing a great deal more. There is, however, no logical argument for giving some aid but not enough. The worst possible policy for El Salvador is to provide just enough aid to keep the war going, but too little to wage it successfully."[9] It's an effective rhetorical ploy. Under the guise of choice—do something, or do nothing, but if we do something, do enough to achieve our goals—it rendered explicit an assumption that often remained implicit: once something is defined as a problem, then it is justified to do whatever is necessary to solve that problem.*

Kissinger had long used some version of this argument to frame crises.[10] In fact, just a few months before presenting his commission's findings, he used the premise to criticize Reagan from the Right. Kissinger had been scheduled to appear on a Sunday morning news show, David Brinkley's *This Week*, when two truck bombs exploded in Beirut, Lebanon, killing 299 US and French soldiers stationed there as part of a "multinational force" to contain the Lebanese civil war. Kissinger didn't miss a beat. He told Brinkley that "we either have to do more or less."[11] It was clear what his choice was. "I do not favor a withdrawal of American forces," he said, urging Reagan to carry out a joint Israel-US strike to punish Syria (which, along with Iran, was backing the anti-Israel forces in Lebanon).

Just a decade out of Vietnam, the United States wasn't yet willing to make a serious military commitment in the Middle East. But there was a place where it could take one of those "tougher stands in order to make others believe in us again," as Kissinger, earlier,

---

* Secretary of State George Shultz bristled at Kissinger's framing Central American policy along these lines, especially Kissinger's suggestion that if the Sandinista government in Nicaragua was identified as a problem, then there should be no limit to the support the White House might give to the Contras: "Henry Kissinger, I guess, argues that we either have to give up or declare nuclear war."

had advised was necessary in the wake of Vietnam. Two days after the Beirut bombing, Reagan ordered US troops to invade Grenada, a small Caribbean island just off the coast of Venezuela. It was billed as a rescue mission, as the *Mayaguez* raid was eight years earlier, this time to save a few hundred US citizens, mostly medical students, from fighting that had broken out on the island between political factions (though the chancellor of St. George Medical College said the students were never in any danger).

The reaction to the invasion, by the press and politicians, was schizophrenic. On the one hand, there was a sense it was nothing but choreographed spectacle (the invasion, said one columnist, gave "American television" one of its "better weeks") meant to distract from the carnage in Beirut, a war, one Democratic senator remarked, that the US "could win."[12] There was something ludicrous about the operation, dubbed "Urgent Fury," which resulted in the granting of "8,612 medals to individual Americans" although there had never been more than "7,000 officers and enlisted soldiers on the island."[13] On the other hand, the Democratic leadership in the House and Senate, after some initial criticism, rallied around the president. The Speaker of the House, Tip O'Neill, called the invasion "justified," as did Representative Thomas Foley. "Years of frustration were vented by the Grenada invasion," said New Jersey Democrat Robert Torricelli, who suggested the triumph helped overcome not just Vietnam but the humiliation of the prolonged 1979–81 Iranian hostage crisis.[14]

"Our days of weakness are over," Reagan said about America's ability to commandeer this small 130-square mile Caribbean island of less than 100,000 people. According to the official US count, 45 Grenadians, 24 Cubans, and 19 Americans died in the assault. "Our military forces are back on their feet and standing tall," said Reagan.*

---

* On April 14, 1986, the Reagan administration launched an air strike on Libya, in response to Libya's involvement in the April 5 bombing of a Berlin nightclub, which

PANAMA

Six years later, Kissinger endorsed George H. W. Bush's December 1989 invasion of Panama. Operation Just Cause—the name given to the invasion of Panama and the capture and removal to the United States of its leader, Manuel Noriega—was a quick, now nearly forgotten war sandwiched between the momentous fall of the Berlin Wall and the consequential first Gulf War. But it was extremely significant since it was the first post–Cold War military operation carried out with the goal of restoring another country's democracy and thus represented a substantial expansion of what constituted a legitimate excuse for going to war.

The campaign didn't start out with such ambitions. For years

---

killed two US soldiers and one Turkish civilian. Secretary of State George Shultz said the US strike was "measured" and "proportionate" to Libya's crime (US planes hit a number of residential buildings, killing an estimated fifteen civilians. Muammar Gaddafi's daughter was also reportedly killed). To justify the reprisal, Shultz cited article 51 of the United Nations charter, which grants nations the right to "self-defense." A nation, Shultz said, "attacked by terrorists is permitted to use force to prevent or preempt future attacks." It was a generous interpretation of the doctrine of self-defense (the United States wasn't attacked by Libya; rather, two of its soldiers were killed in Germany) which most legal scholars at the time disagreed with. Jimmy Carter's former White House counsel, Lloyd Cutler, tried to capture the administration's logic: "As a superpower with global responsibilities, if our forces are attacked in another country, you can construe it as an attack on our territory." The day after the US strike, Kissinger appeared on ABC's *Good Morning America* to voice his "total support" of the raid. Attacking Libya, he said, was "correct" and "necessary." Asked if he was worried about a backlash—increased radicalization, reprisals, or a boost to Gaddafi's stature—he answered: "The question is whose endurance is greater. I believe ours is." The bombing would, Kissinger said, "reduce the incidents of terrorism." Kissinger was also asked what he thought of Reagan's rhetoric. The president had called Gaddafi a "mad dog." "President Reagan has," Kissinger said, "his own exuberant way of communicating with the American public." "Sixty percent of the public agrees with him," Kissinger noted (*Good Morning America*, April 15, 1986, video available at Vanderbilt University Television News Archive; *Washington Post*, April 15, 1986). A case can be made that Shultz's invocation of article 51 was both a vindication of the logic of Kissinger's secret bombing of Cambodia—often justified by Kissinger as self-defense—and a preview of the Authorization to Use Military Force, passed overwhelmingly by the House and Senate on September 14, 2001, which sanctioned not just the invasions of Afghanistan and Iraq but the open-ended Global War on Terrorism. There is, today, no part of the earth that cannot be considered "our territory."

Noriega had been a CIA asset and Washington ally. That began to change in the last years of the Reagan administration, after Seymour Hersh in 1986 published an investigation in the *New York Times* linking Noriega to drug trafficking. It still would be months before the press would break Iran-Contra, but Noriega was deeply enmeshed in the networks involved in that conspiracy, in money laundering, gunrunning, drug trafficking, and intelligence sharing. He worked both sides. He was "our man," as one US diplomat put it, providing key support for the Contras. But he had close ties to Cuba as well. Panama was also a particular focus for the right wing because of the canal: "We built it! We paid for it! It's ours and we are going to keep it!" Reagan repeated in his 1976 primary stump speech, charging Messrs. Kissinger and Ford with wanting to hand the canal over to Panama.

Brent Scowcroft, George H. W. Bush's national security adviser, has said that Bush held a special animus toward Noriega, having worked directly with the Panamanian during his time as director of the CIA. But Panama, Scowcroft said, wasn't high on the administration's agenda when it took office at the beginning of 1989. A "warrant" had been issued for Noriega's arrest and the United States had been encouraging Noriega's opponents to overthrow him. That seemed to be the extent of the White House's interest in the country. "I can't really describe the course of events that led us this way," Scowcroft said, referring to the invasion. "Noriega, was he running drugs and stuff? Sure, but so were a lot of other people. Was he thumbing his nose at the United States? Yeah, yeah."[15]

Events came to a head in late 1989, when the coup that Washington had for months been calling for seemed to be taking place. The White House's response, however, was in "disarray." The intelligence coming in was contradictory and unreliable. "All of us agreed at that point that we simply had very little to go on," Dick Cheney, Bush's secretary of defense, later reported. The United States had lost communication with its would-be rebel-allies. "There was a lot of confusion at the time because there was a lot of confusion in Panama," Cheney said.[16] "We were sort of the Keystone Kops," Scowcroft said, not knowing what to do or who to support. Noriega regained the upper hand.

The tipping point toward military action was domestic politics, as the White House came under intense criticism from politicians and pundits for seemingly having blown an opportunity to remove Noriega from power. Scowcroft recalls the momentum that led to the invasion: "Maybe we were looking for an opportunity to show that we were not as messed up as the Congress kept saying we were, or as timid as a number of people said." The administration had to find a way to respond, Scowcroft said, to the "whole wimp factor."

In the midst of the confusion, it was Kissinger who calmed the waters and urged a tough response. Having established his New York–based consulting firm, Kissinger Associates, a few years earlier, he had been nearly fully rehabilitated. "The Unsinkable Kissinger Bobs Back," was one New York Times headline.* He had reconciled with Dick Cheney, and a number of his protégés had prominent positions in the White House, including Scowcroft, Bush's national security adviser. This was around the time of Beijing's Tiananmen massacre, and Kissinger played a key role guiding the White House's forgiving response.

---

* Here's one account of Kissinger's diverse activities in the late 1980s: "He makes about 20 speeches a year and charges $20,000 for each. Shearson Lehman pays him over $500,000 a year for four luncheon speeches and ad hoc advice. His own company, Kissinger Associates—high-income, low-profile, containing only a handful of specialists—brings in an estimated $5 million in revenues from consulting. Kissinger's former associates, for whom he is mentor, riddle the Bush administration. The deputy Secretary of State, Mr Lawrence Eagleburger, took the position fresh from working for Kissinger Associates. Eagleburger, the Administration's East-West guru, declared an income of $916,989 last year, solely from his work with Kissinger. General Brent Scowcroft, Bush's National Security Adviser, was a deputy to Kissinger in the Nixon administration, a loyal follower and a founder of Kissinger Associates" ("Resurrected and Visible," Australian Financial Review, October 13, 1989).

As the Bush administration fumbled, Kissinger, according to one report, provided two pieces of familiar advice. The first was that "scant" information "was the norm in a crisis." The second was that scant information shouldn't be "an excuse for inaction."[17] And as momentum built for action, so did the pressure to find a suitable justification for action. Shortly after the failed coup, Dick Cheney claimed on PBS's *NewsHour* that the only objectives the United States had in Panama were to "safeguard American lives" and "protect American interests" by defending the passageway from the Atlantic to the Pacific Oceans, the Panama Canal. "We are not there," he emphasized, "to remake the Panamanian government." He also noted that the White House had no plans to act unilaterally against the wishes of the Organization of American States to extract Noriega from the country. The "hue and cry and the outrage that we would hear from one end of the hemisphere to the other," he said, "raises serious doubts about the course of that action."

That was mid-October. What a difference two months would make. By December 20, the campaign against Noriega had gone from accidental—Keystone Kops bumbling in the dark—to transformative: the Bush administration would end up remaking the Panamanian government and, in the process, international law.

Cheney wasn't wrong about the "hue and cry." Every single country other than the United States in the Organization of American States opposed the invasion of Panama. Bush acted anyway. What changed everything was the fall of the Berlin Wall just over a month before the invasion. As the Soviet Union's influence in its backyard (Eastern Europe) unraveled, Washington was left with more room to maneuver in its backyard (Latin America). The collapse of Soviet-style Communism also gave the White House an opportunity to go on the ideological and moral offense.

As with most military actions, the invaders had a number of justifications to offer, but at that moment the goal of installing a "democratic" regime in power suddenly flipped to the top of the list. In adopting that rationale for making war, Washington was in effect radically revising the terms of international diplomacy. At the heart of its argument was the idea that democracy trumped the principle of national sovereignty. Latin American nations, long the target of "regime change" by Washington, immediately recognized the threat and sought to condemn the invasion in the Organization of American States. Their resistance only gave Bush's ambassador to the OAS, Luigi Einaudi, a chance to up the ethical ante. He quickly and explicitly tied the assault on Panama to the wave of democracy movements then sweeping Eastern Europe. "Today we are . . . living in historic times," he lectured his fellow OAS delegates two days after the invasion, "a time when a great principle is spreading across the world like wildfire. That principle, as we all know, is the revolutionary idea that people, not governments, are sovereign."[18]

To be clear, it is not the military intervention that is important about Panama; Washington has been violating sovereignty in Latin America and doing it unilaterally for over a century. Rather, it is the speed with which, *immediately* following the end of the Cold War, Washington moved to legally and openly defend its unilateral action by invoking the ideal of democracy—indeed, to broadcast that ideal in the world's tribunals, like the Organization of American States. Einaudi's remarks hit on all the points that would become so familiar early in the next century in George W. Bush's "Freedom Agenda": the idea that democracy, as defined by Washington, was a universal value, that "history" represented a movement toward the fulfillment of that value, and that any nation or person that stood in the path of such fulfillment would be swept away.

With the fall of the Berlin Wall, Einaudi said, democracy had acquired the "force of historical necessity." It went without saying that the United States, within a year the official victor in the Cold War, would be the executor of that necessity. Bush's ambassador reminded his fellow delegates that the "great democratic tide which is now sweeping the globe" had actually started in Latin America, with human rights movements working to end abuses by military juntas and dictators. The fact that Latin America's freedom fighters had largely been fighting against U.S.-backed anti-Communist right-wing death-squad states (most of them installed and backed during Henry Kissinger's tenure) was lost on the ambassador.

In the case of Panama, "democracy" quickly worked its way up the short list of casus belli. In his December 20 address to the nation announcing the invasion, President Bush gave "democracy" as his second reason for going to war, just behind safeguarding American lives but ahead of combatting drug trafficking or protecting the Panama Canal. By the next day, at a press conference, democracy had leapt to the top of the list. The president began his opening remarks this way: "Our efforts to support the democratic processes in Panama and to ensure continued safety of American citizens is now moving into its second day."[19]

George Will, the conservative pundit, was quick to realize the significance of this new post–Cold War rationale for military action.[20] In a syndicated column (headlined "Drugs and Canal Are Secondary: Restoring Democracy Was Reason Enough to Act"), he praised the invasion for "stressing . . . the restoration of democracy," adding that, by doing so, "the president put himself squarely in a tradition with a distinguished pedigree. It holds that America's fundamental national interest is to be America, and the nation's identity (its sense of its self, its peculiar purposefulness) is inseparable from a commitment to the spread—not the aggressive universalization, but the civilized advancement—of the proposition to which we, unique among nations, are, as the greatest American said, dedicated." Freedom.

That was fast. From Keystone Kops to Thomas Paine in just two months, as the White House seized the moment to change the terms by which the United States engaged the world. In so doing, it overthrew both Manuel Noriega and what, for half a century, had been the bedrock foundation of the liberal multilateral order: the ideal of national sovereignty.

In the mythology of American militarism that has taken hold since George W. Bush's disastrous wars in Afghanistan and Iraq, the actions of his father, George H. W. Bush, are often held up as a paragon of prudence—especially when compared to the later recklessness of Vice President Dick Cheney, Secretary of Defense Donald Rumsfeld, and Deputy Secretary of Defense Paul Wolfowitz. After all, their agenda held that it was the duty of the United States to rid the world not just of evildoers but of evil itself. In contrast, the elder Bush, we are told, recognized the limits of American power. He was a realist, advised by other realists, Kissinger's protégés, including Lawrence Eagleburger and Scowcroft. His circumscribed Gulf War was a "war of necessity," it is said, where his son's 2003 invasion of Iraq was a catastrophic "war of choice."[21]

But the road to Baghdad ran through Panama City, with the 1989 invasion inaugurating the post–Cold War age of unilateral intervention. "Having used force in Panama," Bush's ambassador to the United Nations, Thomas Pickering, recently said, "there was a propensity in Washington to think that force could provide a result more rapidly, more effectively, more surgically than diplomacy."[22] The easy capture of Noriega meant "the notion that the international community had to be engaged . . . was ignored."*

---

* US forces were in and out (with their prisoner Noriega) relatively fast, making Operation Just Cause one of the most successful military actions in US history. At least in tactical terms. There were casualties. More than twenty US soldiers were killed and three to five hundred Panamanian combatants died as well. Disagreement exists over how many civilians perished. In the "low hundreds," the Pentagon's Southern Command said. But others charged that US officials didn't bother to count the dead in El Chorrillo, a poor Panama City *barrio* that US planes indiscriminately bombed because it was thought to be a bastion of support for Noriega. Grassroots human rights organizations claimed thousands of civilians were killed and tens of thousands displaced. As Human Rights Watch wrote, even conservative estimates of civilian fatalities suggested "that the rule of proportionality and the duty to minimize harm to civilians . . .

"Iraq in 2003 was all of that shortsightedness in spades," Pickering said. "We were going to do it all ourselves." And we were going to do it in the name not of national security but of the "civilized advancement" of democracy. Later, after 9/11, when George W. Bush insisted that the ideal of national sovereignty was a thing of the past, when he said nothing—certainly not the opinion of the international community—could stand in the way of the "great mission" of the United States to "extend the benefits of freedom across the globe," all he was doing was throwing more fuel on the "wildfire" sparked by his father.

As a public official, Kissinger repeatedly mocked the principle of sovereignty. "I don't see why we need to stand by and watch a country go communist due to the irresponsibility of its people," he once said of Salvador Allende's 1970 election.[23] But this disregard was always justified by the right of America to defend itself (with "defense" interpreted broadly to cover preemptive actions against anticipated threats). With Panama too, Kissinger, despite what Bush was saying to the press, carefully avoided making mention of democracy (he had just defended China over Tiananmen). Rather, he vaguely invoked the old rationales, a president's prerogative and the like.

But history was getting ahead of him.[24]

---

were not faithfully observed by the invading U.S. forces." That may have been putting it mildly when it came to the indiscriminate bombing of a civilian population. Civilians were given no notice. The Cobra and Apache helicopters that came over the ridge didn't announce their pending arrival by blasting Wagner's "Ride of the Valkyries." The University of Panama's seismograph marked 442 major explosions in the first twelve hours of the invasion, about one major bomb blast every two minutes. Fires engulfed the mostly wooden homes, destroying about four thousand buildings. Some residents began to call El Chorrillo "Guernica" or "little Hiroshima." Shortly after hostilities ended, bulldozers excavated mass graves and shoveled in the bodies. "Buried like dogs," said the mother of one of the civilian dead.

11

Darkness into Light

The cosmic has rhythm, tact, the grand harmony that binds together lovers or crowds in moments of absolute wordless understanding, the pulse that unites a sequence of generations into a meaningful whole. This is Destiny, the symbol of the blood, of sex, of duration. This answers the question of when and whither, and represents the only method of approaching the problem of time. It is felt by the great artist in his moment of contemplation, it is embodied by the statesman in action and is lived by the man of the Spring-time culture. It constitutes the essence of tragedy, the problem of "too late," when a moment of the present is irrevocably consigned to the past. The microcosm contains tension and polarity, the loneliness of the individual in a world of strange significances, in which the total inner meaning of others remains an eternal riddle. Rhythm and tension, longing and fear, characterize the relationship of the microcosm to the macrocosm.

—Henry Kissinger, 1950

Having either condoned, authorized, or planned so many invasions—Indonesia's of East Timor, Pakistan's of Bangladesh, the United States' of Cambodia, South Vietnam's of Laos, South Africa's of Angola, along with Turkey's assault on Cyprus and Morocco's annexation of Western Sahara—Henry Kissinger took the lead in condemning Iraq's 1990 assault on Kuwait. In office, he tried to pull Iraq away from the Soviets by pumping up Baghdad's regional ambitions. As a private consultant and pundit, Kissinger promoted the idea that Iraqis could serve as disposable counterweights to revolutionary Iranians, with the resulting civil war dragging on for years and costing millions of lives. "It's a pity they can't both lose," he is reported to have said.* But now, in the days following Saddam Hussein's August 2 surprise attack, Kissinger insisted that Hussein's annexation had to be reversed.[1]

THE FIRST GULF WAR

George H. W. Bush had launched Operation Desert Shield immediately after Hussein's invasion, sending hundreds of thousands of troops to Saudi Arabia. Taking place less than a year after the quick victory in Panama, Bush's actions helped draw attention away from a worsening domestic economy and the growing savings and loan scandal, in which his son Neil was implicated. But once in Saudi Arabia, what was the US military to do? Contain Iraq? Attack and liberate Kuwait? Or drive on to Baghdad and depose Hussein? There was no clear consensus among foreign policy advisers or analysts.

Prominent conservatives who made their names fighting the Cold War gave conflicting opinions.[2] Jeane Kirkpatrick, for instance, opposed any action against Iraq. As Reagan's ambassador to the UN, Kirkpatrick did much to provide an intellectual foundation for his drive into the Third World. But she didn't think that Washington had a "distinctive interest in the Gulf" now that the Soviet Union was gone. "We have no special relationship with Kuwait. It does not share our values or interests," she said, "Saddam is not directly dangerous to the US or to our treaty allies. He is a danger

---

* This quotation might be apocryphal. But Raymond Tanter, who served on the National Security Council, writes that at a foreign-policy briefing meeting for Republican presidential nominee Ronald Reagan, in October 1980, attended by Kissinger, Kissinger remarked that "the continuation of fighting between Iran and Iraq was in the American interest."

to the independence of other States in the Gulf."* Other conservatives pointed out that, with the Cold War over, it mattered little
whether Iraqi Baathists or Saudi sheiks pumped the oil.³

Kissinger took the point position in countering what he called
America's "new isolationists," that is, those conservatives who were
against taking a strong stand in the Gulf. What Bush did next in
Kuwait, he announced in the very first sentence of his August 19
syndicated column, published in a number of major papers across
the country, would make or break his administration. Anything
short of the liberation of Kuwait would turn Bush's "show of
force"—his quick dispatch of troops to Saudi Arabia—into a
"debacle." The president faced three choices: passively endorse
whatever tepid consensus emerged at the UN, act in league with
other oil-dependent industrial democracies, or "take the lead in
opposing Hussein" in an "effort in which the United States would
bear the principal burden."⁴

Kissinger felt history's urgency. If Bush didn't act, the widespread support he enjoyed would quickly evaporate. Above all, he
needed to avoid a protracted siege, which would sap American will
and strain credibility. Kissinger, who during his tenure at the
White House and State did more than any other single person to
tie the United States to high oil prices and the Saudi regime (as long
as the Saudis kept buying US weapons, contracting US construction firms, and depositing what was left in US banks), was arguing against conservatives like Kirkpatrick, who were making the

---

* In an essay written before Iraq's invasion (but published subsequently in the *National
Interest*), Kirkpatrick even suggested that the United States, with the Cold War over,
might "again become a normal nation—and take care of pressing problems of education, family, industry and technology." Peter Beinart, in *The Icarus Syndrome: A History of American Hubris*, details the attacks of a younger, more bellicose group of
neoconservatives led by figures such as Charles Krauthammer and Paul Wolfowitz
(those who went on to lead the United States into Iraq in 2003) on Kirkpatrick-style
restraint. Kissinger's call for an aggressive response in the first Gulf War helped tip the
intellectual argument in favor of these younger "Wilsonians." And as the number of
US troops increased in Saudi Arabia, even Kirkpatrick began to take a tough line.

"fashionable" argument that it didn't matter who produced the oil. Baiting them in terms they would recognize, he said such advice was nothing short of "abdication." There are, Kissinger said, "consequences" to one's "failure to resist."

Kissinger was among the first, possibly the first, to make the analogy between Hussein and Hitler.[5] He argued that if Iraq's annexation of Kuwait was allowed to stand, the "absolutely inevitable" result would be a series of wars that would threaten the existence of Israel (Hussein, after grabbing Kuwait, suggested that all of the region's occupations should be adjudicated simultaneously, including Israel's control of the occupied territories).[6] In opinion pieces, appearances on network and public TV, and testimony before Congress, Kissinger forcefully argued for intervention, including the "surgical and progressive destruction of Iraq's military assets" and removal of Hussein from power.[7] Sweeping aside the concerns of cautious hawks like Kirkpatrick, Kissinger insisted that there was no turning back: "America has crossed its Rubicon," he said.

Another way to assess how far our expectations have shifted from 1970—how what seemed to be the collapse of the national security state was really the beginning of its reorganization on different, more spectacular, more covert, and, over time, more interventionist footings—is to compare the secrecy with which the bombing of Cambodia was carried out with the visual immediacy of the first Gulf War, conducted to capture and keep the public's attention.

Actually, before making that comparison, it's worth taking a moment to consider the way Panama offered a preview of what was to come. According to one US brigadier general, Operation Just Cause was "extraordinarily complex, involving the deployment of thousands of personnel and equipment from distant military installations and striking almost two-dozen objectives within a

24-hour period of time. . . . Just Cause represented a bold new era in American military force projection: speed, mass, and precision, coupled with immediate public visibility."[8]

One year and one month after that display of "immediate public visibility," on January 17, 1991, Operation Desert Storm was launched. In a way, this war represented the full flowering of the logic behind Kissinger and Nixon's covert air campaign on Cambodia: that the United States should be free to use whatever military force it needs in order to compel the political outcome it seeks. Where Kissinger worked to keep that operation hidden for as long as he could (because he feared the public's reaction), Desert Storm was preceded by a four-month on-air discussion among politicians and pundits (including Kissinger). Where those executing the bombing of Cambodia burned records and fabricated false documents to cover their tracks, Bush led an assault for all the world to see. "Smart bombs" lit up the sky over Baghdad and Kuwait City as the TV cameras rolled. Featured were new night-vision equipment, real-time satellite communications, and cable TV—as well as former US commanders ready to narrate the war in the style of football announcers, right down to instant replays. "In sports page language," said CBS News anchor Dan Rather on the first night of the attack, "this . . . it's not a sport. It's war. But so far, it's a blowout."[9]

And Kissinger himself was everywhere—ABC, NBC, CBS, PBS, and on the radio and in the papers—giving his opinion. "I think it's gone well," he said to Dan Rather on the first night of the bombing.[10] So well, Walter Cronkite felt he had to warn Americans not to be "overly optimistic" or "euphoric."

The next day, January 18, in the CBS studio, Cronkite and Rather engaged in an extended conversation that made them seem less like sports announcers describing live action than veteran color commentators comparing today's game to how it used to be played.[11] The two men concluded that the old big-bellied B-52s that had been used extensively in Vietnam, Laos, and Cambodia and now were being deployed to bomb Baghdad were more effective at sowing terror and generating panic than the lean "hi-tech" missiles the media were fascinated with:

> WALTER CRONKITE: You have seen the B-52s in operation in Vietnam, I have, and they are almost a terror weapon, they are so powerful. They are dropping all of those bombs. My heavens, 14 tons of bomb out of a single airplane—they could very well panic the Iraq army. . . . One thing that's interesting about this, Dan, these bombs come in at a very low rate of speed, comparatively—compared to rocketry and other such things and, as a result, the bomb blast is widespread. It can do an awful lot of surface damage without serious damage to a single target, except right where it lands—blow out a lot of windows, blow out a lot of walls, things of that kind as opposed to the high-speed missiles that are inclined to bury themselves and blow up. . . .
>
> DAN RATHER: I want to pick up on what you were talking about with the B-52s. It's certainly true, anybody who's seen or been through a B-52 raid, it's an absolutely unforgettable, mind-searing experience.
>
> CRONKITE: When you're not underneath it directly.
>
> RATHER: Exactly. And that's when you're able to just sort of observe it. It is a devastatingly effective physical bombing weapon, but also psychologically. That's one of the reasons of going right at the heart of Saddam Hussein's best troops is [to cause] panic and to—to break the back of morale.

Such color commentary, along with the real-time reporting, the night-vision equipment, and camera-carrying smart bombs, allowed for public consumption of a techno-display of apparent omnipotence that, at least for a short time, helped consolidate mass approval. The assault was meant as both a lesson and a warning for the rest of the world. And with instant replay came instant gratification, confirmation that the president had the public's backing.

At midnight January 18, a day into the attack, CBS TV announced a new poll "indicates extremely strong support for Mr. Bush's Gulf offensive." "By God," Bush said in triumph, "we've kicked the Vietnam syndrome once and for all."[12]

Darkness rendered into light, the inherent made manifest, helped along by the counsels of Kissinger, "an ancestral voice prophesying war," as one reporter wrote.[13] And thus, in a short eight years since the Beirut barracks bombing, when Reagan chose not to answer Henry Kissinger's call to fully commit to the Middle East, the United States delivered a stunning display of "shock and awe" (before the phrase was invented). For a moment, then, between the invasion of Panama and the liberation of Kuwait, it seemed as if the reality Kissinger believed he *ought* to live in (where massive bombing would, in Dan Rather's words, "break the back" of its targets) rather than the reality he *had* been living in (where bombing made more problems than the problem that justified the bombing in the first place, including mass radicalization) had come into being. Hussein was easily driven out of Kuwait.

CLINTON AND IRAQ

But he continued in power in Baghdad, creating a problem of enormous proportions for Bush's successor, Bill Clinton. It was the UN that first imposed sanctions on Iraq, which remained in force even after its army was driven out of Kuwait. But it was up to the United States to enforce those sanctions, which included demands that Baghdad allow inspectors in to search for weapons of mass destruction. We now know that Saddam Hussein didn't have such weapons, yet he still refused to cooperate fully with inspectors. A twelve-year siege ensued, with the sanctions greatly damaging Iraq's economy and inflicting unimaginable hardship. That hardship was captured in a now infamous answer Clinton's Secretary of State Madeleine Albright gave to a question put to her in 1996 by the journalist Lesley Stahl, on *60 Minutes*. Stahl asked Albright about the estimated half a million Iraqi children who had died as a result of the sanctions. "I mean," Stahl said, "that's more children than died in Hiroshima." "We think the price is worth it," Albright responded.[14]

By this time, Clinton was sending cruise missiles into Iraq at regular intervals, for various reasons: to punish a Baghdad-backed assassination attempt on George H. W. Bush (twenty-three missiles launched, including three that struck a residential area and killed civilians), to protect the Kurds (forty-six missiles), to force Iraq to cooperate with UN weapons inspectors. This last assault took place in 1998, on the eve of the House impeachment vote related to the Monica Lewinsky affair, and was described by the *New York Times* as "a strong sustained series of air strikes." "More than 200 missiles rained down upon Iraq," the *Times* reported, "without any diplomacy or warning."[15]

Kissinger watched all of this with amusement. In a way, Clinton was following his lead: he was bombing a country we weren't at war with without congressional approval, and one of the reasons he was doing so was to placate the militarist right. For example, in 1997 Clinton tried to appoint Anthony Lake, the former NSC staffer who in 1970 resigned because of his opposition to the invasion of Cambodia, as CIA director. Lake faced resistance in the Senate from many Republicans and more than a few Democrats because he came from the (mildly) dissenting wing of the foreign policy establishment. He not only quit the NSC but, in a 1989 book called *Somoza Falling*, described CIA activities in Nicaragua as "covert actions run amok." To counter opposition to Lake, the Clinton administration in effect repudiated the questioning spirit of the 1970s, giving Kissinger what must have been a gratifying vindication. According to the *New York Times*, the White House tried to sell Lake to Congress "as a man so tough-minded that he lost no sleep when a United States missile aimed at Iraqi intelligence headquarters went awry and killed civilians in 1994."[16] It didn't help.* During three days of confirmation hearings, Lake was grilled on everything from his opinion of the Vietnam War to his having listened to protest music in 1970, with his resignation from Kissinger's NSC over Cambodia painted as "unpatriotic." Lake withdrew his nomination.[17]

Kissinger gave a full airing of his opinion of Clinton's bombing of Iraq shortly after Pol Pot died, in 1998. At a conference commemorating the twenty-fifth anniversary of the accords that ended the Vietnam War,[18] he started, appropriately enough, with Cambodia, defending his actions there, before turning the discussion to Clinton and Iraq:

> I talked with some Clinton Administration person recently when the bombing of Iraq was being contemplated. I said that, in my view, we ought to go after the Republican Guard divisions. "Oh, my God," he said. "Republican Guard divisions? You can't go after the Republican Guard divisions. What we're accusing Iraq of is hiding biological weapons. We can go after every deposit of biological weapons. But we can't go after things that are outside our legal framework."

Washington, Kissinger went on, has to "be able to bring" its "political and military objectives into some relationship to each

---

* Clinton's errant cruise missile strike took place in 1993, not 1994. Out of twenty-four Tomahawk missiles launched at the Iraqi intelligence service for supposedly plotting George H. W. Bush's assassination, three went astray and hit private homes, killing eight civilians as they slept in their beds, including Layla al-Attar, one of Iraq's most famous artists. Another killed the husband and eighteen-month-old child of Zahraa Yhaya, who was twenty-nine at the time. "Please tell the people of America, the mothers of America, that when a missile makes mistakes, it kills people. It kills babies. It kills families sleeping at night, with no war and no warning," she said to the *Los Angeles Times* (July 26, 1993).

other." Weapons of mass destruction aren't really what is at stake in Iraq, he said. The real "problem" is our motivation, or will. "The issue is, do we have a strategy for breaking the back of somebody we don't want to negotiate with? And if we're not able to do that, how can we then avoid negotiating with him? If we are not able to destroy and we are not able to isolate him, we're only going to demonstrate our impotence."

It's that "strategic concept"—the need to be *willing* to break the back of somebody you refuse to negotiate with—that governed what he and Nixon were trying to accomplish in Southeast Asia. "Whether we got it right or not," Kissinger said, "is really secondary."

"Whether we got it right or not, is really secondary." It's not really a remarkable statement, at least not when one considers Kissinger's long-standing insistence that the demonstrative effects produced by one's act of will are more important than the consequences of that act. In any case, Kissinger then made an easy transition from defending his bombing of Cambodia to advising Clinton to bomb Iraq even more. "That approach," he said, referring to the need to align one's military actions with one's political objective, "is the one we still need."

And if Clinton did escalate, what would matter would be the effect more bombing would have not on Iraq but on the United States. Escalation, Kissinger said, would force us to answer this question: "Are we willing to pay this price? And if we are not willing to pay the price, we are back to the Vietnam syndrome of not being able to order our objectives." If we were willing to pay the price, to project the required military force to achieve our goals and to finish what we started, we would be able to overcome our impotence.

At this point, in 1998, Kissinger's opinions are nearly indistinguishable from those of Paul Wolfowitz, William Kristol, Robert Kagan, and other neoconservatives who were then laying the ideological groundwork for the 2003 drive into Iraq. Here is Wolfowitz in 2000, praising Clinton for bombing Iraq without congressional sanction but criticizing him for doing it without a clear sense of purpose: "American forces under President Clinton's command have been bombing Iraq with some regularity for months now," Wolfowitz wrote, without "a whimper of opposition in the Congress and barely a mention in the press."[19] And not just Iraq. "Everyone has become a 'hawk,'" he wrote, cheering Clinton's use of "armed forces in operations involving tens of thousands of troops in Haiti, Bosnia, Kosovo, and Iraq—and to conduct military strikes against Afghanistan and Sudan."*

---

* Kissinger expressed contempt for these interventions for a number of reasons: they were ad hoc, they were justified in the name of "humanitarianism," and they lacked focus, in terms of both immediate objectives and long-term vision. In 1992, he thought the deployment of troops to Somalia, in the last months of the George H. W. Bush's term, a mistake ("We must not seem to be claiming for ourselves a doctrine of universal unilateral intervention," he wrote ["Somalia: Reservations," *Washington Post*, December 13, 1992]). But once the Black Hawk Down incident occurred early in the Clinton administration, he called for swift retaliation. In 1994, he criticized Clinton for sending soldiers to Haiti to restore its elected President Jean-Bertrand Aristide: "I do not favor a military invasion because I can't describe the threat Haiti presents to the United States" ("Kissinger Speaks at Nixon Library," *Los Angeles Times*, July 21, 1994). And the Bosnia conflict seemed to confuse him. The breakup of Yugoslavia started under George H. W. Bush, and Kissinger's ally Lawrence Eagleburger, Bush's deputy secretary of state, came under intense criticism for bungling Washington's response to the crisis. When he was a member of Kissinger Associates, Eagleburger had deep business ties to the Serbs, and some suggested a conflict of interest made him too soft on Slobodan Milosevic ("Eagleburger Anguishes over Yugoslav Upheaval," *New York Times*, June 19, 1992). In 1995, Kissinger said he was opposed to war, arguing that Serbs were not aggressors and that one solution might be to enclose Muslims into their own state (see his appearance on the *Charlie Rose* show, September 14, 1995). Then, once war started, he said it had to be won. He was opposed to the intervention in Kosovo, parting ways with some prominent neoconservatives who were strong for that war. But once fighting started, he agreed with William Kristol that "the war must be won," as John Podhoretz writes, that "victory means that Milosevic is forced to bend to NATO's will—or is driven from power," that Clinton's "conduct of the war has been shameful" and is "weakening NATO's resolve dangerously, and that if the president does not stiffen his resolve and NATO's collective spine in the next month, the alliance's commitment will begin to fall apart" ("This War's Strange Bedfellows," *New York Post*, May 26, 1999). Even as he advanced these criticisms of Clinton, and even as he grew closer to neoconservatives over Iraq, Kissinger still occasionally had ideological disputes with Reaganite "Wilsonians," especially over his defense of China. His last serious pre-9/11 skirmish with neoconservatives took place with the 1999 publication of the third volume of his memoir, *Years of Renewal*. In that book, Kissinger tried to credit détente for bringing about the end of the Cold War.

But, Wolfowitz said, the problem with this new militarism was that it was born out of softness, not hardness, out of "complacency bred by our current predominance." It came too easy and had no real costs. There were, he wrote, in what almost sounded like a complaint, "virtually no American casualties" in Clinton's wars. Clinton did bomb. But his bombing was "facile and complacent," lacking focus. Without a threat that could galvanize America out of its prosperity-induced smugness, we would never be able, to return to Kissinger's phrase, to "order our objectives."

Wolfowitz's opinion that post–Cold War America was too complacent was shared by William Kristol and Robert Kagan, who in an earlier, influential essay published in *Foreign Affairs*, wrote:

> Somehow most Americans have failed to notice that they have never had it so good. They have never lived in a world more conducive to their fundamental interests in a liberal international order. . . . And that is the problem. . . . Today the lack of a visible threat to U.S. vital interests or to world peace has tempted Americans to absentmindedly dismantle the material and spiritual foundations on which their national well-being has been based. . . . The ubiquitous post–Cold War question—where is the threat?—is thus misconceived. In a world in which peace and American security depend on American power and the will to use it, the main threat the United States faces now and in the future is its own weakness.[20]

The echo of Kissinger is clear: power is weakness unless one is willing to use it. There is, however, a subtle difference worth point-

---

Robert Kagan offered an extremely negative review of the book in *The New Republic* ("The Revolutionist: How Henry Kissinger Won the Cold War, or So He Thinks," June 21, 1999). Kagan was particularly upset over Kissinger's attempt to take credit for the 1975 Helsinki human rights accords (which neoconservatives view as a repudiation of amoral realpolitik).

ing out. In the past, Kissinger tended to focus on *our* actions as the galvanizing agent: *we* had to take a tough stand; *we* had to act furiously; *we* needed to avoid inaction to prove that action was possible. His discussion of dangers the United States faced tended to be abstract, represented as disorder or instability. He never amped the danger into a primal threat to the nation's existence. Post–Cold War militarists, in contrast, stressed the external menace as the animator, an existential evil that lurks beyond our border whose function seems to be to remind us that existential evil lurks beyond our border. It was 9/11 that brought the two positions together.

THE SECOND GULF WAR AND BEYOND

Between 1998 and the fall of 2001, the fight against radical Islam was not high on the list of reasons neoconservatives said we needed to carry out regime change in Iraq. Some invoked national security, insisting that Hussein was hiding weapons of mass destruction. Others said the arrangement left in place by the first Gulf War had become unsustainable. A decade of lobbing missiles into Iraq, killing innocents, and enforcing punitive sanctions had destabilized the region, created an unsustainable situation that was captured in the callous comment by Secretary of State Albright that half a million starving Iraqi children was a price worth paying to contain Hussein.* America's policy toward the whole region had to

---

* In July 2003, Assistant Secretary of Defense Paul Wolfowitz, an architect of the invasion of Iraq, explained to Tim Russert on *Meet the Press* that the unsustainability of "containment" was the major reason for war—not supposed Iraqi links to Al Qaeda or WMDs: "Let me say a couple of things, Tim. People act as though the cost of containing Iraq is trivial. The cost of containing Iraq was enormous, 55 American lives lost, at least, in incidents like the Cole and Kobar Towers, which were part of the containment effort, billions of dollars of American money spent. . . . And worst of all, if you go back and read Osama bin Laden's notorious fatwa from 1998, where he calls for killing Americans, the two principal grievances were the presence of those forces in Saudi Arabia, and our continuing attacks on Iraq, 12 years of containment was a terrible price for us, and for the Iraqi people it was an unbelievable price, Tim. . . . And I

change, but for that to happen, the region first had to change. And for the region to change, Saddam Hussein had to go. The solution to the problem created by the first Gulf War was a second Gulf War.

Then 9/11 happened, producing, among policy and opinion makers, a perfect marriage of strategy (what to do with the Middle East) and sentiment (the stimulant that comes from confronting an existential threat).*

Kissinger was an early supporter of a bold military response to 9/11. On August 9, 2002, he openly endorsed the policy of "regime change" in Iraq in his syndicated column, acknowledging that such a policy was "revolutionary." "The notion of justified pre-emption," he wrote, "runs counter to modern international law." That revolution is necessary, he argued, because of the novelty of the "terrorist threat," which "transcends the nation-state." But, Kissinger said, "there is another, generally unstated, reason for bringing matters to a head with Iraq": to "demonstrate that a terrorist challenge or a systemic attack on the international order also produces catastrophic consequences for the perpetrators, as well as their supporters."[21] That secular Baathists were the enemies of Islamic jihadists and that Iraq neither perpetrated 9/11 nor supported the perpetrators of 9/11 didn't enter into the equation. After all, being "right or not is really secondary" to the main issue: being willing to do something.

Less than three weeks later, on August 26, 2002, Vice President Dick Cheney, who during the Ford presidency had repeatedly sidelined Kissinger, laid out his full case for why the United States

---

think one of the things that would have come by waiting [to depose Hussein], frankly, is more instability for the key countries in our coalition, including Arab countries."

* It wasn't just neoconservatives who thought that 9/11 might provide meaning to post–Cold War America, as political theorist Corey Robin points out. For George Packer, America's patriotic response to the attacks awakened in him "alertness, grief, resolve, even love." For David Brooks, 9/11 was "a cleanser, washing away a lot of the self-indulgence of the past decade" (Corey Robin, *Fear: The History of a Political Idea* [2004], pp. 157–58).

had to invade Iraq, speaking before the national convention of Veterans of Foreign Wars. "As former Secretary of State Kissinger recently stated," said Cheney, directly quoting Kissinger's column, there is "an imperative for pre-emptive action."[22]

Judging from his writings, the attacks on the World Trade Center and the Pentagon invigorated Kissinger, bringing him close to the neocon position that an external threat might clear away the main obstacle to an effective foreign policy: weak-willed domestic opinion. He did, though, worry that the window of opportunity wouldn't stay open long. He advised Bush to act fast "while the memory of the attack on the United States is still vivid and American-deployed forces are available to back up the diplomacy."[23]

Kissinger announced that "time is of the essence," as it always is in such cases. Specifically, in September 2002, he urged the White House to follow up its "success" in Afghanistan by launching what he called "phase two" of a global antiterrorist campaign. The removal of Saddam Hussein from power would be just the beginning of this phase. "The issue is not whether Iraq was involved in the terrorist attack on the United States," he wrote, brushing away distractions. Rather, he said, the United States needed to "return Iraq to a responsible role in the region." After that was done, the United States needed to move on to "the destruction of the global terrorist network." Kissinger identified Somalia and Yemen as possible targets.[24]

Kissinger, as he did when he made the case for action in Panama and Kuwait, avoided making moral or idealist arguments to justify what he was now envisioning as global war. But there was no way to launch the kind of expansive, never-ending response he was promoting that wouldn't have resulted in an inflation of justifications. Recall George H. W. Bush's "Keystone Kops" stumbling into democracy promotion to validate the quick invasion of Panama, a minor and relatively inconsequential country. What started out as an execution of a warrant for Manuel Noriega's arrest evolved, within just a few months, into the wild-fire advance of a "great principle," a "revolutionary idea." The same inflation occurred in Iraq on a greater scale, especially once it was found that Hussein wasn't actually hiding weapons of mass destruction.

In 2005, about two and a half years after the United States attacked Iraq, Michael Gerson, Bush's speechwriter, went to visit Kissinger in New York.[25] This was after Fallujah and Abu Ghraib, after the Blackwater massacres and the torture, after it became clear that the real beneficiary of the US invasion of Iraq would be revolutionary Iran, after revelations about cooking the intelligence and manipulating the press in order to neutralize opposition to the invasion. It was that strange, surreal moment when public support for the war was plummeting and Bush's justifications for waging the war were expanding. America's "responsibility," Bush announced earlier that year at his second inaugural address, was to "rid the world of evil."

Gerson helped write that speech and he asked Kissinger what he thought of it. "At first I was appalled," Kissinger said, but then he came to appreciate it for instrumental reasons. "On reflection," as Bob Woodward recounted the conversation in *State of Denial*, Kissinger "now believed the speech served a purpose and was a very smart move, setting the war on terror and overall U.S. foreign policy in the context of American values. That would help sustain a long campaign." Means and ends. Ends and means. Realism to idealism and back again.

Kissinger, at that meeting, gave Gerson a copy of an infamous memo he wrote for Nixon in 1969 and asked him to pass it along to Bush. "Withdrawal of U.S. troops will become like salted peanuts to the American public," Kissinger warned Nixon. "The more U.S. troops come home, the more will be demanded." Don't get caught in that trap, Kissinger told Gerson, for once withdrawals start, it will become "harder and harder to maintain the morale of those who remain, not to speak of their mothers."

Kissinger then reminisced about Vietnam, reminding Gerson that incentives offered through negotiations needed to be backed up by credible threats—and that for the former to be effective the latter had to be unrestrained. He recounted one of the many "major" ultimatums he gave to the North Vietnamese, warning of the "dire consequences" they would face if they didn't make the concessions needed for the United States to withdraw from Vietnam with honor. They didn't.

"I didn't have enough power," Kissinger said.

Kissingerism without Kissinger

Men become myths.
—Henry Kissinger, 1954

Henry Kissinger ended his latest book, *World Order*, published in 2014, on a note of humility. "Long ago, in youth," its very last paragraph reads, "I was brash enough to think myself able to pronounce on 'The Meaning of History.' I now know that history's meaning is a matter to be discovered, not declared. It is a question we must attempt to answer as best we can in recognition that it will remain open to debate." Elegiac and vaguely rueful, it's an evocative coda to this book—and to his career. Kissinger is ninety-two.

But Kissinger here is feigning a recantation of something that he is in fact affirming. Few readers would have recognized the allusion to his undergraduate thesis; fewer still would know of the author's immersion in German metaphysics. So they would not have recognized that Kissinger was describing himself as having humbly grown into agnosticism when in fact Kissinger has been agnostic about history's meaning at least since his early twenties.

The driving argument of his thesis was exactly to insist that the meaning of history wasn't to be "declared" but to be "discovered" and that our freedom as conscious beings depends on the recognition that history has no predetermined meaning, a recognition that in turn allows us to carve out more room to maneuver, just a bit more freedom. "The riddle of time opens up for Man, not to be classified as a category of Reason as Kant attempted," he wrote in youth and seems to believe still in age. "Time represents a denotation for something inconceivable. It expresses itself in the eternal becoming." "History discloses a majestic unfolding," and the only meaning it holds is the meaning "inherent in the nature of our query," the questions we, in our solitude, put to the past.

Kissinger here, his plaintive endnote notwithstanding, isn't offering an autumnal apologia. The book admits no mistakes and claims no responsibility for his part in rallying the nation to invade Iraq. He downplays his role as an informal consultant to George W. Bush and Bush's foreign policy team, omitting that he met regularly with Dick Cheney and that, in 2005, he wrote that "victory over the insurgency is the only meaningful exit strategy."[1] There is no discussion of the long-term effects of his Middle East policies: yoking Washington to Riyadh; his bolstering of Pakistani intelligence, which in turn cultivated the jihad; his playing off Iraq and the Kurds; and then, as a private citizen after the fall of the shah, his cheerleading as Iranians and Iraqis slaughtered each other.

Kissinger remains consistent that one shouldn't look to history to find the causes of present problems or the origins of blowback. Too much information about the past makes for paralysis. As Bush's hawkish ambassador to the UN, John Bolton, recently said, past decisions are "irrelevant to the circumstances we face now." What is relevant is how we act to contain the current threat. "If we spend our time debating what happened 11 or 12 years ago," Dick Cheney insists, "we're going to miss the threat that is growing and that we do face." "I won't talk about the past," Jeb Bush said, when asked if he would address his brother's foreign policy if he ran for the presidency himself. "I'll talk about the future." Never let yesterday's catastrophes get in the way of tomorrow's actions. Rather than learning from the past to understand the present, Kissinger still sees the primary function of history as a way to imagine the future: maybe some combination of the 1648 Peace of Westphalia and the 1815 Congress of Vienna, he suggests, would be a good fusion model to contain Islam and balance power among competitive allies. "Words of wisdom," said Nicholas Burns, a former diplomat and Bush official and now Harvard professor.

Kissinger's reputation, since he left office in 1977, has had its ups and downs. The early 1990s were good years, as Bill Clinton, a Democrat, embraced him. The two men had their differences over military policy but they agreed on economics, particularly the need to push through the North American Free Trade Agreement, which Kissinger, unofficially, helped negotiate.[2] The former statesman was, writes the economist Jeff Faux, "the perfect tutor for a new Democratic president trying to convince Republicans and their business allies that they could count on him to champion Reagan's vision."[3] But then later in the decade, Pol Pot's death and Pinochet's arrest in London stirred old ghosts, reminding the public of Kissinger's actions in Cambodia and Chile. Shortly after, Christopher Hitchens published a best-selling indictment of Kissinger, calling for his prosecution as a war criminal.

9/11 drew Kissinger close to the George W. Bush administration. He was even named by Bush to be the chair of the official investigation into the attacks. But a number of 9/11 widows were suspicious of Kissinger Associates' business dealings with the gulf kingdom, believing Saudi Arabia to be a sponsor of Al Qaeda. Kissinger met with a delegation of widows as a courtesy but was "stunned" when they insisted he reveal the names of his clients, according to one of the widows present at the encounter. "He seemed stricken and became unsteady," spilling his coffee, which he blamed on a bad eye.[4] (Kissinger's "client list" has been one of the most sought-after documents in Washington since at least 1989, when Senator Jesse Helms unsuccessfully demanded to see it before he would consider confirming Brent Scowcroft as the head of the NSC and Lawrence Eagleburger as deputy secretary of state. "We can look at [the list] up in the secure room of the fourth floor of the Capitol," Helms said, to no avail.)[5] The day after meeting with the widows, Kissinger resigned from the commission.

In 2004, a federal judge dismissed, on jurisdictional grounds, a lawsuit filed against him by the family of a Chilean military officer who was killed in an attempted kidnapping that Kissinger helped organize. Kissinger's public standing once again rebounded.[6] There are still rumors that he can't travel to this or that country out of fear that he would be arrested, but with Hitchens's death in 2011, Kissinger outlived one of his most relentless critics.

More recently, Hillary Clinton's review of *World Order* in the *Washington Post* must have been satisfying. Earlier, as a law student at Yale in the spring semester of 1970 (a year before she met Bill Clinton), Hillary Rodham was at the center of what she called "the Yale-Cambodia madness," a series of protests that started around the "New Haven Nine" Black Panther trial but escalated when Nixon, on April 30, announced the invasion of Cambodia. On May 1, the day after Nixon's speech, a 2006 article in the *Yale Alumni Magazine* recounts, "Vietcong flags filled the air; gas masks were distributed. Streaming banners and impromptu chants abounded: 'Seize the Time!' 'End U.S. imperialism around the world!'"[7]

Whatever Hillary Clinton might then have felt about Kissinger's war on Cambodia, she has made her peace. In her review, Clinton admitted that "Kissinger is a friend," that she "relied on his counsel," and that he "checked in with me regularly, sharing astute observations about foreign leaders and sending me written reports on his travels." The "famous realist," she said, "sounds surprisingly idealistic." Kissinger's vision is her vision: "just and liberal."[8]

No former national security adviser or secretary of state has wielded, after leaving office, as much influence as has Kissinger, and not just with his advocacy for increasingly spectacular shows of military strength. Especially after the Reaganites gave up the White House to George H. W. Bush, who appointed many of Kissinger's close allies to top foreign policy posts, Kissinger, through Kissinger Associates, became a global power broker. Throughout the 1980s and 1990s, he acted as a shadow emissary to China, lunched with Mexico's president to get what became Nafta moving, boxed "isolationists" like Jeane Kirkpatrick into a corner to provide intellectual support for neoconservative internationalism, and consulted with Latin American governments on how best to privatize their industries.

Detractors have criticized Kissinger for having used the contacts he made as a government official as a private consultant. Others have said that his consultancy work is a conflict of interest with his influence as an opinion maker (not only did Kissinger, until recently, appear regularly on network and cable shows, he has sat on the boards of major news corporations).[9] Another criticism is that Kissinger Associates has profited from the consequences of Kissinger's foreign policies. In 1975, for example, Kissinger, as secretary of state, worked with Union Carbide to set up its chemical plant in Bhopal, India, working with the Indian government and helping secure a loan from the Export-Import Bank of the United States to cover a major portion of the plant's construction.[10] Then, after the plant's 1989 chemical leak disaster, Kissinger Associates represented Union Carbide, helping to broker, in 1989, a $470 million out-of-court settlement for victims of the spill. The payout was widely condemned as paltry in relation to the scale of the disaster.[11] The spill caused nearly four thousand immediate deaths and exposed another half million people to toxic gases. In Latin America and Eastern Europe, Kissinger Associates also profited from what one of its consultants called the "massive sale" of public utilities and industries, a sell-off that, in many countries, was initiated by Kissinger-supported dictators and military regimes.[12]

And then there is the odd role Kissinger continues to play in this country's foreign policy debate, with defense intellectuals and journalists regularly penning essays reconsidering Kissinger's legacy and prescribing a neo-Kissingerian tonic for today's troubles, though they have trouble defining what exactly such a policy would look like. Often Kissingerism is defined in negative terms. It's not the reckless adventurism of the neocons (though, as I've tried to show, it actually is). And it's not Barack Obama's pragmatic overcorrection, a foreign policy that mistakes power for purpose (though, again, Kissinger himself did exactly that). That Kissingerism is so hard to pin down is, I think, an effect of Kissingerism, of Kissinger's rehabilitation of the national security state and the relentless militarism that goes with it. Constant, unending war—be it fought with neocon zealotry or Obama's dronelike efficiency—has done more than coarsened thought and morality. It has brought about a "semantic collapse," a dissociation of words and things, belief and action, in which ethics are unmoored from their foundation and abstractions are transmuted into their opposite: in Clinton's review of Kissinger's last book, "idealists" are "realists" and everybody is a "liberal"—and Henry Kissinger is our avatar.

At this point in his life, however, Kissinger is as much pure affect as he is power broker. The gestures Clinton mentioned in her review—I rely on his counsel; he checks in with me and gives me reports from his travels—are ceremonial, meant to bestow gravitas.* Kissinger himself has become the demonstrative effect, whatever substance there was eroded by the constant confusion of ends and means, the churn of power to create purpose and purpose defined as the ability to project power. Evidence continues to mount that his diplomacy was, on its own terms, a failure; cables continue to be released that show his callousness in the face of, and often his complicity in, mass atrocities. "Fired by the discovery of some factual error," the intellectual historian Stuart Hughes wrote of Oswald Spengler's critics, "they have dashed off to meet him on a field of battle where he never had the slightest intention of putting in an appearance." Kissinger, too, enjoys some sort of Spenglerian immunity. Neither fact, reason, nor all those declassified documents revealing sordid doings of one kind or another can touch him. Just four days after he wrote his August 2002 column urging Bush to quickly take "pre-emptive action" to bring about "regime change" in Iraq, the *Times* ran an article citing Kissinger as a realist gadfly to the neocons' dream of toppling Hussein, in an article headlined "Top Republicans Break with Bush on War Strategy."[13] Kissinger, it seems, can simultaneously be himself and his negation. Talk about unity of opposites.

It's not all spectacle though. There are a few skeptical reporters around who, occasionally, pierce the facade, usually by bringing up either Chile or Cambodia. One is Todd Zwillich, who in 2014 did an hour-long interview with Kissinger for NPR's *The Takeaway.*

---

* It's now a ritual among our political class to seek out Kissinger and engage in some form of public banter with him, as Samantha Power, Barack Obama's ambassador to the United Nations, recently did when the two diplomats went to a Yankee game together. Power, the author of a Pulitzer-Prize-winning book, *A Problem from Hell*, that earned her a reputation as a fierce opponent of genocide, jokingly asked Kissinger why he became a Yankee fan. "Was that in keeping with a realist's perspective on the world? Was that where victories were likely?" Power continued, referring to herself: "The human rights advocate, of course, falls in love with the Red Sox, the downtrodden, the people who can't win the World Series." "Now we are the downtrodden," replied Kissinger, a man implicated in three of the genocides—Cambodia, Bangladesh, and East Timor—that Power wrote about.

Kissinger was largely on autopilot for the first half of the discussion, giving his opinions on the world's hot spots. But he was caught off guard when Zwillich brought up the 1973 coup in Chile. The former secretary of state tried to deflect: "Let me tell you something here—it's an issue that our audience cannot possibly know much about. This happened over 40 years ago." "With all due respect to you," Kissinger told Zwillich, "it's not an appropriate subject." But the host kept pushing the question, leading Kissinger to cite Obama's efforts to overthrow Assad in Syria and his ouster of Gaddafi in Libya to validate his actions in Chile.

Then Zwillich mentioned Cambodia.

"Cambodia!" Kissinger cried, in despair more than anger.[14] He went on to rehearse the same arguments—the areas bombed were mostly uninhabited; it was North Vietnam that first violated Cambodia's sovereignty; the United States had a right to defend itself—he had been making for years. But this time he added something new. He justified Cambodia by pointing to Barack Obama's drone strikes. The current administration," he said, "is doing it in Pakistan, Somalia."

Here, then, is a perfect expression of American militarism's unbroken circle. Kissinger is invoking today's endless, open-ended war to justify what he did in Cambodia and Chile (and elsewhere) nearly half a century ago. But what he did nearly half a century ago created the conditions for today's endless wars.*

---

* Technically, according to Chase Madar, a lawyer and expert in international law, the drone strikes in Pakistan, Yemen, and Somalia (as well as all the many battles in the open-ended global counterinsurgency, or COIN) are broadly justified by the Authorization to Use Military Force (AUMF), passed by the House and Senate on September 14, 2001. The drone strikes in Afghanistan have a slightly different legal rationale, found both in the AUMF and Article 51 of the UN Charter, which grants nations the right to "self-defense." Notably, this was the UN article whose invocation by Secretary of State George Shultz to justify the 1986 bombing of Libya in retaliation for the Berlin nightclub bombing defined the whole world as US territory. More recently, Barack Obama has asked Congress for a new authorization to use military force to fight the Islamic State, a request that would leave in place without alteration the 2001 AUMF.

It's not so much that Kissinger's justification for bombing Cambodia set actual juridical precedents used by government lawyers to sanction today's global counterinsurgency campaign and drone strikes. Then, as now, legal rationales are often pasted on after the fact. It's more that by executing such an assault, and getting away with it, Kissinger provided a broad set of effective *political* arguments to justify war: when called on by Congress or the public to account for his actions, he invoked the right to self-defense, the effectiveness of his policies ("except" for being illegal, he asked the Pike Committee in 1975, "there is nothing wrong with my operation?"), and the need to deploy enough military force to establish credibility and achieve our political goals.

Perhaps the most influential argument Kissinger made to validate his war on Cambodia was the need to destroy enemy "sanctuaries." Over and over again, while in office and out, he has insisted that bombing and cross-border raids were required to protect American lives (often, when doing so, greatly exaggerating the numbers of US soldiers killed: "500 Americans a week," Kissinger said in 1991).[15] That argument was outside of the mainstream of international law in 1970, so much so it prompted Thomas Schelling's public break with Kissinger. Today, it is unquestioned. The goal of denying "safe haven" to terrorists is, write Micah Zenko and Amelia Mae Wolf in *Foreign Policy*, "the premise for the war in Afghanistan and for the expansion of drone operations into Pakistan, Yemen, and Somalia. Most recently, it has underlined the rationale for initiating an open-ended war to degrade and destroy the Islamic State."[16] As it did in Southeast Asia, the premise mystifies more than it clarifies, deflecting attention away from the fact that such aggressive militarism often worsens the problem—while turning the whole world into a battlefield. Fourteen years, and counting, at a cost of four trillion dollars, and counting, the global war on terror has acted as an accelerant, leaving behind a series of failed or failing states (among them, Iraq and Libya) and taking an organization, Al Qaeda, which had been mostly contained to Afghanistan, and transforming its cause into a worldwide danger.

It doesn't matter. "If you threaten America, you will find no safe haven," Barack Obama has said, allowing Kissinger his retroactive absolution: Obama does it.

There's a remark by Hannah Arendt in *The Origins of Totalitarianism* where she describes administrators of the British Empire as "monsters of conceit in their success and monsters of modesty in their failure." Arendt is referring specially to the Empire's higher aristocratic officers, a new kind of imperialist who became one with the imperial system. Unlike older forms of conquest, European expansion starting in the late nineteenth century "was not driven by the specific appetite for a specific country but conceived as an endless process in which every country would serve only as a stepping-stone for further expansion." The particular vices or virtues of these administrators mattered little, for "once he has entered the maelstrom of an unending process of expansion, he will, as it were, cease to be what he was and obey the laws of the process, identify himself with anonymous forces that he is supposed to serve in order to keep the whole process in motion; he will think of himself as mere function, and eventually consider such functionality, such an incarnation of the dynamic trend, his highest possible achievement."[17]

In a way, Kissinger achieved such a fusion between self and system; his personal ascendance became indistinguishable from the restoration of the imperial presidency, his personal success as exceptional as the nation he served. The melding is so complete that Kissinger can't imagine criticism of his policies as anything other than criticism of what he thinks America should be. "If we want to bring America together in the crisis that we face," he recently said, "we should stop conducting these discussions as a civil war," that is, stop trying to hold public officials responsible for the actions they take in the name of national defense.

Arendt said that imperial officials who have achieved such an overidentification of self and system "had to be perfectly willing to disappear into complete oblivion once failure had been proved, if for any reason they were no longer 'instruments of incomparable value,'" as London's consul general in Cairo called the bureaucrats who carry out a "policy of Imperialism." Rarely, though, did Kissinger ever have to consider this fate. For a while in 1970, after the invasion of Cambodia, Kissinger, joking about the criticism he faced from former Harvard colleagues, talked about quitting the White House and joining the faculty at Arizona State. He seemed resigned, one reporter said, "to finishing his teaching career in the academic boondocks."[18] But Kissinger evolved and adapted, surviving the Cambodia hearings, Watergate, and the Church Committee investigation, never losing his incomparable value, especially when it came to justifying war.

Far from disappearing into oblivion, he endures. And after Kissinger himself is gone, one imagines Kissingerism will endure as well.

NOTES

PRELUDE: ON NOT SEEING THE MONSTER

1. Fred Kaplan, *The Wizards of Armageddon* (1991), describes Schelling's influence on Vietnam strategy.
2. For the Harvard delegation, see "Friends Said 'No' to Kissinger," *Boston Globe*, May 10, 1970; Michael Kinsley, "Eating Lunch at Henry's," *Inside the System*, ed. Charles Peters and Nicholas Lehmann (1979), p. 197; David Warsh, "Game Theory Suggests Quick Action on Greenhouse Effect Is Remote," *Washington Post*, June 13, 1990; "Cambodia Act Called 'Sickening,'" *Hartford Courant*, May 10, 1970; "Harvard Visit to Kissinger 'Painful,'" *Boston Globe*, May 9, 1970.

INTRODUCTION: AN OBITUARY FORETOLD

1. A. J. Langguth, *Vietnam: The War, 1954–1975* (2000), p. 564.
2. Walter Isaacson, *Kissinger* (1992), p. 31; Robert Dallek, *Nixon and Kissinger: Partners in Power* (2007), p. 33.
3. Henry Kissinger, "The Meaning of History (Reflections on Spengler, Toynbee, and Kant)," AB honors thesis, Harvard University, 1950 (held by Widener Library, Harvard; henceforth cited as MH), p. 23.
4. Kissinger's undergraduate thesis was written under the direction of William Yandell Elliott, who applied Kantian thought to diplomatic history. But by the time he arrived at Harvard, Kissinger had a prior engagement with Continental philosophy, under the tutelage of Fritz Kraemer, a Prussian

anti-Nazi conservative whom Kissinger met while he was stationed as an infantry private at Camp Claiborne, Louisiana. Kraemer held a number of graduate degrees, including one from the University of Frankfurt in 1931, just around the time Max Horkheimer, Theodor Adorno, and other social theorists formed what is now known as the Frankfurt School. Astute readers will clearly recognize in Kissinger's writings themes and arguments often associated with the Frankfurt School, and Kraemer might have been a link. "Over the next decades," Kissinger said at his 2003 funeral, "Kraemer shaped my reading and thinking, influenced my choice of college, awakened my interest in political philosophy and history, inspired both my undergraduate and graduate theses." Bruce Kuklick, in *Blind Oracles: Intellectuals and War from Kennan to Kissinger* (2006), notes that there were a number of scholars critical of positivism at Harvard at the time Kissinger was an undergraduate, including Henry Sheffer and W. V. O. Quine.

5. Quoted in Hanes Walton Jr., James Bernard Rosser Sr., and Robert Louis Stevenson, *The African Policy of Secretary of State Henry Kissinger* (2007), p. 16.

6. MH, pp. 326–27.

7. MH, p. 348.

8. MH, p. 9.

9. For the use of "tragedy," see my introduction to a recent edition of William Appleman Williams, *The Contours of American History* (2011).

10. Frank Costigliola, *The Kennan Diaries* (2014), p. 541.

11. Henry Kissinger, "Peace, Legitimacy, and the Equilibrium (A Study of the Statesmanship of Castlereagh and Metternich), PhD thesis, Department of Government, Harvard University, 1954, published in 1957 as *A World Restored: Metternich, Castlereagh and the Problem of Peace, 1812–1822*. Page 213 for the quotation.

12. Oriana Fallaci, *Interview with History* (1976), p. 44.

13. "The New Establishment," *Vanity Fair*, October 1994.

14. Michael Glennon, *National Security and Double Government* (2014); Scott Horton, *Lords of Secrecy* (2005). See also, Matthew Dickinson, *Bitter Harvest: FDR, Presidential Power and the Growth of the Presidential Branch* (1999); Douglas Stuart, *Creating the National Security State: A History of the Law that Transformed America* (2009); Garry Wills, *Bomb Power: The Modern Presidency and the National Security State* (2011); Harold Koh, *The National Security Constitution* (1990).

15. Morton Kondracke, "Leaning on the Left," *New York Times*, March 15, 1992.

16. Daniel Patrick Moynihan, in a speech to the American Council on Education on October 8, 1970, seems to be the first to use the term "adversary culture," which he said was "entrenched in higher education." He went on: "The intellectuals' propensity to condemn in the sixties what they helped formulate in the fifties has only helped to further the breach between the public and the

university." Early neoconservative attempts to formulate the concept tended to stress psychological explanations having to do with the softness and prosperity of bourgeois society, in which young people seek "meaning" through protest. See Norman Podhoretz, "The Adversary Culture and the New Class," in *The New Class?*, ed. B. Bruce-Biggs (1979); Irving Kristol, "The Adversary Culture of Intellectuals," *Encounter*, October 1979. More recently, Paul Hollander revived the concept in the wake of 9/11 and cast a wide net: "Adherents of the adversary culture can be found in a wide variety of settings, organizations and interest groups. They include postmodernist academics, radical feminists, Afrocentrist blacks, radical environmentalists, animal rights activists, pacifists, Maoists, Trotskyites, critical legal theorists and others. They often have different political agendas but share certain core convictions and key assumptions: all are reflexively and intensely hostile critics of the United States or American society and, increasingly, of all Western cultural traditions and values as well. The most important among their beliefs is that American society is deeply flawed and uniquely repellent—unjust, corrupt, destructive, soulless, inhumane, inauthentic and incapable of satisfying basic, self-evident human needs. The American social system has failed to live up to its original historical promise and, they insist, is inherently and ineradicably sexist, racist and imperialist" ("The Resilience of the Adversary Culture," *National Interest* [2002]).

17. Kissinger, *For the Record* (1981), p. 124.
18. Interview with ABC News, June 22, 2014; available at http://www.realclear politics.com/video/2014/06/22/cheney_pay_attention_to_current_threat _cant_debate_what_happened_12_years_ago.html.
19. Cambodia: Kissinger, *Ending the Vietnam War* (2003), p. 470; Chile: Kissinger, *Years of Upheaval* (1982), p. 383; the Kurds: Kissinger, *Years of Renewal* (1999), pp. 576–96; Timor: transcript of August 1995 confrontation between Kissinger and journalists Amy Goodman and Allan Nairn; available at http://etan.org /news/kissinger/ask.htm.
20. "Faith, Certainty and the Presidency of George W. Bush," *New York Times*, October 17, 2004.
21. "Strains on the Alliance," *Foreign Affairs*, January 1963.

1: A COSMIC BEAT

1. "The Salad Days of Henry Kissinger," *Harvard Crimson*, May 21, 1971.
2. James Mann, *The Rise of the Vulcans* (2004), p. 77.
3. All quotations from Spengler taken from 1926 translation, by Charles Francis Atkinson, of *The Decline of the West*, hereafter cited as DW. This sentence is from p. 425.
4. DW, p. 17.
5. MH, p. 15.

6. MH, p. 17. A good way to understand the influence that Spengler's critique of positivism had on Kissinger is to consider a short book the liberal Arthur Schlesinger published in 1967, *The Bitter Heritage: Vietnam and American Democracy, 1941–1966,* which set out what has since become known as the "quagmire thesis." America, Schlesinger said, slipped into Vietnam by accident; the war was a "triumph of the politics of inadvertence." "Our present entanglement," he argued, stemmed not from "deliberate consideration" but rather from "a series of small decisions," one misstep after another, "until we find ourselves entrapped today in that nightmare." Schlesinger offered no theory of history that could explain this absentmindedness, no way to account for how, exactly, the most powerful and prosperous nation in world history, at the apex of its attainment and creativity, might stumble like a drunk down a blind alley and wake up lost in the rice paddocks of Southeast Asia, bankrupting itself in an unwinnable war. Kissinger, unlike Schlesinger, did have a theory and he got it from Spengler: purposeless war is a symptom of civilizational decline, and the descent begins imperceptibly. States might continue to amass and project power, but at some point in their evolution, at the height of their success and complexity and largely because of that success and complexity, they lose a sense of self-understanding.

7. The quotation regarding objective laws comes from Morgenthau's classic 1947 work, *Politics among Nations,* offered as a simplified definition of what political realists believe, one that Morgenthau immediately qualifies.

8. H. Stuart Hughes, *Oswald Spengler* (1991), p. 70. John Farrenkopf, in his book on Spengler, *Prophet of Decline: Spengler on World History and Politics* (2001), p. 41, writes: "Spengler criticizes cause-and-effect historical analysis because it implicitly denies that cultures have the capacity to burst forth as foci of pristine and nonderivative cultural creativity and vitality. According to the mechanistic, causal approach, 'everything follows, nothing is original.'"

9. Isaacson, *Kissinger,* p. 68, wrongly suggests that Kissinger "sidled away" from this critique of causality. He didn't, expressing variations of it throughout his career, as we shall see.

10. Henry Kissinger, *White House Years* (2011), p. 56.

11. MH, pp. 13–14; 75; 102; 105; 194; for the quotations on causality and militarism.

12. For these two memos, see the William Y. Elliott Papers at the Hoover Institution Archives, box 28.

13. Sigmund Diamond, *Compromised Campus: The Collaboration of Universities with the Intelligence Community, 1945–1955* (1992), p. 140. Most Kissinger biographers, when they discuss Kissinger's Harvard mentor, William Elliott, focus on his "flamboyance," downplaying his very close ties with domestic and national intelligence agencies and his unapologetic advocacy in favor of domestic surveillance. Diamond's chapter "Kissinger and Elliott" does a good

job (based on declassified US government documents) at tracing the complicated nexus of Harvard Yard and Langley, at the center of which was Elliott, a
committed Cold Warrior who suggested (in a 1958 article that he inscribed
to J. Edgar Hoover) that an "Atlantic Round Table for Freedom," based on
the "Round Table of Arthurian legend" that held "the West against Hun and
Moslem," be established, composed of "ten outstanding Companions," or
modern "Knights."

14. Among the most interesting of these early articles are: "American Policy and
Preventive War," *Yale Review* (1955); "Military Policy and Defense of the 'Grey
Areas,'" *Foreign Affairs* (1955); "Force and Diplomacy in the Nuclear Age," *Foreign Affairs* (1956); "Reflections on American Diplomacy," *Foreign Affairs*
(1956); "Controls, Inspection and Limited War," *Reporter* (1957); "Missiles and
the Western Alliance," *Foreign Affairs* (1958); "The Policymaker and the Intellectual," *Reporter* (1959); "As Urgent as the Moscow Threat," *New York Times
Magazine* (1959); and "The Search for Stability," *Foreign Affairs* (1959).

15. Kissinger, "Military Policy and Defense of the 'Grey Areas.'"

16. Henry Kissinger, *Nuclear Weapons and Foreign Policy* (1957), p. 190.

17. The term "grey areas" to refer to the nations outside of Europe was first used
by Secretary of the Air Force Thomas Finletter in February 1951 (later
expanded on in his 1954 *Power and Policy*). Interestingly, Kissinger, in his 1951
memos cited above, criticized the "grey area" concept, associating it with
Washington's tendency, as evinced in Korea, to allow the Soviets to dictate
where and when it would fight. But Kissinger's evolution into a nuclear strat-
egist, and his advocacy of limited, tactical nuclear war, allowed him to embrace
the idea of fighting in "grey areas": if Washington could back up its conventional forces with the credible threat of nuclear power when it fights in,
say, Indochina, then it wouldn't necessarily be ceding the advantage to
Moscow.

18. Kissinger, "Force and Diplomacy in the Nuclear Age."

19. Kissinger, *Nuclear Weapons and Foreign Policy*, p. 7.

20. Kissinger, "Peace, Legitimacy, and the Equilibrium," p. 7.

21. Kissinger, *Nuclear Weapons and Foreign Policy*, pp. 236; 249.

22. Henry Kissinger, *Necessity for Choice* (1961), p. 15.

23. James and Diane Dornan, "The Works of Henry A. Kissinger," *Political Science Reviewer* (Fall 1975), p. 99.

24. Arthur Schlesinger Jr., *Journals: 1952–2000* (2007), p. 84.

25. "Reflections on Cuba," *Reporter*, November 22, 1962, p. 21.

26. "Strains on the Alliance," *Foreign Affairs*.

27. Ellsberg, *Secrets: A Memoir of Vietnam and the Pentagon Papers* (2003), p. 229.

28. According to Ellsberg, Kissinger by 1967 was expressing, at academic confer-
ences and in private conversations, "a point of view that was well in advance of
that of any other mainstream political figure at that point." Washington's "only
objective" should be to ensure a "decent interval" between US withdrawal from

South Vietnam and the country's complete takeover by troops from the North (*Secrets*, p. 229). See William Safire, *Before the Fall* (1975), p. 160, for the quote.

29. "Educators Back Vietnam Policy," *New York Times*, December 10, 1965.
30. "Harvard Debates Oxford on Vietnam," *New York Times*, December 22, 1965.
31. Robert Shrum, *No Excuses* (2007), p. 15.

2: ENDS AND MEANS

1. MH, p. 321.
2. Isaacson, *Kissinger*, p. 76.
3. For the transcript, see the William Y. Elliott Papers at the Hoover Institution Archives, box 55.
4. Halberstam, "The New Establishment." For the quotation in the footnote, see MH, pp. 13–14.
5. The story was first told in detail by Hersh, in *The Price of Power*, and has been verified by Richard Allen and confirmed, in passing, by Kissinger himself (see citations later in chapter). Walter Isaacson's biography, *Kissinger*, supports every detail of Hersh, but suggests that "what Kissinger provided was not serious spying" but a "willingness to pass along tales and tidbits." This assertion in no way contradicts Hersh's description of events. See also Ken Hughes, *Chasing Shadows: The Nixon Tapes, the Chennault Affair, and the Origins of Watergate* (2014), especially n. 7, pp. 175–77, which provides additional evidence that confirms Kissinger's involvement.
6. Marvin Kalb and Bernard Kalb, *Kissinger* (1973), pp. 15–16.
7. Kalb and Kalb, *Kissinger*, p. 18.
8. Isaacson, *Kissinger*, p. 127.
9. Hersh, *Price of Power*, p. 14.
10. "The American Experience in Southeast Asia: Historical Conference," September 29, 2010; transcript available at: http://www.state.gov/p/eap/rls/rm/2010/09/148410.htm.
11. Isaacson, *Kissinger*, p. 133.
12. Isaacson, *Kissinger*, p. 131.
13. Ibid.
14. Interview with Richard Allen, Ronald Reagan Oral History Project, Miller Center, University of Virginia, May 28, 2002; available at http://millercenter.org/president/reagan/oralhistory/richard-allen.
15. Hersh, *Price of Power*, p. 21.
16. Hughes, *Chasing Shadows*, p. 46.
17. Hughes, *Chasing Shadows*, p. 47.
18. http://whitehousetapes.net/transcript/nixon/525-001; Ken Hughes, "LBJ Thought Nixon Committed Treason," History News Network, June 15, 2012;

and Robert Parry, "The Dark Continuum of Watergate," June 12, 2012; http://consortiumnews.com/2012/06/12/the-dark-continuum-of-watergate/.

19. *FRUS: Soviet Union*, October 1971–May 1972, vol. 14, doc. 126, p. 446.
20. "Henry Kissinger & the Nixon-Chennault-Thieu Cabal of 1968," H-Diplo Discussion, April 19, 2011; http://h-net.msu.edu/cgi-bin/logbrowse.pl?trx=vx&list=h-diplo&month=1104&week=c&msg=v18g74TLByTCI2MqcwPN%2bQ&user=&pw=.
21. Kissinger, *A World Restored*, p. 326.
22. Kissinger, "Reflections on American Diplomacy," p. 39.
23. Kissinger, *A World Restored*, p. 327.
24. In Issacson, *Kissinger*, p. 132.
25. *Nixon: The Triumph of a Politician, 1962–1972* (1989), p. 231.

3: KISSINGER SMILED

1. H. R. Haldeman, *The Ends of Power* (1978), p. 83.
2. *Foreign Relations of the United States, 1969–1976*, vol. 6, Vietnam, January 1969–July 1970 (2006), p. 96.
3. Quoted in Barbara Zanchetta, *The Transformation of American International Power in the 1970s* (2013), p. 32.
4. Kalb and Kalb, *Kissinger*, especially ch. 5, "Henry's Wonderful Machine," is still among the best discussions of the transformation of the NSC under Kissinger and Nixon. See p. 80 for the quotation. Also, Hersh, *Price of Power*, chapter 2, "A New NSC System," describes the transformation. Both the Kalbs and Hersh are also still the most useful sources for the bureaucratic infighting and personality conflicts involved in the transformation.
5. Safire, *Before the Fall*, p. 190.
6. Kalb and Kalb, *Kissinger*, p. 91.
7. Hersh, *Price of Power*, p. 87.
8. William Shawcross, *Sideshow: Kissinger, Nixon, and the Destruction of Cambodia* (1979), p. 271.
9. "Kissinger Tapes Describe Crises, War and Stark Photos of Abuse," *New York Times*, May 27, 2004.
10. Hersh, *Price of Power*, p. 63.
11. H. R. Haldeman, *The Haldeman Diaries* (1994), p. 51.
12. Hersh, *Price of Power*, p. 121.
13. Bob Woodward and Carl Bernstein, *The Final Days* (1976), p. 191.
14. Shawcross, *Sideshow*, p. 29.
15. Joan Hoff, *Nixon Reconsidered* (1995), p. 219.
16. Kalb and Kalb, *Kissinger*, p. 156.
17. *Diplomacy* (1994), p. 704.
18. Isaacson, *Kissinger*, p. 275.
19. Schlesinger, *Journals*, p. 322.

20. Melvin Small, *The Presidency of Richard Nixon* (1999), p. 28.

21. *Cluster Munitions Monitor 2010*, p. 13.

22. http://www.japanfocus.org/-Ben-Kiernan/3380.

23. See "Bombs over Cambodia," *Walrus* (Toronto), October 2006, pp. 62–69, and n. 38 of Kiernan and Owen's "Roots of U.S. Troubles in Afghanistan: Civilian Bombing Casualties and the Cambodian Precedent," *Asia-Pacific Journal*, available at http://www.japanfocus.org/-Ben-Kiernan/3380. See also the maps found on the Web page of Yale University's Cambodian Genocide Program: http://www.yale.edu/cgp/us.html.

24. http://www.voanews.com/content/a-13-2009-02-02-voa34-68796482/411754 .html.

25. State Department inspectors determined that the defoliation was "caused by a deliberate and direct overflight of the rubber plantations." Independent investigators, in consultation with US authorities, including Senator Frank Church, suggested that the CIA targeted the plantations in order to destabilize the Sihanouk government. See Wells-Dang, "Agent Orange in Laos and Cambodia: The Documentary Evidence," in *Indochina News* (Summer 2002), available here: http://www.ffrd.org/indochina/summer02news.html#ao. See also A. H. Westing, E. W. Pfeiffer, J. Lavorel, and L. Matarasso, "Report on Herbicidal Damage by the United States in Southern Cambodia," December 31, 1969, in Thomas Whiteside, *Defoliation* (1970), pp. 117–32; and Arthur H. Westing, "Herbicidal Damage to Cambodia," in J. B. Neilands et al., *Harvest of Death: Chemical Warfare in Vietnam and Cambodia* (1972), pp. 177–205.

26. E-mail communication, but see his "The US Bombardment of Cambodia, 1969–1973," *Vietnam Generation* 1 (Winter 1989): 4–41, for the numbers.

27. Quoted in Ellsberg, *Secrets*, p. 418.

28. http://legaciesofwar.org/resources/cluster-bomb-fact-sheet/; http://www.trust .org/item/20130829191627-4qtnw/?source=search; Jerry Redfern and Karen Coates, *Eternal Harvest: The Legacy of American Bombs in Laos* (2013).

29. Kissinger, "Peace, Legitimacy, and the Equilibrium," pp. 539–543, for the quotations in this chapter.

30. See Rick Perlstein, *The Invisible Bridge: The Fall of Nixon and the Rise of Reagan* (2014), pp. 331; 523–24.

31. "The American Experience in Southeast Asia: Historical Conference."

32. TelCon, Conversation between Henry Kissinger and Nick Thimmesch, April 9, 1973.

4: NIXON STYLE

1. "Conversation among President Nixon, the President's Assistant for National Security Affairs (Kissinger), and the Assistant to the President (Haldeman), April 17, 1971, *Foreign Relations of the United States, 1969–1976*, vol. 32: SALT I, 1969–1972 (2010), p. 447.

2. Dale Van Atta, *With Honor: Melvin Laird in War, Peace, and Politics* (2008), p. 157.
3. Gerald S. Strober and Deborah Hart Strober, *Nixon: An Oral History of His Presidency* (1994), p. 172.
4. Strober and Strober, *Nixon*, p. 173.
5. Robert Dallek, *Nixon and Kissinger: Partners in Power* (2007), p. 262.
6. Miller Center, University of Virginia, Presidential Recordings Program, Conversation between Nixon, Kissinger, and Haldeman on Wednesday, November 17, 1971; available at http://whitehousetapes.net/transcript/nixon/620-008.
7. Miller Center, University of Virginia, Presidential Recordings Program, Conversation between Nixon and Goldwater, November 10, 1971; available at http://whitehousetapes.net/transcript/nixon/014-017.
8. Colin Dueck, *Hard Line: The Repubican Party and U.S. Foreign Policy since World War II* (2010), p. 160.
9. Haldeman, *The Ends of Power*, p. 94.
10. Derek Shearer, "An Evening With Henry Kissinger," *Nation*, March 8, 1971.
11. Schlesinger, *Journals*, p. 325.
12. Kalb and Kalb, *Kissinger*, p. 97.
13. MH, p. 102.
14. "Douglas Brinkley and Luke A. Nichter, "Nixon Unbound," *Vanity Fair*, August 2014.
15. Shearer, "An Evening With Henry Kissinger."
16. Jonathan Schell, *The Time of Illusion* (1976), p. 115.
17. Isaacson, *Kissinger*, p. 279.
18. *Haldeman Diaries*, p. 244.
19. Dallek, *Nixon and Kissinger*, p. 261.
20. Fredrik Logevall and Andrew Preston, eds., *Nixon in the World* (2008), p. 11.
21. John Day Tully, Matthew Masur, and Brad Austin, *Understanding and Teaching the Vietnam War* (2013), p. 89.
22. *Haldeman Diaries*, p. 500.
23. Larry Berman, *No Peace, No Honor: Nixon, Kissinger, and Betrayal in Vietnam* (2001), p. 123.
24. *Haldeman Diaries*, p. 435.
25. Kissinger, *Ending the Vietnam War*, p. 254.
26. Berman, *No Peace*, p. 129.
27. "The American Experience in Southeast Asia: Historical Conference."
28. Berman, *No Peace*, p. 127.
29. Van Loi Lưu, Anh Vu Nguyen, *Le Duc Tho-Kissinger Negotiations in Paris* (1996), p. 230.
30. David Halberstam, Letter to the Editor, *New York Magazine*, February 17, 1975.
31. Schlesinger, *Journals*, p. 362.

32. Ken Hughes, "The Paris 'Peace' Accords Were a Deadly Deception," January 31, 2013, *History News Network*; available at http://historynewsnetwork.org/article/150424.

33. "The Cambodian Issue: President or King," *Washington Post*, March 30, 1973.

34. Berman, *No Peace*, pp. 8, 9, 258, for this and the following quotations.

5: ANTI-KISSINGER

1. Hersh, *Price of Power*, p. 127.

2. For the "McNamara revolution," see James E. Hewes Jr., *From Root to McNamara: Army Organization and Administration*, Washington: Center of Military History (1975). Stephen Talbot, "The Day Henry Kissinger Cried," *Salon*, December 5, 2002, tells of his encounter with Kissinger and Kissinger's mocking reaction to McNamara discussed in the footnote; available at http://www.salon.com/2002/12/05/kissinger_3.

3. For Sitton's opinions of McNamara's system, see his oral history, cited above.

4. For the Wheeler, Knight, and Abrams quotations, see U.S. Congress, Senate Committee on Armed Services, *Bombing in Cambodia: Hearings, Ninety-Third Congress*, 1973, pp. 15; 132–133; and 343.

5. Spengler, *DW*, p. 29.

6. For an example, see Brooks Adams, *The Law of Civilization and Decay* (1895). For analysis, see John Patrick Diggins, *The Promise of Pragmatism: Modernism and the Crisis of Knowledge and Authority* (1994); Arthur Herman, *The Idea of Decline in Western History* (1997); Jackson Lears, *No Place of Grace: Anti-Modernism and the Transformation of American Culture, 1880–1920* (1981).

7. For two influential Ellsberg essays from the 1950s, see "Theory of the Reluctant Duelist," *American Economic Review* (1956), and "Risk, Ambiguity, and the Savage Axioms," *Quarterly Journal of Economics* (1961).

8. MH, p. 36.

9. Ellsberg, *Secrets*, p. 237. Hersh, *Price of Power*, and Kalb and Kalb, *Kissinger*, also discuss these surveys.

10. Kissinger, *White House Years*, p. 39.

11. Henry Kissinger, "Domestic Structure and Foreign Policy," *Daedalus* (Spring 1966).

12. Ellsberg, *Secrets*, p. 347.

13. Michael A. Genovese, *The Watergate Crisis* (1999), p. 9.

14. Barbara Keys, "Henry Kissinger: The Emotional Statesman," *Diplomatic History* 35 (2011): 587–609.

15. Isaacson, *Kissinger*, p. 328.

16. Also, Nixon and Haldeman never stopped reminding Kissinger that he was Jewish and that "spies" tended to be Jewish (as they speculated Ellsberg might be). Scholars have suggested that Kissinger felt pressure to prove his loyalty. Nixon: "All right. I want a look at any sensitive areas around where Jews are

involved. . . . The Jews are all through the government, and we have got to get in those areas. We've got to get a man in charge who is not Jewish to control the Jewish." Later, the Pentagon Papers episode led Nixon to appreciate the loyalty of African Americans: "But the Negroes, have you ever noticed? There are damn few Negro spies."

17. Presidential Recordings Project, Miller Center, University of Virginia, Nixon Conversation, June 17, 1971, 525-001; available at http://millercenter.org /presidentialrecordings/rmn-525-001.
18. "Haldeman Talks," *Newsweek*, February 27, 1978.
19. Ellsberg, *Secrets*, p. 328–29.
20. Tim Weiner, *Enemies: A History of the FBI* (2013), p. 282.
21. Isaacson, *Kissinger*, p. 768.
22. Isaacson, *Kissinger*, pp. 580–81.

6: THE OPPOSITE OF UNITY

1. Kissinger, "Peace, Legitimacy, and the Equilibrium," p. 542.
2. US Department of State, Office of the Historian, Memorandum from the President's Assistant for National Security Affairs (Kissinger) to President Ford, May 12, 1975, document 280; available at: https://history.state.gov/historical documents/frus1969-76v10/d280.
3. Kissinger, *Years of Upheaval*, p. 46.
4. For what follows, US Department of State, Office of the Historian, "Memorandum of a Conversation," Peking, November 12, 1973, including Mao Tse-tung, and Henry Kissinger, among others, document 58; available at: https://history .state.gov/historicaldocuments/frus1969-76v18/d58.
5. This *New Yorker* essay was introduced into the Senate record during its hearings to confirm Kissinger as Secretary of State. See *Hearings before the Committee on Foreign Relations, United States Senate . . .* (1973), pp. 306–7.
6. John Lewis Gaddis, *We Now Know: Rethinking Cold War History* (1997), p. 187.
7. The late Philip L. Geyelin, a longtime Kissinger observer at the *Washington Post*, wrote that after eight years in power, Henry Kissinger "had very little to show for his grand designs. No administration in memory had left for its successors such a backlog of unfinished foreign business: SALT II, the Middle East, the Panama Canal treaty, the Greek-Turkish conflict over Cyprus, the hardest half of the 'opening' to China, an Atlantic Alliance languishing for lack of American attention, a sleeping giant of an international energy crisis" (*The Atlantic Monthly*, February 1980).
8. US Department of State, Office of the Historian, FRUS, no. 358, Telegram from State to Embassy in Philippines, December 2, 1976; available at https://history .state.gov/historicaldocuments/frus1969-76ve12/d358.
9. For Ford and Kissinger's green-lighting the invasion, see the analysis and declassified documents, from which the quotations are drawn, at the National

Security Archive, "East Timor Revisited: Ford, Kissinger and the Indonesian Invasion, 1975–1976"; available at http://www2.gwu.edu/~nsarchiv/NSAEBB /NSAEBB62/.

10. Gary Bass has written the definitive account of this episode, his 2013 *The Blood Telegram: Nixon, Kissinger, and a Forgotten Genocide*.

11. Thomas Borstelmann, *The Cold War and the Color Line* (2009), p. 228.

12. For the "tar baby" policy, see Walton, Rosser, and Stevenson, *African Policy of Secretary of State Kissinger*; Anthony Lake, *The Tar Baby Option: American Policy toward Southern Rhodesia* (1973); Ryan Irwin, *Gordian Knot: Apartheid and the Unmaking of the Liberal World Order* (2012).

13. Piero Gleijeses, *Conflicting Missions: Havana, Washington, Africa, 1959–1976* (2003), p. 353.

14. See also Shannon Rae Butler, "Into the Storm: American Covert Involvement in the Angolan Civil War, 1974–1975," PhD diss., Department of History, University of Arizona, 2008.

15. Gleijeses, *Conflicting Missions*, p. 355.

16. The National Security Archive makes available many of the Angola documents at http://www2.gwu.edu/~nsarchiv/NSAEBB/NSAEBB67/.

17. House of Representatives, Committee on International Relations, Subcommittee on Africa, *United States–Angolan Relations* (1978), p. 13.

18. John Stockwell, *In Search of Enemies* (1978). See also Butler, "Into the Storm."

19. Gleijeses, *Conflicting Missions*, p. 390.

20. Piero Gleijeses, *Visions of Freedom: Havana, Washington, Pretoria, and the Struggle for Southern Africa, 1976–1991* (2013), p. 281.

21. Gleijeses, *Visions of Freedom*, p. 10.

22. "Remarks at the Annual Dinner of the Conservative Political Action Conference," January 30, 1986, in *The Public Papers of the Presidents of the United States: Ronald Reagan, 1986* (1988), pp. 104–05.

23. "Memorandum of Conversation," December 17, 1975, Paris, *Foreign Relations of the United States, 1969–1976*, vol. 27 (2012), document 302, p. 812.

24. Rashid Khalidi, *Brokers of Deceit: How the U.S. Has Undermined Peace in the Middle East* (2013), p. 2; Yaqub, "The Weight of Conquest: Henry Kissinger and the Arab-Israeli Conflict," in Logevall and Preston, *Nixon in the World*, p. 228.

25. Richard W. Cottam, *Iran and the United States* (1989), p. 150.

26. For senior diplomat George Ball holding Kissinger responsible for the 1979 Iranian Revolution, see Schlesinger, *Journals*, p. 458.

27. Andrew Scott Cooper, *The Oil Kings: How the U.S., Iran, and Saudi Arabia Changed the Balance of Power in the Middle East* (2011), p. 21.

28. *The Wall Street Journal* (July 25, 1974) reported Hanover Trust was estimating that "about $1 billion to $1.5 billion of new 'petrodollar' funds is available for investment each week," a "major portion likely would be sopped up by various governmental actions, including the direct investment of funds into spe-

cial U.S. Treasury securities." "Wouldn't the federal Reserve love it," as one economist put it, "if they got all the credit from Congress for a drop in interest rates when it was really the Arabs" who did it by pumping the money they took from US consumers back into the economy. By the mid-1970s, "as much as $50 to $60 million [of Iranian deposits] a day passed through Chase," which in turn loaned the money back to Iran to fund "big industrial projects," which in turn paid interest back to Chase. The new petrodollar interface also reflected a changing relationship between Washington and the developing world. As the historian Christopher Dietrich argues, Kissinger used the energy crisis to respond to third-world economic nationalism in a way that prioritized a "free-market vision of globalization, one that undercut broader visions of international economic justice." Where nationalists from energy importing countries demanded that petrodollars be distributed through a public institution, like the International Monetary Fund, as a kind of third-world Marshall Plan to capitalize industrial production, Kissinger successfully insisted on recycling oil wealth through private capital markets and private investment banks. Kissinger argued that "to play politics with the international economy was irrational and dangerous." There's an irony here, for it was exactly Kissinger's "free-market vision" that gave rise to the "irrational and dangerous" forces that would lead the assault on détente. In the U.S., the rapid increase of energy costs and influx of petrodollars empowered "independent" resource extractors that would become a key economic constituency of the fast-growing New Right (such as the Texas Hunt brothers or today's more well-known Koch brothers). They were "independent" in the sense that they weren't part of the corporate oil titans—Standard, Gulf, Texaco, and so on—that dominated energy production and that had largely resigned themselves to the fact of nationalization of oil production in countries like Libya and Venezuela. "The companies are dumb enough for socialism," Kissinger said in 1975, of the corporate establishment's willingness to work with OPEC. But those corporations might have provided the ballast for Kissinger's broader vision of global political stability. The "independents," on the other hand, would unite with other sectors of the New Right behind Ronald Reagan to tear down Détente and drive back into the third world. For the Kissinger's "dumb enough" quote, see National Archives, RG 59, Records of Henry Kissinger, Box 10, Classified External Memoranda of Conversations, January–April 1975, available at: http://history.state.gov/historicaldocuments/frus1969-76v37/d39#fn1). Dietrich, "Oil Power and Economic Theology: The United States and the Third World in the Wake of the Energy Crisis," *Diplomatic History*, forthcoming (quotation from personal correspondence with author). For the quotations and discussion in the footnote, see Cooper, *The Oil Kings*, pp. 107; 127–34; 137; 139; 183; for Iran paying for US military R and D, see Cooper, *The Oil Kings*, p. 147, who interviewed former Secretary of Defense James Schlesinger. Daniel Sargent, *A

Superpower Transformed: The Remaking of American Foreign Relations in the 1970s (2015), pp. 138–40; 183–86; "In Oil Riches for Arabs, a Silver Lining," *New York Times*, March 10, 1974; Stephen Walt, *The Origins of Alliance* [2013], p. 127. For the "oil price floor" plan, see "Compromise Seen on Kissinger Oil Floor Price Plan Cook," *Los Angeles Times*, February 7, 1975; "Kissinger Presents Oil Plan to Faisal," *Baltimore Sun*, February 16, 1975; Cooper, *The Oil Kings*, p. 225, and Steven Schneider, *The Oil Price Revolution* (1983). For the role of the "independent" energy sector in funding the domestic "Sagebrush Rebellion" and pushing Reagan to reopen the third world, making possible the eventual take-back of nationalized industries, see Ferguson and Rogers, *Right Turn*, pp. 89–96.

29. "Memorandum of Conversation," Henry Kissinger, Richard Helms, Harold Saunders, July 23, 1973, Washington, *Foreign Relations of the United States, 1969-1976*, vol. 27, Iran, Iraq, 1973-1976 (2013), document 24, p. 83.

30. "Minutes of Senior Review Group Meeting," July 20, 1973, *Foreign Relations of the United States, 1969-1976*, vol. 27, Iran, Iraq, 1973-1976 (2013), document 23, p. 70.

31. "Meeting between the Shah of Iran and the Secretary of Defense," July 24, 1973," *Foreign Relations of the United States, 1969-1976*, vol. 27, Iran, Iraq, 1973-1976 (2013), document 26, p. 91.

32. Mark Kesselman, *Introduction to Comparative Politics* (2009), p. 603.

33. Zulfikar Ali Bhutto, Pakistan's prime minister in 1975, was a supporter of the 1971 military assault on Bangladesh. In early 1975, he met in Washington with Ford and Kissinger to discuss a restoration of military aid. After the meeting, Kissinger told Ford that Bhutto "was great in '71." "That was one of Nixon's finest hours," he said, of Nixon's support for Pakistan as it committed what his own ambassador considered genocide ("Memorandum of Conversation, February 5, 1975," from the National Security Adviser's Memoranda of Conversation Collection at the Gerald R. Ford Presidential Library, available online).

34. "A feature of the Kissinger-Shah relationship," writes Andrew Scott Cooper in *The Oil Kings*, "was its emphasis on oral agreements and the absence of a paper trail."

35. Diego Cordovez and Selig S. Harrison, *Out of Afghanistan: The Inside Story of the Soviet Withdrawal* (1995), pp. 15–16.

36. Selig S. Harrison, "How the Soviet Union Stumbled into Afghanistan," in Cordovez and Harrison, *Inside Story*.

37. Some writers, like Steve Coll in *Ghost Wars* (2005), downplay the CIA role in supporting the Islamist groups that eventually coalesced around Osama bin Laden as Al Qaeda, saying that "CIA archives contain no record of any direct contact between a CIA officer and bin Laden during the 1980s." Assuming that Coll had complete access to the CIA's archives, and assuming that those archives contain a complete record of all the CIA's covert activities, focusing

on establishing responsibility for the action of one individual misses the larger
context: the networks built, the arms supplied, the turbocharging of the
ISI. According to the journalists Donald L. Barlett and James B. Steele
("The Oily Americans, *Time*, May 13, 2003), the CIA in Afghanistan ran
"one of its longest and most expensive covert operations, supplying billions
of dollars in arms to a collection of Afghan guerrillas fighting the Soviets."

7: SECRECY AND SPECTACLE

1. See Perlstein, *Invisible Bridge*, pp. 523–24.
2. William Shannon, "On His Own Terms," *New York Times*, September 13, 1973. Kissinger testified in closed executive session and in a public hearing. The transcript of the public hearing is published as *Nomination of Henry A. Kissinger: Hearings, Ninety-Third Congress* (1973). See p. 29 for the quote.
3. Kissinger, *Ending the Vietnam War*, p. 123.
4. See the documents at "East Timor Revisited," on the NSA Web site: http://www2.gwu.edu/~nsarchiv/NSAEBB/NSAEBB62/.
5. Michael Howard Holzman, *James Jesus Angleton* (2008), p. 301.
6. Geraldine Sealey, "Hersh: Children Sodomized at Abu Ghraib, on Tape," *Salon*, July 15, 2004; available at http://www.salon.com/2004/07/15/hersh_7/.
7. The indispensable Michael Paul Rogin, "'Make My Day': Spectacle as Amnesia in Imperial Politics," *Representations* 29 (Winter 1990), for the relationship of spectacle to secrecy.
8. *Hearings*, p. 356.
9. *New York Times*, "Excerpts From Transcript of the Proceedings on Impeachment," July 31, 1974.
10. Perlstein, *Invisible Bridge*, p. 524. See also United States Congress, *Bombing in Cambodia: Hearings, Ninety-Third Congress, First Session* (1973); Miraldi, *Seymour Hersh*, p. 166; *Time*, August 5, 1974.
11. Perlstein, *Invisible Bridge*, p. 428.
12. Berman, *No Peace*, p. 279.
13. Ford Library, National Security Adviser, NSC Meetings File, box 1. Top Secret; Sensitive. The meeting was held in the White House Cabinet Room; available at https://history.state.gov/historicaldocuments/frus1969-76v10/d285#fn1.
14. Ford Library, National Security Adviser, NSC Meetings File, box 1, chronological file. Top Secret; Sensitive. The meeting was held in the White House Cabinet Room. Available at https://history.state.gov/historicaldocuments/frus1969-76v10/d295#fn1.
15. Kissinger, *Years of Renewal*, p. 563.
16. Isaacson, *Kissinger*, p. 651.
17. Thomas Paterson et al., *American Foreign Relations: Volume 2: Since 1895* (2014), p. 417.

18. Butler, "Into the Storm," p. 137.

19. I have found no secondary accounts of the Cienfuegos "crisis" supporting the assertion that the Soviets were building a major military installation that didn't rely on Kissinger's account of the crisis, either the memos he produced at the time or his subsequent writing. Hersh's *The Price of Power* deals with the affair, basing its conclusions on testimony to Congress: "Intelligence experts in the State Department, the CIA, and even the Pentagon saw no tangible evidence of a major installation. In their opinion, Cienfuegos was meant to be a rest-and-recreation facility for Soviet submarines that would permit the Soviet navy to lengthen its normal overseas tours." Colonel John Bridge, identified by Hersh as the chief of the Soviet area office of the Defense Intelligence Agency, "testified that 'they [the Soviets] have established—we say it is a facility, at Cienfuegos, which might support naval operations, including those of submarines. It is by no means to be construed, I think, as a formal full-scale base. It is a support facility, a possible support facility.' As for the barracks, he testified, they were built of wood, obviously temporary facilities for crew stopovers. The concrete buoys which so alarmed Kissinger had been in place since 1968, well before the arrival of the Russians. . . . Similarly, the new dock Kissinger had noticed enclosed 'a small area, perhaps . . . a swimming area, or something like that.' The water was far too shallow for any other use, one officer said." In the *New York Times*, Tad Szulc ("White House Charge on Cuba Puzzles U.S. Officials," September 30, 1970) wrote: "American officials said today that the United States had only dubious and dated information to indicate that the Soviet Union might be planning to build a strategic submarine base in Cuba. For this reason, these officials, who include members of the intelligence community, said they were at a loss to explain why the White House chose last week to warn Moscow against the establishment of such a base." Also from Szulc: "Officials said there was still no evidence of suspicious construction activities, despite flights by U-2 surveillance planes." See also "Soviet Naval Activities," *CQ Almanac 1971*, which described hearings on the matter held by the House Foreign Affairs Subcommittee on Inter-American Affairs. Colonel Bridge is quoted here as saying: "I must make it very clear that we have absolutely no indication that any submarine ever entered Cienfuegos harbor." Bridge also makes clear that the main piece of intelligence was the guesswork related to what sport Cubans played: "Our people place some significance on the fact that a soccer field was built there—and it quite obviously by all description is a soccer field—because soccer is not a sport that is common to Cuba. A baseball diamond, we would have said, you would expect to find baseball diamonds." See also Dallek's account, *Nixon and Kissinger*, pp. 230–31.

20. Hersh, *Price of Power*, p. 257; Kalb and Kalb, *Kissinger*, p. 211. Dallek, *Nixon and Kissinger*, pp. 229–30, also suggests that Kissinger was posturing for Nixon. Nixon nursed a grudge against Castro, whose revolution he believed

cost him the 1960 presidential election by allowing JFK an opening to run to his right. Nixon also had deep ties to the anti-Communist Cuban exile community (two of the Watergate burglars were anti-Castro Cuban exiles and at least two others were anti–Cuban Revolution activists who had been involved in the failed Bay of Pigs invasion) and soon after his 1969 inaugural had stepped up covert operations against Castro and Cuba. In 1977, *Newsday* reported that "with at least the tacit backing of U.S. Central Intelligence Agency officials, operatives linked to anti-Castro terrorists introduced African swine fever virus into Cuba in 1971. Six weeks later an outbreak of the disease forced the slaughter of 500,000 pigs to prevent a nationwide animal epidemic. A U.S. intelligence source told *Newsday* last week he was given the virus in a sealed, unmarked container at a U.S. Army base and CIA training ground in the Panama Canal Zone, with instructions to turn it over to the anti-Castro group." Former CIA agent Howard Hunt reportedly "mentioned something about planning for the second phase of the Bay of Pigs around the beginning of Nixon's second term," which if true, was yet another idea—along with restarting the bombing of North Vietnam and imposing an austerity budget on the United States—derailed by Watergate. William M. LeoGrande and Peter Kornbluh in their recent book, *Back Channel to Cuba: The Hidden History of Negotiations between Washington and Havana* (2014), write that Kissinger helped moderate Nixon's hostility toward Castro, a process interrupted by Castro's Angola intervention, discussed in this chapter.

21. For Cuba in Angola and Kissinger's reaction, see Gleijeses, *Visions of Freedom* and *Conflicting Missions*, and Kornbluh and LeoGrande, *Back Channel to Cuba*. For the quotations, see Memorandum of Conversation, Ford, Kissinger, and Scowcroft, February 25, 1976. Available here: http://nsarchive.gwu.edu/NSAEBB/NSAEBB487/docs/01%20-%20Memorandum%20of%20Conversation,%20February%2025,%201976,%20Ford%20Library.pdf.

22. Still, the United States might indeed have "cracked the Cubans," as Kissinger said he wanted to do. On October 6, 1976, CIA- and FBI-supported Cuban exiles, led by a notorious anti-Castro activist named Orlando Bosch, bombed Cubana flight 455, after it had just taken off from Barbados, killing all seventy-three passengers—fifty-seven Cubans, eleven Guyanese, and five North Koreans—and all five crew members. At the very least, the CIA knew of the plans of the group (which went by different names, among them "Condor") to bomb a Cuban airliner as early as June. There are, however, two pieces of evidence suggesting that Kissinger didn't sanction this bombing. The first is that Bosch apparently had also targeted Kissinger for execution in retribution for attempting to normalize relations with Cuba, at least according to another CIA-linked anti-Castro Cuban trying to ingratiate himself with Washington. The second is that Kissinger authored a memo immediately after the bombing that said that Washington "had been planning to suggest Bosch deportation before Cubana Airlines crash took place for his suspected involvement in other

terrorist acts and violations of his parole. . . . Suspicion that Bosch involved in planning Cubana Airlines Crash led us to suggest his deportation urgently." Bosch wasn't, however, deported. See Ann Louise Bardach, *Cuba Confidential: Love and Vengeance in Miami and Havana*, p. 190.

23. National Archives, Nixon Presidential Materials, White House Tapes, Oval Office, Conversation No. 517-4; available at http://history.state.gov/historical documents/frus1969-76ve10/d101#fn1.

24. See the declassified documents at the National Security Archive, "Nixon: Brazil Helped Rig Uruguayan Elections," at http://www2.gwu.edu/~nsarchiv/NSAEBB /NSAEBB71/.

25. Kissinger's congratulation was in a November 24, 1973, cable made available by WikiLeaks: https://www.wikileaks.org/plusd/cables/1973STATE231341_b .html. For sources related to the discussion on Guatemala in the footnote, see the following documents found in the *Foreign Relations of the United States, 1969–1976, Volume E-10, Documents on American Republics, 1969–1972* (available at https://history.state.gov/historicaldocuments/frus1969-76ve10 /ch10): Document 343: Memorandum from the President's Deputy Assistant for National Security Affairs (Haig) to the President's Assistant for National Security Affairs (Kissinger), Washington, November 16, 1970; Document 346: Memorandum from Arnold Nachmanoff of the National Security Council Staff to the President's Assistant for National Security Affairs (Kissinger), Washington, November 23, 1970; Document 348: Telegram 22560 from the Department of State to the Embassy in Guatemala, February 10, 1971; Document 355: Memorandum for the Record, Washington, August 16, 1971; Document 356: Paper Prepared by the Central Intelligence Agency, Washington, undated; Document 357: Memorandum from Arnold Nachmanoff of the National Security Council Staff to the President's Assistant for National Security Affairs (Kissinger), Washington, August 19, 1971; Document 358: Memorandum for the Record, Washington, September 16, 1971; Document 364: Memorandum from William J. Jorden of the National Security Council Staff to the President's Assistant for National Security Affairs (Kissinger), Washington, September 28, 1972. Along with Cambodia, Kissinger is most defensive about his role in destabilizing Chilean democracy. He has consistently blamed Allende for provoking the coup against him, once even misquoting Zhou Enlai to suggest that the Chinese premier believed that Allende had brought about his own downfall as a result of his own reckless policies. In the official memorandum of the November 1973 conversation, Zhou says, "It was good because it could show a bad thing could be turned into good account. That is our way of seeing this thing. We told them about this, but they didn't believe us. That kind of phenomenon was caused by themselves. We give only limited support to Latin American countries' revolutions. We are still learning"—the Chinese premier was suggesting that the coup would usefully end Chile's misplaced faith in bourgeois democracy.

Kissinger in his memoir refigures these remarks to read: "We told them about [the risks], but they didn't believe us. That kind of phenomena was caused by themselves. . . ." For the original (translated and transcribed) conversation, see National Archives, Nixon Presidential Materials, NSC Files, Kissinger Office Files, box 100, Country Files, Far East, Secretary Kissinger's Conversations in Peking, November 1973 (available here: http://history.state.gov /historicaldocuments/frus1969-76v18/d59#fn1). See *Years of Upheaval*, p. 405, for Kissinger's use of it.

26. For Kissinger's "harder line," see National Archives, Nixon Presidential Materials, White House Tapes, Oval Office, Conversation No. 517-4. No classification marking; available at http://history.state.gov/historicaldocuments /frus1969-76ve10/d42#fn1. At this point, there is not much more to say about Kissinger's involvement in Chile. His defenders will continue to defend, to read the evidence in the narrowest possible way so as to achieve maximum plausible denial. As chair of the interagency 40 Committee, Kissinger helped organize a comprehensive program of destabilization that financed anti-Allende newspapers, channeled money through third parties to opposition unions, increased aid to the military, sabotaged the economy, ran "black operations to divide and weaken" Allende's coalition, and provided funds to the conservative National Party to create the paramilitary group Patria y Libertad, a death squad. "Our hand doesn't show on this one," Nixon said to Kissinger shortly after the coup. But over the years, leaked and declassified US documents have shown Nixon and Kissinger's fingerprints everywhere. See Scott Horton's post, "The Case against Kissinger Deepens," July 6, 2010, on Kissinger's admitting that the CIA did, in fact, kill General René Schneider in 1970 in order to prevent Allende's coming to power, in an operation in which Kissinger continues to deny involvement: http://harpers.org/blog/2010/07/the-case-against -kissinger-deepens-continued/. See the documents at the National Security Archive's "Kissinger and Chile: The Declassified Record, http://www2.gwu .edu/~nsarchiv/NSAEBB/NSAEBB437/.

27. "Kissinger Defends 1970s Latin American Policy," an AP story published in the *Michigan Daily*, October 5, 2004.

28. See the US documents collected at the National Security Archive's "New Declassified Details on Repression and U.S. Support for Military Dictatorship," at http://www2.gwu.edu/~nsarchiv/NSAEBB/NSAEBB185/. All the documents cited in this chapter, unless otherwise indicated, can be found at the National Security Archive Web site.

29. There is no indication, in the transcript of the conversation, that Kissinger had a private sidebar with Pinochet during their meeting. But Kissinger made sure to handpick that meeting's note taker, his trusted aide William Rogers. "I could work with him afterwards," he had said. The note taker for his meeting with Guzzetti, who did record that Kissinger had a "word alone" with the admiral, was Luigi R. Einaudi, a career diplomat.

30. Http://www.desaparecidos.org/notas/2008/01/los-militares-argentinos-calcu .html.

31. For Condor, see J. Patrice McSherry, *Predatory States: Operation Condor and Covert War in Latin America* (2005), and John Dinges, *The Condor Years: How Pinochet and His Allies Brought Terrorism to Three Continents* (2004). For the documents cited below, including those related to Kissinger's meeting with Cavajal and Pinochet, along with Letelier's murder, see the National Security Archive: http://www2.gwu.edu/~nsarchiv/NSAEBB/NSAEBB312/.

32. "Leader's Torture in the '70s Stirs Ghosts in Brazil," *New York Times*, August 4, 2012.

33. "Militares brasileiros tiveram aula em instituto americano sobre como praticar tortura," *O Globo*, October 12, 2014; available at http://oglobo.globo.com /brasil/militares-brasileiros-tiveram-aula-em-instituto-americano-sobre -como-praticar-tortura-14789322#ixzz3Ok1djNjO.

34. For Mujica, see Telesur English, "Mujica Opens Health Unit in Jail Where He Was Tortured," November 11, 2014; available at http://www.telesurtv.net /english/news/Mujica-Opens-Health-Unit-in-Jail-Where-He-Was-Tortured -20141111-0055.html. For Bachelet: "Former Chilean Military Officers Jailed for 1974 Death of President Bachelet's Father," *Guardian*, November 21, 2014.

35. House of Representatives, Committee on International Relations, Subcommittee on Africa, *United States-Angolan Relations* (1978), p. 13. See also Kevin Danaher, *The Political Economy of U.S. Policy toward South Africa* (1982), pp. 132–33.

8: INCONCEIVABLE

1. Miller Center, University of Virginia, Presidential Recordings Project, Nixon Conversation 620-008; available at: http://millercenter.org/presidential recordings/rmn-620-008.

2. John Kenneth White, *The New Politics of Old Values* (1990), p. 15. For Kissinger's ongoing opinion of Reagan in the footnote, see Schlesinger, *Journals*, pp. 512, 519, 538; " 'Off Record' Kissinger Talk Isn't," *New York Times*, April 20, 1986.

3. "Reagan Launches Attack on Ford, Kissinger," *Daily News*, March 5, 1976.

4. Ronald Reagan Paid Political Broadcast, March 31, 1976, 9:30 p.m.–9:59 p.m., Vanderbilt Television News Archives.

5. "Reagan Appeals for G.O.P. Crusade," *New York Times*, May 23, 1968.

6. For détente, see Louisa Sue Hulett, *Decade of Détente: Shifting Definitions and Denouement* (1982); Alexander Florey Woolfson, "The Discourse of Exceptionalism and U.S. Grand Strategy, 1946–2009," PhD diss., London School of Economics, 2012; Michael B. Froman, *The Development of the Idea of Détente: Coming to Terms* (1991). "Top Secret, Memorandum of Conversation," February 9, 1973, White House, Collection: Kissinger Transcripts; accessed via Proquest's Digital National Security Archive database.

7. Kissinger, *Years of Renewal*, p. 37.
8. For détente as a possible solution to the economic crisis of Keynesianism, see Thomas Ferguson and Joel Rogers, *Right Turn: The Decline of the Democrats and the Future of American Politics* (1986).
9. Ronald Reagan Paid Political Broadcast, March 31, 1976.
10. Elmo Zumwalt, *On Watch* (1976), p. 319.
11. Ronald Reagan Paid Political Broadcast, March 31, 1976.
12. For the 1968 quotation, see Brian P. Janiskee and Ken Masugi, eds., *The California Republic: Institutions, Statesmanship, and Policies* (2004), 248.
13. Cited in Lou Dubose and Jake Bernstein, *Vice: Dick Cheney and the Hijacking of the American Presidency* (2006), p. 209.
14. J. Peter Scoblic, *U.S. vs Them: Conservatism in the Age of Nuclear Terror* (2008), p. 94.
15. Anne Hessing Cahn and John Prados, "Team B: The Billion Dollar Experiment," *Bulletin of Atomic Scientists*, April 1993 (This is actually two separate articles under the combined title. The quote comes from Cahn's essay). See also Cahn's *Killing Détente: The Right Attacks the CIA* (2010).
16. The Bamford quotation comes from Jeff Stein, "Bush Team Sought to Snuff CIA Doubts," *San Francisco Chronicle*, October 26, 2005, as does the preceding quotation.
17. Jerry Wayne Sanders, *Peddlers of Crisis: The Committee on the Present Danger and the Politics of Containment* (1983), p. 198.
18. Cahn, *Killing Détente*, p. 186
19. Barry Werth, in *31 Days: The Crisis That Gave Us the Government We Have Today* (2006), p. 341, writes that Team B "became the rallying point for opposition to détente and arms control"; "Rumsfeld and Cheney drove the SALT II negotiations into the sand at the Pentagon and the White House," and "the vaunted Nixon-Kissinger realism in foreign affairs was at last stalled, if not defeated." See also Laura Kalman, *Right Star Rising: A New Politics, 1974–1980* (2010).
20. For the "morality plank," see Robert Merry, *Sands of Empire: Missionary Zeal, Foreign Policy, and the Hazards of Global Ambition* (2008), p. 165.
21. "A Tough Warning from the Right-Wing," *Washington Post*, January 26, 1975.
22. Schlesinger, *Journals*, p. 439.
23. Kissinger, *Years of Renewal*, p. 37.
24. John Chamberlin," "Kissinger Gave Up on Military Might," appearing in, among other papers, Lebanon, Pennsylvania's *Daily News*, and Coshocton, Ohio's *Tribune*, June 6, 1975.
25. Department of State, *Bulletin*, vol. 73, no. 1880 (July 7, 1975). See also Sargent, *A Superpower Transformed*, pp. 165–97. Jeane Kirkpatrick would later in a famous essay, "Dictators and Double Standards" (published in *Commentary* in late 1979), focus on the increasing use of the word "interdependence" by

liberals and internationalists as an example of their post-Vietnam crisis of confidence and moral abdication.

26. Daniel T. Rodgers, *Age of Fracture* (2011), p. 25.

27. Rodgers, *Age of Fracture*, p. 39.

28. *Public Papers of the Presidents of the United States: Ronald Reagan, 1984* (1986), p. 1002.

9: CAUSE AND EFFECT

1. "In an Interview, Pol Pot Declares His Conscience Is Clear," *New York Times*, October 23, 1997.

2. Cited in Shawcross, *Sideshow*, pp. 394–95.

3. Shawcross, *Sideshow*, p. 396.

4. "A Death in Cambodia; Evil Has Its Reasons," *Guardian*, April 17, 1998.

5. *Does America Need a Foreign Policy*, p. 264, for example.

6. There are defenses of Kissinger's Cambodia policy. For a useful summary of such arguments, as well as a convincing rebuttal, see James Tyner, *The Killing of Cambodia: Geography, Genocide, and the Unmaking of Space* (2008).

7. "Possible Bombing of Cambodia," Top Secret, Memorandum of Conversation, February 9, 1973. National Archives. Nixon Presidential Materials Staff. National Security Council Files; accessed via the Digital National Security Archive.

8. National Archives, Nixon Presidential Materials, Henry A. Kissinger Telephone Conversation Transcripts, box 19, chronological file. No classification marking; available at: https://history.state.gov/historicaldocuments/frus1969-76v10/d27#fn1.

9. Ben Kiernan, *How Pol Pot Came to Power: Colonialism, Nationalism, and Communism in Cambodia, 1930–1975* (2004), p. 390. The historian Tony Judt, himself a passionate anti-Communist and debunker of justifications of left-wing repression, put it bluntly: "Absent the forcible involvement of Cambodia in the Vietnam War, we would never have heard of Pol Pot" (See "What Have We Learned, If Anything," *The New York Review of Books*, May 1, 2008).

10. For the following discussion and quotations, see Ben Kiernan, *The Pol Pot Regime: Race, Power, and Genocide in Cambodia under the Khmer Rouge, 1975–1979* (2014), especially pp. 16–25. Ben Kiernan, "The American Bombardment of Kampuchea, 1969–1973," *Vietnam Generation* 1:1, Winter 1989, p. 8.

11. For the quotations, see Kiernan, *The Pol Pot Regime*, pp. 21–23, and *How Pol Pot Came to Power*, pp. 350, 371.

12. Kissinger, *Diplomacy*, p. 694.

13. Kissinger, *White House Years*, p. 45.

14. Kissinger, *Years of Renewal*, pp. 501, 514.

15. Memcon, Kissinger, and Swank, Bangkok, 9 February 1973, cited in Philip Dunlop, "Sideshow Revisited: Cambodia and the Failure of American Diplomacy, 1973," MA Thesis, University of British Columbia (201), p. 26. Available here: https://circle.ubc.ca/bitstream/handle/2429/24240/ubc_2010_spring _dunlop_philip.pdf?sequence=1. See also Kiernan, "The American Bombardment," p. 35.

16. National Archives, Nixon Presidential Materials, NSC Files, Kissinger Office Files, box 75, Kissinger Conversations at Zavidovo, May 5–8, 1973. Top Secret; Sensitive; Exclusively Eyes Only; available at http://history .state.gov/historicaldocuments/frus1969-76v15/d112#fn1.

17. For the "murderous thugs" quotation in the footnote, see "Memorandum of Conversation, 'Secretary's Meeting with Foreign Minister Chatchai of Thailand,' November 26, 1975, 1:00 p.m., State Department, Secret/Nodis"; available at http://www2.gwu.edu/~nsarchiv/NSAEBB/NSAEBB193/HAK-11-26 -75.pdf. For the "homicidal clique" quotation, see Kissinger, *Years of Renewal*, p. 499.

18. *Commentary* (1952), review of H. Stuart Hughes's *Oswald Spengler: A Critical Estimate*.

19. Hughes, *Oswald Spengler*, p. 72.

10: ONWARD TO THE GULF

1. "Adviser with No One to Advise," *Washington Post*, April 14, 1980.

2. *Official Report of the Proceedings of the Thirty-Second Republican National Convention Held in Detroit, Michigan* (1980), pp. 373–77.

3. "The Special Ops Surge," January 16, 2014, Tomdispatch.com, http://www .tomdispatch.com/blog/175794/tomgram%3A_nick_turse,_secret_wars _and_black_ops_blowback/. See also Linda Bilmes and Michael Intriligator, "How Many Wars Is the US Fighting Today?," *Peace Economics, Peace Science, and Public Policy* (2013).

4. Danaher, *The Political Economy of U.S. Policy*, p. 132, cites a number of sources describing Kissinger's use of Israel and South Africa as proxies in Angola in 1973. And Harold Koh, *The National Security Constitution* (1990), p. 53, notes that then director of the CIA, George H. W. Bush, refused to confirm in testimony that Washington actually cut off all assistance to its Angolan rebels.

5. See Schlafly's remarks: http://reagan2020.us/remembering/schlafly.asp. See also her book, coauthored with Chester Ward, *Kissinger on the Couch* (1975).

6. *Report of the National Bipartisan Commission on Central America* (1984), p. 93.

7. "Latin Panel's Soviet Finding Is Challenged by Moynihan," *New York Times*, January 13, 1984.

8. *New York Times* columnist Tom Wicker on the Kissinger Commission: "President Reagan's decision to set up a 'bipartisan' national commission to underpin his unpopular Central American policy is bad news for more reasons than the rebirth of Henry Kissinger. . . . The plan extends the already worrisome practice of turning over hard-fought political issues to supposedly blue-ribbon, non-governmental commissions. When such a panel delivers what appears to be an arbitrator's Solomonic decision in substitute for the political judgments of Congress and the president, the result is dangerous to oppose and even difficult to modify." Considering Kissinger's actions in Chile, Wicker said, "a less appropriate person to act as arbiter of policy anywhere in Latin America could not be found this side of General Pinochet" ("Hiding behind Henry," *New York Times*, July 19, 1983). As late as 1989, Vice President Dan Quayle was invoking the Kissinger Commission to justify an ongoing hard line: "I believe it was best spelled out in the Kissinger Report, which was produced in the early 1980s by former Secretary of State Henry Kissinger."

9. *Report*, p. 102.

10. See *Los Angeles Times*, April 26, 1986, for Shultz's comment in the footnote.

11. "They Can't Just Sit There Any Longer," *Washington Post*, October 24, 1983.

12. "TV: Reports and Debates on Crisis," *New York Times*, October 27, 1983.

13. "Medals Outnumber G.I.'s in Grenada Assault," *New York Times*, March 30, 1984.

14. "O'Neill Now Calls Grenada Invasion 'Justified,'" *New York Times*, November 9, 1983.

15. Interview with Brent Scowcroft, Miller Center, University of Virginia, November 12–13, 1999; available at http://millercenter.org/president/bush/oralhistory /brent-scowcroft.

16. "Panama Crisis: Disarray Hindered White House," by Andrew Rosenthal and Michael Gordon, *New York Times*, October 8, 1989.

17. "Resurrected and Visible," *Australian Financial Review*, October 13, 1989.

18. "Remarks to Organization of American States" (December 22, 1989), reprinted in *Panama: A Just Cause*, U.S. Dept. of State Current Policy document no. 1240, p. 3.

19. "Press Conference with President Bush," *Federal News Service*, December 21, 1989.

20. Richard Haass, *War of Necessity, War of Choice: A Memoir of Two Iraq Wars* (2009); George Will, "Drugs and Canal Are Secondary: Restoring Democracy Was Reason Enough to Act," *Philadelphia Inquirer*, December 22, 1989.

21. Likewise, the moderation of George W. Bush's secretary of state, Colin Powell, has often been contrasted favorably with the rashness of the neocons in the post-9/11 years. As the chairman of the Joint Chiefs of Staff in 1989, however, Powell was a strong supporter of the invasion. It was Powell who pushed for a more exalted name to brand the war with, one that undermined the very idea of those "limits" he was theoretically trying to establish. Following Pentagon

practice, the operational plan to capture Noriega was to go by the meaningless name of "Blue Spoon." That, Powell wrote in *My American Journey* (1995), was "hardly a rousing call to arms. . . . [So] we kicked around a number of ideas and finally settled on . . . Just Cause. Along with the inspirational ring, I liked something else about it. Even our severest critics would have to utter 'Just Cause' while denouncing us." Yet since the pursuit of justice is infinite, it's hard to see what your exit strategy is once you claim it as your "cause" (recall that George W. Bush's original name for his Global War on Terror was to be Operation Infinite Justice).

22. For Pickering's remarks, see Jordan Michael Smith, "Noriega's Revenge," *Foreign Policy* (December 19, 2009).

23. Richard Fagen, "The United States and Chile," *Foreign Affairs*, January 1975.

24. The contradiction in denying sovereignty to other nations while claiming it for one's own is obvious. But the contradiction can be managed as long as the double standard is justified, as Kissinger prefers, by the interests of state, by the need to establish international legitimacy and stability (and that justification, as we have seen, need not be considered amoral: a greater good can be achieved when great powers are allowed to create an orderly, stable, and peaceful interstate system). Problems emerge once denial of sovereignty is sanctioned by "democracy" and "human rights." The idea that there exists a "universal jurisdiction" of justice that trumps national sovereignty, as Einaudi lectured Latin Americans, opens up a Pandora's box, a threat that Kissinger immediately recognized: Kissinger supported the invasion of Panama to overthrow Noriega but objected to the "legality of the present legal proceedings" against Noriega in the United States. "I have some question whether you can try a foreign leader under American law for acts he didn't commit on American soil." It was an interesting question, said Kissinger, and it was indeed. Captured by the US military, Noriega was illegally transferred to the United States (Washington had no extradition treaty with Panama to justify the removal of Noriega), put on trial in Miami in April 1992 in the US District Court for the Southern District of Florida, and convicted in September for drug trafficking, racketeering, and money laundering—crimes that he committed prior to Panama's being "at war" with the United States. In 1998, the principle of "universal jurisdiction" advanced again when the British detained Augusto Pinochet in response to a Spanish extradition request, for crimes committed against Spanish citizens in Chile. This action moved Kissinger to write an essay in *Foreign Affairs* (July/August 2001) defending his old ally, titled "The Pitfalls of Universal Jurisdiction." "The ideological supporters of universal jurisdiction," Kissinger wrote, want to "criminalize certain types of military and political actions and thereby bring about a more humane conduct of international relations." It was a "dangerous precedent," he wrote, referring to efforts to extradite former leaders. The essay reads like a brief for his own defense, for just two months after it was published, on September 10,

2001, the children of Chilean general René Schneider filed a suit in federal court in Washington charging Kissinger and cohorts with "summary execution" of their father. Judge Rosemary Collyer, a former Reagan administration official appointed to the bench by George W. Bush, dismissed the suit on technical and jurisdictional grounds, including upholding the defense's argument that since Kissinger was acting as the national security adviser of the United States, the proper defendant of the suit would be the United States government, and the United States, based on the doctrine of sovereign immunity, is exempt from such suits. Since then, however, other countries have opened legal investigations of Kissinger's activities. Returning to the case of Noriega, Kissinger's protégé Scowcroft was also opposed to the idea of putting the Panamanian leader on trial, for much the same reason as Kissinger was: "In the late Reagan administration, Noriega was indicted, which I thought was a strange way to behave. I thought that the United States indicting foreign officials, over whom we had no jurisdiction, was really an aberration. So I didn't take that very seriously. President Bush did. He kept mentioning the indictment of Noriega, and I kept saying, 'You can't do that. You can't do that. You have no jurisdiction. It's a foreign official. They're unindictable anyway.'" Noriega is still in prison, now in Panama, having completed his term in the United States and then, on different charges, in France. For Scowcroft, see his interview cited earlier. For Kissinger's opinion of Noriega's transfer to the United States, see "Soviets Intervened on Autonomy Issue, Kissinger Suggests," *The Globe and Mail*, January 26, 1990.

11: DARKNESS INTO LIGHT

1. For the Tanter remark, see his *Rogue Regimes* (1990), p. 48.
2. "Conservatives Are Leading Murmurs of Dissent," *Washington Post*, August 24, 1990.
3. "Doves Grow Talons in Cold War About-Face," *Australian Financial Review*, August 23, 1990. For the Kirkpatrick essay mentioned in the footnote, see "A Normal Country in a Normal Time," *The National Interest* (September 1990).
4. "US Has Crossed Its Mideast Rubicon—and Cannot Afford to Lose," *Los Angeles Times*, August 19, 1990.
5. "Confrontation in the Gulf," *New York Times*, August 13, 1990.
6. Ibid.
7. "If you look at the United States in the postwar world," Kissinger told a reporter a few years after the first Gulf War, "we always stopped military actions too soon." At this point, he sounded less like America's top diplomat emeritus and more like a disappointed tourist: "We didn't go to Hanoi, we didn't go to Pyongyang, we didn't go to Baghdad." "I personally thought," he said, "we should have forced the overthrow of Saddam." Georgie Anne Geyer, "Should

the U.S.-Led Coalition Have Driven on to Baghdad?," *Denver Post*, October 16, 1994. For the quotation in the text, see "The President and His Hasty Hawks," *New York Times*, August 22, 1990.

8. General John Brown, introduction, *Operation Just Cause* (2004), p. 3.
9. John Mueller, *Public Opinion in the Gulf War* (1994), p. 162.
10. *CBS Evening News*, January 17, 1991 (transcript available via LexisNexis).
11. *CBS Evening News*, January 18, 1991 (transcript available via LexisNexis).
12. March 1, 1991, Remarks to the American Legislative Exchange Council; available at http://www.presidency.ucsb.edu/ws/?pid=19351.
13. "Right Fears Bush May Have Gone Too Far," *Guardian*, August 20, 1990.
14. Quoted in, among other places, John Dower, *Cultures of War* (2011), p. 92.
15. "Attack on Iraq," *New York Times*, December 17, 1998.
16. "Deep Scars Are Expected in Senate Hearings," *New York Times*, February 3, 1997.
17. *Nomination of Anthony Lake to Be Director of Central Intelligence, Hearing before the Select Committee on Intelligence of the United States Senate* (1998); Anthony Lewis, "Again, Scoundrel Time," *New York Times*, March 21, 1997.
18. "The Paris Agreement on Vietnam: Twenty-Five Years Later," conference transcript, Nixon Center, Washington, DC, April 1998; available at https://www.mtholyoke.edu/acad/intrel/paris.htm.
19. In *Present Dangers* (2000), ed. Robert Kagan and William Kristol, p. 311.
20. William Kristol and Robert Kagan, "Toward a Neo-Reaganite Foreign Policy," *Foreign Policy* (July–August 1996).
21. Published widely through the *Los Angeles Times* Syndicate International; available at http://www.sfgate.com/opinion/openforum/article/The-Politics-of-Intervention-Iraq-regime-2784793.ph.
22. Transcript available at http://transcripts.cnn.com/TRANSCRIPTS/0208/26/se.01.html.
23. "Phase II and Iraq," *Washington Post,* January 13, 2002; available at http://www.henryakissinger.com/articles/wp011302.html.
24. "Phase II and Iraq."
25. The following meeting of Gerson and Kissinger is recounted in Bob Woodward, *State of Denial* (2007), pp. 408–10.

EPILOGUE: KISSINGERISM WITHOUT KISSINGER

1. Henry Kissinger, "Lessons for an Exit Strategy," *Washington Post*, August 12, 2005.
2. Kissinger had started taking an active role in bringing the various parties who would write that trade treaty together during the George H. W. Bush administration. And all of Kissinger's allies in the White House, including Mack McLarty, who would soon join Kissinger Associates, pushed Clinton to prior-

itize Nafta over the health care legislation that Hillary Clinton was working on. It was Kissinger who came up with the idea of having past presidents stand behind Clinton as he signed the treaty. Reagan was sick and Nixon still non grata, but "flanked by former presidents Bush, Carter and Ford at a White House ceremony, Mr. Clinton delivered an impassioned speech," the *Wall Street Journal* reported. No such presidential backdrop was assembled to help support Hillary Clinton's health care proposal, which by August 1994 was dead.

3. Jeff Faux, *The Global Class War* (2010), p. 21.
4. Kristen Breitweiser, *Wake-Up Call: The Political Education of a 9/11 Widow* (2006), pp. 137–40.
5. "Kissinger's Client List Sought," *USA Today*, March 16, 1989.
6. "Second-guessing the methods by which the Executive Branch chose to deal with a new Socialist regime in Chile in the 1970s vis a vis their effect on foreign citizens," Judge Rosemary Collyer wrote in her opinion, "is not the proper role of this Court." It would be impossible for the court, she said, to "measure and balance a myriad of thorny foreign and domestic political considerations, i.e., the magnitude of any threat to the United States and its democratic allies from the spread of Marxism to Chile. The Court lacks judicially discoverable and manageable standards to resolve these inherently political questions." And besides, since Kissinger was acting as the national security adviser of the United States, the proper defendant of the suit would be the United States government, and the United States, based on the doctrine of sovereign immunity, is exempt from such suits.
7. Paul Bass and Doug Rae, "The Story of May Day 1970," *Yale Alumni Magazine* (July–August 2006).
8. "Hillary Clinton Reviews Henry Kissinger's *World Order*," *Washington Post*, September 4, 2014.
9. For conflicts of interest, see "Henry Kissinger's Entangling Ties," *New York Times*, December 3, 2002; Fairness and Accuracy in Reporting, "Henry Kissinger: The Walking, Talking Conflict of Interest," October 31, 1989 (http://fair.org/extra-online-articles/henry-kissinger/); "Tricky World of Mr. Kissinger," *Orlando Sentinel*, September 20, 1989; for conflicts of interest regarding his lobbying on Chinese and Latin American Policy, see Isaacson, *Kissinger*, 746–48.
10. For Kissinger's 1975 support, see the cables released by WikiLeaks, including (1) February 4, 1975, cable from Delhi embassy to State Department detailing Union Carbide's avoidance of Indian funding and corporate structure requirements for foreign subsidiaries; (2) August 22, 1975, cable from Delhi requesting review of Union Carbide's loan application; (3) September 11, 1975, cable from Kissinger about review of Union Carbide loan application; (4) September 25, 1975, US ambassador indicates Union Carbide negotiations as one of the "success stories" in US government's campaign to weaken regulations on foreign investment in India; (5) November 18, 1975, cable from Kissinger to Delhi embassy detailing approval of and content of Eximbank loan to

Union Carbide ($1,260,000 credit covering 45 percent of plant's construction costs); and (6) January 6, 1976, cable from Kissinger to Delhi indicating terms of the approved loan and the $2.8 million in US goods and services Union Carbide will purchase to construct the Bhopal plant. The above cables can be found at https://wikileaks.org/plusd/cables/1975NEWDE01606 _b.html; https://wikileaks.org/plusd/cables/1975NEWDE11369_b.html; https ://wikileaks.org/plusd/cables/1975STATE216298_b.html; https://www.wikileaks .org/plusd/cables/1975NEWDE12918_b.html; https://wikileaks.org/plusd/cables /1975STATE272385_b.html; and https://www.wikileaks.org/plusd/cables/1976 STATE001679_b.html.

11. For Kissinger's role in brokering the settlement, see the 1988 letter obtained by the environmental reporter Rob Edwards, found here: http://www .downtoearth.org.in/dte/userfiles/images/JRD-Tata-letter-to-PM-May-31, -1988.jpg. The *New York Times* reports that Kissinger's firm had an account with Union Carbide ("Nominee for Deputy Post at State Is Challenged on Consulting Ties," March 16, 1989).

12. In Argentina, Kissinger Associates helped implement the economic policies that led to that country's 2002 collapse (Eagleburger advised the Argentine Economy Ministry's team); elsewhere, it actively lobbied against "protectionism," urging Latin American nations to lower tariffs and subsidies, in a way helping to implement what Kissinger in his 1980 speech at the Republican National Convention said should be US policy. "Privatisation Groundswell," *Australian Financial Review*, June 7, 1990; "Argentina's Big-Name, High-Dollar Advocates," *Washington Post*, April 11, 2002.

13. August 6, 2002.

14. http://www.thetakeaway.org/story/transcript-kissinger-talks-isis-confronts -his-history-chile-cambodia/.

15. In Kiernan, *The Pol Pot Regime*, p. 24.

16. "The Myth of the Terrorist Safe Haven," *Foreign Policy*, January 26, 2015.

17. Hannah Arendt, *Origins of Totalitarianism* (1973), p. 215.

18. *The Bryan Times*, June 2, 1970.

ACKNOWLEDGMENTS

When I mentioned to friends and colleagues that I was writing a book about the legacy of Henry Kissinger's foreign policy, many often made mention of Christopher Hitchens's *The Trial of Henry Kissinger*. I think then that here would be the place to point out that I see my interest in Kissinger as somewhat antithetical to Hitchens's 2001 polemic. *The Trial of Henry Kissinger* is a good example of what the great historian Charles Beard, in 1936, dismissed as a "devil theory of war," which blames militarism on a single, isolatable cause: a "wicked man." To really understand the sources of conflict, Beard said, you had to look at the big picture, to consider the way "war is our own work," emerging out of "the total military and economic situation." In making the case that Kissinger should be tried—and convicted—for war crimes, Hitchens didn't look at the big picture. Instead he focused obsessively on the morality of one man, his devil: Henry Kissinger. It must have been a fun book to write, giving the author the satisfaction of playing the people's prosecutor. Yet aside from assembling the docket and gathering the accused's wrongdoing in one place, *The Trial of Henry Kissinger* is not very useful and is actually counterproductive; righteous indignation doesn't provide much room for understanding. Hitchens burrows deep into Kissinger's dark heart, leaving readers waiting for him to come out and tell us what it all means. That is, besides the obvious: Kissinger is a criminal. But Hitchens never does. In the end, we learn more about the prosecutor than the would-be prosecuted. The book provides no insights into the "total situation" in which Kissinger operated and makes no effort to explain the power of his ideas or how those ideas tapped into deeper intellectual currents within American history. Hitchens depicts Kissinger as a ravager of American values, so out of place in his adopted democratic land it was as if Wagner had wandered into a production of Aaron Copland's *Appalachian Spring*, muscled the baton from the conductor, and added a little Götterdämmerung to the square dances and fiddles.

Hitchens is by far the most damning of Kissinger's chroniclers, but he is not alone in missing the point. Most students of Kissinger find it hard to say anything about Kissinger that isn't about Kissinger. He is such an outsized figure that he eclipses his own context, leading his many biographers, critics, and admirers to focus nearly exclusively on the quirks of his personality or his moral failings. Seymour Hersh's *The Price of Power: Kissinger in the Nixon White House*, published in 1983, did capture the secretive world of the national security apparatus as it was functioning during the Vietnam War, and his study of Kissinger's paranoia reads like a (somewhat innocent) prelude to the all-pervading surveillance and counterterrorism state we now live under. But Hersh, writing in the early 1980s, couldn't know the long-term effects—not only of specific policies but of how Kissinger's imperial existentialism enabled a later generation of militarists who, in the 1990s, took us, after a quick detour through Central America and Panama, deeper into the Gulf, and then, after 9/11, into Afghanistan and Iraq. *Kissinger's Shadow*.

Friends, family, and colleagues helped with this book, including reading all or parts of the manuscript, answering questions, assisting with the research, or just talking about the topic. I owe a large debt to Marilyn Young, Ben Kiernan, Bob Wheeler, Carolyn Eisenberg, Chase Madar, Corey Robin, Jim Peck, David Barreda, Matt Hausmann, Cos Tollerson, Rachel Nolan, Christy Thornton, Barbara Weinstein, Philip Gourevitch, Ada Ferrer, Sinclair Thomson, Josh Frens-String, Maureen Linker, Kate Doyle, Esther Kaplan, Nick Arons, Richard Kim, Roane Carey, Jean Stein, Katrina van den Heuvel, Tom Hayden, Arno Mayer, Bev Gage, Chris Dietrich, Kirsten Weld, Peter Kornbluh, Susan Rabiner, Mario del Pero (for his helpful book on Kissinger, *The Eccentric Realist*), Mark Healey, Ernesto Semán, Tannia Goswami, and Toshi Goswami.

I don't know if there is a devil theory of publishing, but there should be, for Sara Bershtel explains it all. Or at least she does for me. Sara's intense reading and much needed skepticism turned a jumble of a manuscript ("I think you are saying something important," she remarked about the first draft, "I just don't understand what it is.") into a passable finished product. Thank you. Thanks also to all the others at Metropolitan Books, including Connor Guy, Roslyn Schloss, Riva Hocherman, Maggie Richards, and Grigory Tovbis.

This book is for Manu Goswami and Eleanor Goswami Grandin. Eleanor will be three when it is published.

INDEX

ABOUT THE AUTHOR

GREG GRANDIN is the author of *The Empire of Necessity*, which won the Bancroft Prize; *Fordlandia*, a finalist for the Pulitzer Prize and the National Book Award; as well as *Empire's Workshop*, *The Last Colonial Massacre*, and *The Blood of Guatemala*. A professor of history at New York University and a recipient of fellowships from the Guggenheim Foundation and the New York Public Library, Grandin has served on the UN Truth Commission investigating the Guatemalan Civil War and has written for the *Los Angeles Times*, *The Nation*, *The London Review of Books*, and *The New York Times*. He lives in Brooklyn.